Defining Acts

efining Acts

Drama and the Politics
of Interpretation
in Late Medieval England

RUTH NISSE

University of Notre Dame Press
Notre Dame, Indiana

Copyright © 2005 by University of Notre Dame
Notre Dame, Indiana 46556
All Rights Reserved
www.undpress.nd.edu

Manufactured in the United States of America

Library of Congress Cataloging-in-Publication Data
Nisse, Ruth.
Defining acts : drama and the politics of interpretation in
late medieval England / Ruth Nisse.
p.   cm.
Includes bibliographical references and index.
ISBN 0-268-03601-2 (alk. paper)
ISBN 0-268-03602-0 (pbk. : alk. paper)
1. English drama—To 1500—History and criticism.   2. Political plays, English—
History and criticism.   3. Mysteries and miracle-plays, English—History and
criticism.   4. Politics and literature—Great Britain—History—To 1500.
5. Literature and society—Great Britain—History—To 1500.   6. Theater—Political
aspects—England—History—To 1500.   7. Social problems in literature.   I. Title.
PR643.P64N57   2004
822'.109358—dc22
2004027604

∞ *This book is printed on acid-free paper.*

to my parents

Gerald Shklar and
Judith N. Shklar (ז״ל)

c o n t e n t s

acknowledgments

This project was supported by a grant-in-aid from the University of Nebraska-Lincoln and a year's fellowship from the Stanford Humanities Center; many thanks to Keith Baker, Bliss Carnochan, Susan Dunn, and the staff and fellows at Stanford for a wonderful intellectual experience.

The manuscript and rare book librarians at the Cambridge University Library, the British Library, and the Green Library at Stanford University provided expert and friendly assistance with my research. I offer thanks to Tim Johnson at the University of Minnesota's rare book library for kindly making photocopies on short notice and to Kathy Johnson and the Interlibrary Loan staff at the University of Nebraska for their ongoing help. I would also like to thank my research assistant Dennis Kuhnel for helping me to prepare the bibliography.

Barbara Hanrahan, Rebecca DeBoer, and the staff at the University of Notre Dame Press have been a joy to work with; I thank them and my excellent copy editor, Elisabeth Magnus. An earlier version of chapter 2 appeared in the *Journal of Medieval and Early Modern Studies,* 28:2 (1998): 431–56; a small portion of chapter 1 appeared in "Reversing Discipline: The *Tretise of Miracles Pleyinge,* Lollard Exegesis, and the Failure of Representation," in the *Yearbook of Langland Studies* 11 (1997): 163–94. I thank these journals for permission to reprint this material.

It is a pleasure to thank my colleagues and friends whose generous support made it possible for me to write this book. The members of the

Medieval-Renaissance group at the University of Nebraska offered helpful comments on various parts of the project. The students in my medieval drama classes at both Nebraska and Stanford reminded me of why this kind of study is rewarding. Sarah Beckwith, Robert L. A. Clark, Bruce Holsinger, Deeana Klepper, Lisa Lampert, Victoria Morse, Bill North, Paul Olson, Sally Poor, Fiona Somerset, Paul Strohm, and Jennifer Summit all read various parts of the manuscript; I am grateful for their valuable ideas, insights, and suggestions. I am especially indebted to my fabulous neighbor Sarah Kelen, who patiently read and discussed everything, sometimes in several versions.

Laura Severt King's brilliant work on early drama has inspired me since graduate school, and I thank her for sharing it with me. My thinking about this project and everything else has benefited from the unique intellectual perspectives of Adnan Husain, Amelia Montes, Clarissa Campbell Orr, Miri Rubin, Tom Schultheiss, Pegatha Taylor, and Blakey Vermeule. Willis Johnson is, in the most profound sense, my guide in all things Hebrew. Omar Gassama's thoughtfulness and wise cheer helped me through the final stages of this project.

It was my good fortune as a graduate student at Berkeley to study medieval literature with Anne Middleton, whose intellectual generosity, exemplary scholarship, and commitment to learning are a constant inspiration. I thank my aunts Iris Ballon and Ruth Schachter for being endless sources of loving wisdom and humor. My mother first introduced me to the ideas that she lived and breathed, the most precious possible gift; to her and my father I dedicate this book with love and gratitude.

Ah the old questions, the old answers,
there's nothing like them!

—Samuel Beckett, *Endgame*

In the York pageant *Christ before Herod,* performed annually on the Feast of Corpus Christi by the listers' craft guild, the famously ranting king of Judea returns Jesus to Pilate, declaring:

> "Wherfore schulde we flaye hym or fleme hym
> We fynde it noʒt in rollis of recorde;
> And sen þat he is dome, for to deme hym,
> Ware þis a goode lawe for a lorde?
>
> (399–402)[1]

While Herod's conclusion is of course an elaboration of the Gospel of Luke's narrative of this event, it is also a moment of supreme irony in regard to the relationship between writing and performance in medieval theater. The pageant's humor, such as it is, derives from the tyrant's entering the scene threatening to stab, crush, or chain up everyone in sight but exiting, after his frustrating encounter with the silent "dumb" Savior, worrying about legal precedents. No adequate logic is available to deal with the problem, either from Jesus' own words or from the recorded law; the trial begins in deafening bluster yet ends in deafening silence. In another sense, however, Herod's remark about the absence of writing to support an unjust punishment conjures up the immense "rolls of record" that, unbeknownst to him, precisely direct that Jesus must be brutally tormented and killed in the story onstage in York. The Gospels, the books of the Hebrew prophets and the psalms reinterpreted as prefigurations of the Christian event, and centuries of Western theological texts and commentaries on every aspect of the Incarnation determine this pageant's outcome and, together with the specific performance itself, its range of meanings. The great eleventh-century theologian Anselm of Canterbury, for example, provides one such piece of writing: in *Why God Became Man,* he offers the elegant formulation that "Christ, along with the Father and the Holy Spirit, had determined the way in which he would demonstrate the exaltedness of his omnipotence should be none other than through his death."[2] This book investigates how playwrights in late medieval England met the challenge of translating this kind of paradox—God's simultaneous power and vulnerability—and the many other problems that ultimately derive from the hermeneutic methods of scholastic biblical commentaries and dialectics, into a vernacular theatrical language.

Defining Acts seeks to bridge the gap between the question asked in Herod's "tumbling" English alliterative verse, an inventive piece of theatrical amplification, and the kind of incisive academic Latin answer proposed by Anselm. By reading medieval drama in relation to its many theological, political, and literary intertexts, I explore the ways in which these "rolls of record" become unrolled as elements of public theatrical performances, available to new audiences. My larger purpose is to show how the surviving texts of the medieval stage, urban pageant cycles as well as traveling "miracles" and morality plays, reveal a dramatic idiom deeply invested in practices of interpretation. In these works the reading of Scripture, literary texts, bodies, and signs initiates a dialogue between performance and locale that reflects the social production of meaning in the fourteenth and fifteenth centuries. The study further considers the development of urban biblical drama, first performed at York and Beverley on Corpus Christi in the 1370s, as a hermeneutic vocabulary in its own right. No sooner did the vernacular drama's methods of interpretation appear than they were subjected to the critiques, dour and outrageous respectively, of an anonymous Wycliffite tract known as the *Tretise of Miraclis Pleyinge* (c. 1400) and Chaucer's *Miller's Tale.* Later in the fifteenth century, other dramatic works like the Croxton *Play of the Sacrament* offered their own theatrical refinements and rejections of the cycles' urban ideology and stagecraft.

Any book that claims to deal with "medieval English drama" must naturally begin with a number of caveats. The combined textual and performance histories of the body of works commonly called by this name make the prospect of working on even the most complicated of medieval authors—William Langland comes to mind—seem alluring in its simplicity.[3] All of the dramatic texts that I consider are recovered by their modern editors from single manuscripts, several of which are marked by layers of revision postdating the English Reformation.[4] Urban communities, altering the plays to accord with Protestant beliefs, continued to perform cycle plays after the Reformation, well into the Elizabethan era.[5] Moreover, the extant information about performances of medieval plays, culled from civic records, monastic accounts, and the gentry's household books among other sources, is at best fragmentary, at worst misleading.[6]

The great York cycle of Corpus Christi plays is the most fully documented medieval English production. The surviving register of plays assembled between 1463 and 1477 (now BL MS Additional 35290) provides a text, while a plethora of records from city governors and individual craft guilds preserved in York's *Memorandum Books* provides accounts of how the city itself became a stage with pageant wagons processing through its streets. Even so, the problems are obvious: there is only so much, for example, that the extant text can tell us about the earlier years of the cycle, "fossilized" in Richard Beadle's word, in the plays.[7] The manuscript was in continuous use, bearing the traces of generations of annotators; the main scribe, foreseeing this, left blank spaces for unregistered plays, three of which were filled in by one John Clerke and another hand in the mid–sixteenth century.[8] The records' many silences, furthermore, leave us with no real way to recapture the metamorphosis by which the texts were fashioned into performances—the magical process hilariously mangled by Shakespeare's "Rude Mechanicals" in *A Midsummer Night's Dream*.

The manuscript of the East Anglian N-Town plays (BL MS Cotton Vespasian D. viii) is a late-fifteenth-century compilation of pageants from various earlier sources arranged in cycle form, often with little coherence. As Alan Fletcher writes of the "archaeology" of the collection's layers, the text is best understood according to the medieval theory of *compilatio* or communal authorship, by which the main scribe organized his materials into an inclusive work that could be used according to the needs of various playing communities.[9] The Towneley plays are preserved in the manuscript most difficult both to interpret and to date (Huntington Library MS HM 1), with estimates ranging from the end of the fifteenth century to the middle of the sixteenth. A compilation of plays arranged in artificial cycle form, the manuscript includes versions of some of the York plays, plays from independent sources, and, most notably, the works of what appears to be a singular mid-fifteenth-century playwright-reviser, known, according to his legitimating "author-function" (to use Foucault's term), as the "Wakefield Master."[10] In addition to the controversies over authorship generated by the plays either written or revised by the "Master," several including internal references to the Wakefield area, the critical response to the manuscript has attempted to account for a number of missing leaves, probably containing Marian plays and other material removed after the Reformation.[11]

Even from this brief account of some of the texts of medieval drama, it should be clear that studies of this material must rely on a certain amount of speculation and imagination, especially when it comes to performance. The reader of a collection of medieval plays must often attempt both to re-create the public spectacle of a summer feast day celebration and to decipher a series of references to annual liturgical events — Candlemas or Easter festivities, for instance — prompted by the cycle form's invocations of the entire church calendar.[12] Much of the interpretive work on medieval drama has naturally focused on the feast of Corpus Christi itself, instituted by the church in 1264 to celebrate the eucharistic miracle by which bread and wine become Christ's flesh and blood and, in St. Gregory's terms, "one thing is made of visible and invisible."[13] V. A. Kolve's *Play Called Corpus Christi,* notably, sets forth a connection between the sacrament's "eternal power" and a formal theory of scriptural history, as reproduced in the cycle plays' episodic structure. The meaning of the plays is essentially determined by the structure of the high medieval biblical gloss's dialogue of text and commentary on a page of Scripture. In this system, any biblical text always points to the end of history: "Figures and their fulfillment, the mimesis of total human time."[14] Jerusalem the city, for example, as represented by York or any English city, is always the heavenly Jerusalem of eschatology.

Whereas Kolve stresses the implications of an allegorical understanding of Old and New Testament histories on medieval ideas about penance and salvation, Mervyn James's influential structuralist account interprets Corpus Christi in terms of ritual practices that expressed "the opposites of social wholeness and social differentiation" through the "natural symbol" of the human body.[15] For James, the plays function as a way of resolving the "tensions" that arose among the craft guilds, a diachronic ritual in distinction to the synchronic, hierarchical Corpus Christi procession in which city and church officials carried the host through the city. More recent assessments, partly in acknowledgment of the fragmentary manuscript evidence, have rejected such totalizing schemes in favor of localized studies and the critical methodologies of cultural history. Gail McMurray Gibson, for example, analyzes fifteenth-century East Anglian culture in terms of an "incarnational aesthetic" that puts the Corpus Christi, in the form of a suffering human body, at the center of drama and spiritual practice alike.[16] Sarah Beckwith centers her exploration of the drama's theology exclusively on York's Corpus Christi cycle, reading the entire event as a "sacramental theater" by which the Eucharist's dialectic of visibility and invisibility shapes and enacts the city's social self-understanding.[17]

This study moves away from a sharp focus on the Eucharist and its symbolic field by engaging with drama as one of the main forms of a broader fifteenth-century vernacular theology. I am interested above all in the "politics of interpretation," the process by which poet-playwrights, players, and spectators brought specifically hermeneutic problems to a public stage in order to negotiate their potential communal consequences. The opening chapter of *Defining Acts,* "Drama after Chaucer," introduces the concept of drama as a translation of scholastic hermeneutic practices into public performance, drawing out the political implications of these methods of reading for urban communities. To this end, I begin with the best-known medieval text that embraces the dangers and pleasures of theatrical representation, Chaucer's *Miller's Tale.* Like the vehemently antitheatrical *Tretise of Miraclis Pleyinge,* Chaucer's fabliau hinges on the shifting boundaries between "ernest" and "game" in civic theater and the potential for exegesis to challenge ideas of social and sexual identity. My reading of the *Miller's Tale* serves as an entry into the fourteenth-century controversies over the meaning of the "literal" or "historical" level of the Bible. The "literal" is the sense most accessible to all readers, including laypeople, as opposed to the "allegorical" interpretations marked as the realm of clerical privilege. The *Treatise* itself best captures the problem of the "literal sense" at the core of civic theater: written by two exponents of vernacular translation of Scripture and lay exegesis, the tract nevertheless argues that public plays are incapable of conveying allegorical meaning and that they even corrupt biblical narrative into a carnal spectacle that actually threatens to reenact a history of Jewish and pagan error. Reading this text against a variety of dramatic records, theological tracts, and chronicles, I use its often self-contradictory argument as a starting point to investigate how contemporary dramatic performances actually represented questions of biblical authority and interpretation.

The next two chapters turn to the Passion sequence of the earliest surviving English mystery cycle to consider civic theater as a form of political and historical discourse that invents and defines its community. The York plays align a civic rhetoric of "common profit" and consensus with the radical ideas propounded by the fourteenth-century Wycliffite sermons of a "common" will and "common" understanding of English Scripture among laypeople. In the *Entry into Jerusalem* play, a committee of stage-aldermen who go to meet Jesus must perform a collective textual exegesis before they can welcome him into the city. Likewise, in the plays of Pilate and Herod's tyranny, misrule is figured as deeply flawed interpretation. At the same time that they invent this new theatrical idiom, the York playwrights attempt to reconcile the patriarchal civic authority that they celebrate with a female mysticism that claims its own kind of political power. Especially in the wake of Catherine of Siena's and Bridget of Sweden's potentially destabilizing revelations about ecclesiastical and political rulers, clerical "discernment of spirits," the assessment of the legitimacy of visionary experience, had become a central issue of English spirituality. The *Dream of Pilate's Wife* from the middle of the Passion sequence encompasses the entire problem: the plays, at once influenced by women's visionary texts but resistant to women's authority, use the discourse of "discernment" to present the dangers of a series of false visions. My analysis of gender politics concludes with a very different work, the anomalous *Mary Play* from the hybrid N-Town cycle. In this series of pageants strongly influenced by vernacular Bridgettine devotion, a strikingly positive picture of the visionary woman author emerges in the education of the Virgin into a prophet and poet—a female "novus David."

Chapter 3, "Labor's End," argues that the "Wakefield Master" plays, which revise some elements of the York cycle, constitute a political critique of the earlier work's ideology of labor. If the earlier plays, put on by labor guilds, engage contemporary anxieties about the proximity of their own advertising of work and commodified "made objects" to idolatry, the Wakefield Master's unique theatrical idiom takes these ideas to more radical conclusions. The two Shepherds' Plays are in fact works in the *Piers Plowman* tradition that respond to urban theater by staging both the politics and hermeneutics of competing Franciscan, Langlandian, and Wycliffite versions of Christian poverty. In reaction to the York cycle's celebration of a visible, public, oligarchic exegesis, the Wakefield plays introduce a radical interiority as their site of interpretation. The *First Shepherds' Play* reinscribes the spiritual Franciscan ideal of prophecy as the mark of apostolic poverty; the chaotic Wakefield *Buffeting* further explores the capacity of labor to generate idolatry in scenes of extreme physical and metaphysical violence.

In Chapter 4, I similarly interpret the grotesque anti-Judaic Croxton *Play of the Sacrament* as an antiurban play, put on in the environs of Norwich for an audience at once part of an urban economy and wary of its implications for their collective, "local" identity. While the Jews had been expelled from England in 1290, the figure of the "hermeneutic Jew," the multifaceted foil of Christian exegesis, remained central to English eschatology. Drawing on a long history of debate over Jewish exegesis, especially in the commentaries of Nicholas of Lyra, I situate the play among contemporary views of Jews as models and antimodels of community. The play, itself representative of a kind of "diasporic theater," is produced as a direct critique of the politics of urban drama. The Croxton play promotes a sense of space and body radically different from that of the mystery cycles: Heraclea/Aragon, the ultimately decimated site of the miracle, is urban space, whereas the "Babwell Mill" episode, a strange comic interlude, defines local space. The jarring contrasts between the two, and finally between both and an ideal Jerusalem, are central to the play's treatment of the Jews as urban "aliens."

My concluding chapter focuses on the politics of interpretation and devotion in a little-studied late-fifteenth-century morality play, *Wisdom*. This allegorical text, a dramatization of Walter Hilton's *Epistle on the Mixed Life* and *Scale of Perfection* as well as several continental mystical texts, demonstrates the dangers of encouraging the English gentry to read and interpret ambiguous language. While Hilton's *Epistle*, a manual for lay devotion, cautions its audience of wealthy book owners not to abandon social duties for a wholly contemplative life, *Wisdom* deals with the very different danger of a gentry who could potentially appropriate and misread multivalent mystical texts to serve their own political ends. In *Wisdom*, Lucifer, who tempts the Soul into vice, represents a willfully bad reader: by interpreting the metaphors of the mystical idiom literally, he, not unlike Chaucer's Absolon, "de-allegorizes" devotional writing into corrupt legal, sexual, and political discourses. In a most timely insight, *Wisdom* warns all of us how easily the figural language of the spirit can be transformed into the slogans of a misruled ruling class.

As this summary makes clear, my project participates in the current reappraisal of fifteenth-century literature, that vexing body of works usually associated with the cultural decline and "dullness" directly preceding the English Renaissance.[18] Nicholas Watson has claimed that the striking originality of fourteenth-century English theological writing, as exemplified by masterpieces as diverse as Julian of Norwich's *Showings*, the alliterative *Pearl*, and the long Wycliffite sermon cycle, was stifled after the archbishop of Canterbury, Thomas Arundel, promulgated the anti-Wycliffite *Constitutions* in 1409.[19] In a modification of this view, Fiona Somerset argues that the *Constitutions*, which in theory not only forbade unlicensed translation of Scripture but sought to limit all forms of lay education and reading, had far less impact outside the universities than their stated scope.[20] While scholars continue to dispute the severity of the *Constitutions'* practical effects and the evident bleakness of Watson's catalog of fifteenth-century vernacular productions, the dramatic texts have remained outside the disciplinary boundaries of the discussion. At one level, this makes sense insofar as theatrical performances took place with some form of clerical approval and their scripts were transmitted more or less openly. As I demonstrate in this study, however, a variety of dramatic works take up the most urgent issues surrounding the practices of vernacular theology and indeed offer their own contributions to exegetical discourse. This new style of English theology emerges, then, within the frame of orthodox religious celebration, yet outside the clerical educational institutions that Arundel's legislation most urgently sought to police.[21]

The few plays that I have selected as the subject of this book address the fifteenth-century controversies over the laity's access to English Scripture and exegesis at the heart of both Wycliffite and decidedly non-Wycliffite writers. The problems of women's visionary experience and its translation into devotional texts are familiar to Julian's *Showings* and *The Book of Margery Kempe*; the relationship between poverty and prophecy preoccupies Langland's *Piers Plowman*; and the theological crisis precipitated by the expulsion of the Jews haunts any number of Middle English works, from *Cursor Mundi* to *The Siege of Jerusalem* and Chaucer's *Prioress's Tale*. In a moving account of theater's cultural work, Joseph Roach writes: "Performance . . . stands in for an elusive entity that it is not, but that it must vainly aspire both to embody and replace. Hence flourish the abiding yet vexed affinities between performance and memory, out of which blossom the most florid nostalgias for authenticity and origin"[22] Not only did late medieval performers represent biblical time and space according to an imagined ideal, but men represented women, Christians represented Jews, artisans represented the merchant oligarchs who ruled their city. The project of staging the originary narrative of Christianity itself became, in hermeneutic theater, a pageant of contingent authorities in dialogue not just with the rivals they temporarily impersonated but with the texts that gave shape to these impersonations. While the longings of medieval performances are distant from our own, the desire for legibility that unifies these plays is with us still.

Drama after Chaucer

The *Miller's Tale* and
the Failures of Representation

"In Pilate's voys he gan to crie / And swoor, "By armes, and by blood and bones" (3124–25).[1] With these lines, Chaucer describes the eruption of the drunken Miller into the *Canterbury Tales* as he temporarily drowns out the Monk's voice with his own colorful account of the Incarnation, moving ever deeper into Christ's body from visible to invisible parts. The moment also marks the inception of theatrical identity in the poem, as the Miller's new "voys" transforms him into someone between his peasant "self" and the mystery plays' tyrant.[2] In the records of the York Corpus Christi plays, a trace remains of a millers' play, the *Division of Christ's Garments.* Although the text is lost, the subject is an intriguing one.[3] In the York *Crucifixion* play, the soldiers who have just executed Christ draw lots for his clothing just as the Canterbury pilgrims do for the privilege of telling the first tale, proclaiming that "The schorte cutte schall wynne, þat wele ȝe woote, / Whedir itt falle to knyght or knave" (295–96).[4] Pilate, however, takes part in the action only in the Towneley *Play of the Dice,* the one surviving play devoted wholly to the gambling episode: when he loses the egalitarian game of dice, he bellows "unbychid, unbayn!"

(roughly "cursed mutineers!") and simply pulls rank, demanding and receiving the seamless garment (369).[5]

The Pilate whose voice the Miller adopts is presumably some version of this figure, a ruler who not only uses his power and "voice" to subvert a game of chance and grab an object of desire but actually rewrites biblical narrative in the process.[6] Pilate is here simultaneously an exemplar of illegitimate authority and theatricality, the potential of performance to change even the most established gospel script. The Miller's similar intervention in the *Canterbury Tales,* as he plays a role even more hypermasculine than that of the Knight or the "manly" Monk, introduces a work that considers precisely the relationship between Scripture, power, and theatricality. The *Miller's Tale* turns to contemporary theater as a rejoinder to the idealized ancient Athenian tournament in the *Knight's Tale,* questioning the notion of "natural" social and sexual identities in a drama where not only knaves play knights and men play women (and perhaps vice versa), but humans play God.

All of these issues are captured by the *Miller's Tale*'s most striking image of a thing unseen, "Goddes pryvetee," Chaucer's much-discussed pun on God's genitals and his secrets. "Goddes pryvetee," that which cannot be represented from either God's divinity *or* his humanity, is also the central theme of the *Tretise of Miraclis Pleyinge,* the Wycliffite polemic against biblical theater roughly contemporary with the *Canterbury Tales.* If Chaucer frames the dangers of representation his work will reveal with the warning that "the Millere is a cherl," the second of the *Tretise*'s authors describes "the pleyinge of the fleysh with the spirit" in the following terms: "[A]s felawchip of a thral with his lord makith his lord dispisid, so myche more pleyinge with the miraclis of god makith hem dispisid, sithen pleyinge to comparisoun of the mervelouse werkis of God is fer more cherl than any man may ben cherl of a lord" (108).[7] This is one in a long series of metaphors that the text deploys to describe the impossibility of representing Scripture onstage in its full hermeneutic complexity. The bodies of actors may stand in for the literal characters of biblical narrative, but without the frame of exegetical method, the clerical study of the sacred page with its ordering of spiritual interpretations, theater becomes the most dangerous form of what St. Augustine called "carnal" misreading. In *On Christian Doctrine,* Augustine had warned of "the ambiguities of metaphorical words":

> To begin with, one must take care not to interpret a figurative expression literally. What the apostle says is relevant here: "the letter kills but the spirit gives life." For when something meant figuratively is interpreted as if it were meant literally, it is understood in a carnal way. No "death of the soul" is more

aptly given that name than the situation in which the intelligence, which is what raises the soul above the level of animals, is subjected to the flesh by following the letter. A person who follows the letter understands metaphorical words as literal, and does not relate what the literal word signifies to any other meaning. . . . It is, then, a miserable kind of spiritual slavery to interpret signs as things, and to be incapable of raising the mind's eye above the physical creation so as to absorb the eternal light.[8]

The actors and audience of biblical drama, according to the *Tretise*'s account, participate in an extreme version of this spiritual error of misreading. By "playing," they become subject to an absolute confusion of literal with allegorical meanings, history with eternity, illusion with reality. Yet the passage above from the *Tretise* on the dangers of "fellowship" is itself not wholly metaphorical, signaling as Chaucer does the political danger, the actual disordering of relations between lord and "churl" that could result from the metaphysical chaos of theater.

In both the *Miller's Tale* and the *Tretise of Miracles Pleyinge,* biblical theater most threatens to get out of control at the intersection of hermeneutics and politics, in its continual exchanges between the narratives presented onstage and the communities responsible for the productions. As these authors understand, the performance of dramatic cycles on the Feast of Corpus Christi in York, Coventry, and other emerging cities marks a historical moment when civic governing bodies receive and apply ideas of reading and interpretation previously limited to the clergy and academic debates. V. A. Kolve demonstrated that the "mystery cycles" were conceived as representations of salvation history according to typological or allegorical principles, spectacles that could theoretically encompass and link the seven ages of the church from Creation to Doomsday, including the community's own role as it performed the work in the present moment.[9] The audience, likewise, ideally experienced the plays as visual representations of what Erich Auerbach called figural allegory in its "full historicity," "the interpretation of one worldly event through another."[10] For example, the York *Flood* play theoretically positions the "comic" conflict between Noah and his wife over her refusal to get aboard the ark as an aspect of the Old Testament "figure" that signals, through static typological references, its New Testament "fulfillment" in Jesus' baptism and the Last Judgment. The typological scheme is fulfilled dramatically in the representation of both events later in the sequence of plays.

As the *Tretise* contends over and over with its own exegetical readings, however, the temporal paradigm of allegoresis can never be translated into a spatial vocabulary, even one as elaborate as the York plays' mapping of biblical narrative onto the theater of the city itself. According to the Wycliffite polemic, the scheme of typology collapses under the weight of its own stagecraft as the embodied and manifestly literal nature of theater erases the multivalent scholastic text. Corpus Christi theater is, after all, *about* the body in the Eucharist, the product of what Gail Gibson calls the late medieval "incarnational aesthetic" that valorizes Christ's suffering flesh above his divine power, the visible over the invisible.[11] Like the great works of "affective mysticism" translated into English for a lay audience in this period—most prominently the Franciscan *Meditations on the Life of Christ*—mystery plays invite the audience to imagine themselves as eyewitnesses of biblical narrative and to empathize with the sufferings of all the figures in the Passion. For example, the *Meditations* describes Jesus' experience in vivid terms: "But in what battle is He tormented? You will hear and see. One of them seizes him (this sweet, mild, and pious Jesus), another binds him, another attacks him, another scolds Him, another pushes him, another blasphemes Him, another spits on Him, another beats Him, another walks around him, another questions him."[12] In the *Meditations'* style of devotional experience, imagination effectively suspends the temporal or historical difference at the basis of exegetical logic.

Exactly by this medium of vision and emotion, the Wycliffite polemicists argue, the plays "reverse discipline," both in the sense of indulging the bodily pleasures of the audience and in the more specialized sense of disrupting the order established by scriptural exegesis. In the *Tretise,* the implicit violence of discipline is directed toward the proper reception of text: "the verry vois of oure maister Crist is herd as a scoler herith the vois of his maister, and the yerd of God in the hond of Crist is seyn" (95). Hugh of St. Victor's *Didascalicon,* the widely circulated handbook of monastic reading practices, describes how exegesis proceeds according to "the order which exists in the disciplines" of the levels of interpretation; the student begins by thoroughly learning the foundation of history, the "literal" sense of the scriptural text, before moving on to the "spiritual" senses of allegory and tropology.[13] In an analogy that the *Tretise* repeats several times, players of "miracles" or biblical scenes are like the Jews who tortured Christ: "[S]ithin thes miraclis pleyeris taken in bourde the ernestful werkis of God, no doubte that ne they scornen God as diden the Jewis that bobbiden Crist, for they lowen at his passioun as these lowyn and japen of the miraclis of God" (97). As opposed to the *Tretise's* central image of the ideal reader who obeys Christ as a child obeys a cane-wielding schoolmaster, the actors' violence here resembles students pummeling their teacher. Unable to project the text's true spiritual and ethical meanings, the actors simply reenact the brutal tortures of Christ for the bloodthirsty amusement of the audience; and like the "Jews" of medieval Christian exegetical ideology, they apprehend only the literal sense of Scripture, which they further degrade to a "carnal" spectacle. The body being beaten up in the plays of the buffeting of Christ is, as this text emphasizes, *only* a human body; since it cannot represent Christ in his humanity and divinity, it becomes a mockery, a parody of Scripture. In the *Tretise,* these reversals are the essence of "play," the opposite of discipline, and carry far-ranging social consequences for the community performing such representations.

The *Tretise*'s Wycliffite argument, then, runs against the very thing that characterizes medieval social thought in the modern imagination, the metaphoricity of the body. As Miri Rubin writes of the "natural symbol" of Corpus Christi: "The mystical body had become so public, so exposed, so much a locus of desire and power, that it was a sort of public good, which patricians hastened to appropriate, at least on occasions which they controlled."[14] The Wycliffite *Tretise*'s claims speak to an acute awareness of this symbolic manipulation, an alarmed sense that the organic idiom behind the civic ideology of Corpus Christi naturalizes as an illusory communal body a fragile, unstable people always in danger of "reversing Christ" and regressing into its "Jewish" or pagan origins. While the vernacular plays work to confirm economic and political identities, therefore, they erase the historical identity, accessible only through the reception and interpretation of English Scripture, necessary for the true "conversion" and salvation of every level of the community.

The *Tretise* and the *Miller's Tale,* so radically different in tone, nonetheless complement each other perfectly in their portrayals of theater's failure to convey the layers of meaning generated by biblical exegesis and the inevitable triumph of the literal sense and the body. While the *Tretise*'s most emphatic point is that "we shulden not maken oure pleye and bourde of tho miraclis and werkis that God so ernestfully wrought to us" (94), Chaucer ends his *Prologue* to the *Miller's Tale* with the disclaimer that the "Avyseth yow, and put me out of blame; / And eek men shal nat maken ernest of game" (3185–86). A little-examined episode from the Peasants' Revolt of 1381 helps to explain why Chaucer and his Wycliffite contemporary, while holding opposite views of the value of fiction, invoke an already violated boundary between "ernest" and "game" as the main ethical challenge to theatrical representation.[15]

According to the version of events recorded by John Gosford, the almoner of the Abbey of Bury St. Edmunds, in the evening of 14 June—the day after the Feast of Corpus Christi—the East Anglian rebels, led by the clerk, John Wrawe and including many Bury townspeople, captured the "traitor" Prior John de Cambridge and proceeded to subject him to a kind of real-life or "snuff" Passion play.[16] According to Gosford, the rebels, following the script of the "perfidious Jews'" buffeting of Christ on the night of the Last Supper, led the prior to Newmarket, where they "ridiculed and heckled him, sometimes genuflecting before him saying 'ave raby,' sometimes toasting him without drinking-cups, sometimes giving him a slap demanding 'prophetiza quis est qui percussit te' (Prophesy! Who is it that struck you?)."[17] The following day, having beheaded the prior, the rebels used his head in an even more bizarre pageant together with the remains of the chief justice, John Cavendish. Thomas Walsingham's *Historia Anglicana* here agrees with Gosford:

> As no one opposed them, they entered the town and marched around as if in a procession, carrying the said prior's head high on a lance in full view of the townsmen until they reached the pillory. Then, in recognition of the previous friendship between the prior and John Cavendish and to pour scorn on both, they held together the two heads on the tops of the lances as if they were talking or kissing each other—an absurdly improper action. Later, when they were tired of such jests, they placed both heads above the pillory again.[18]

If the first of these accounts seems to lend itself a bit too neatly to the monk's own hagiographic impulse, it nonetheless captures the same idea as the second (which it was probably intended to counter in the textual version of the revolt): that the rebels appropriated the forms of an urban Corpus Christi celebration as a working political vocabulary.[19] In the puppet show the rebels perform, the heads apparently represent not just their former hated and feared "selves" but a pair of mystery play characters—interchangeably the tyrants Pilate and Herod reaching their accord, or Judas betraying Jesus with a kiss. As in the *Tretise*'s objections to theatrical representation, there is no stable relation, in the rebels' "jest," between the body and the figure it evokes; the body is simply an arbitrary sign. Stripped of their offices and so desacralized, the prior and the chief justice become props for this "churls'" theater of the absurd. For the monastic historian providing the account, exegesis in the hands of laypeople, unanchored by its textual frame, quite literally turns into revolutionary violence.

By enacting any version of a Corpus Christi procession and play, the Bury rebels further took the "improper" action of defining themselves as an autonomous community already in possession of the very liberties that they were demanding from the abbey.[20] Like the enfranchised towns of York or Beverley, Bury in 1381 temporarily had a "civic" Corpus Christi celebration, literally over the prior's dead body. Walsingham's fulsome praise of John of Cambridge includes, however, a strange detail: "[T]his prior," he writes, "was a worthy and artistic man, surpassing in the sweetness of his voice and his musical skill the Thracian Orpheus, the Roman Nero, and the British Belgabred."[21] John's *own* theatrical "voys," that is, which links him to both paganism and secular tyranny, is in this odd aside a potential cause of his downfall at the hands of a mob. He is perhaps Orpheus, dismembered by crazed rustics likened to Ovid's "savage women"; but, at the same time, he is Nero, who famously forced his subjects to attend his theatrical performances, where, according to Suetonius, he played "goddesses and heroines" as well as male roles.[22] In Chaucer's *Monk's Tale,* following the *Roman de la rose,* Nero's tyranny ends when "the peple roos upon hym on a nyght" (2527), thus transforming the Roman historians' accounts of Servius Galba's military coup into a justifiable popular revolt. While Walsingham discusses the prior's voice in one sentence in a chronicle that condemns the 1381 rebels at great length, even this trace of theater is as profoundly destabilizing as the *Tretise* contends, throwing its subject's authority and identity into question.

Chaucer's Miller has often been seen as a representative of the peasants and artisans who led the 1381 uprising, a "cousin," in Paul Olson's words, "to the revolt's Jack the Miller" preserved in the letters recorded by Knighton's and Walsingham's chronicles.[23] Lee Patterson, in the most extensive of these interpretations, finds the Miller's disruptive uses of language aimed at oppressive clerical practices.[24] Seth Lerer, reading the *Miller's Tale* against the backdrop of Ricardian spectacle and popular revolt, eloquently contends that "the Miller's threats are of a violent and decentering *theatricality:* one that too easily can spill from pageant wagon on to public square, one that can use the strategies of civic celebration against themselves and, in the process, undermine both the communal values that the Corpus Christi dramas were designed to celebrate and the courtly values that Ricardian theatrics were designed to affirm."[25] None of the recent historicist or Marxian accounts, however, specifically relates the Miller's class consciousness to his talents as "a jangeler and a goliardeys," an actor and a master of deceptive, ironic language. While the Miller is undoubtedly a "glutton of words," these two terms, taken together, more specifically identify him with poetic performance and composition: *jangeler* (windbag and gossip) also suggests the French *jogleor* (minstrel, from Latin *joculator*), and *goliardeys* links him to the authors of the satiric twelfth-century Latin "Golias" poems.[26] Robin the Miller's style of ecclesiastical satire, however, reflects upon the act of performance itself. Even as he tells a tale that demonstrates the literalizing dangers of biblical drama as forcefully as the *Tretise,* he attests to theater's socially transformative power.

In the course of his many-layered performance, the Miller not only speaks in Pilate's voice but sees with Alison's "likerous [e]ye" (3244), defying the very idea of a natural identity with the theatrical figures of his desires. As recent readings of the *Miller's Tale* suggest, Robin identifies with Alison, the object of male desire, as she presides over the wounding effeminizing of the men around her.[27] The violence that Pilate only threatens in his ranting appearances in the mystery plays the fabliau carries out. In Marshall Leicester's terms, the Miller's revolt against the knight and the knightly ideal of representation enclosed in Theseus's amphitheater lies in his "'bisexuality'—the ability to play any of the roles normally allotted by patriarchy to either of the sexes."[28]

The action in the *Miller's Tale* takes place on or around a stage, Alison's and John's "shot-window," which, with its crucial hinge controlling and limiting vision and access, is itself a model for how the mind works, an architecture of the imagination. The image of the "window" is a common metaphor in devotional texts for sensual experience in the imaginative process: one treatise warns against "stirrings" that come from outside "bi windows of þi bodily wittes."[29] Furthermore, all the pleasures in the tale — including Alison's and Nicholas's "myrthe and solas" (3654) in bed — are theatrical. As on the contemporary stage deplored by the *Tretise,* actors and viewers are interchangeable. The "shot-window" is coterminous with Alison's "hole" (3732) and "nether yë" (3852), so that in this narrative of continual displacements and reflections the stage is also the final eye, the spectator. If "Goddes pryvetee" is the sacred thing that cannot be seen, then the heroine's famously ambiguous vagina or anus is the "eye" that sees everything.

The sheer density of reference in the *Miller's Tale* to biblical episodes staged in mystery plays imbues the entire narrative with a sense of the instability of exegetical categories, both literal and figurative.[30] The "legende and a lyf / bothe of a carpenter and of his wyf" (3141–42) — at once John and Alison, Noah and his difficult Uxor, Joseph and Mary, and apparently Oswald the Reeve and Mrs. Oswald — fittingly ushers in the real problem of the biblical stage, the impossibility of representing the incarnation of Christ with a human body. Just as the *Tale* toys with the dangerous difference between the Virgin Mary's body and the body of someone — female or male — playing the role of Mary, between the *porta clausa* and the ambiguous sometimes-closed, sometimes open shot-window, the narrative's main crisis is marked by a trace of Christ's body. Absolon's ill-fated kiss is, among many other things, the climax of his exegetical error of attempting not just to read literally but to enact theatrically the Song of Songs, the one book of the Old Testament to which patristic and subsequent tradition denied a "true" literal or historical meaning.[31] His unusual name underlines that, of David's sons, he is *not* King Solomon, despite his claim, just before the kiss, to be "a lord at alle degrees" (3724). For a very brief moment of the *Miller's Tale,* the logic of exegesis asserts itself independently from the actors' expressed desires when Alison offers Absolon a kiss on two distinct levels, allegorical and literal: "For Jhesus love, and for the love of me" (3717). From his impossible attempt to play the part of the divine *Sponsus* (Bridegroom) with his mangled love lyrics, Absolon, down on his knees before the window, "with his mouth" (3734) suddenly becomes the *Sponsa* (Bride), the human contemplative who could imagine the mystical "kiss of his [God's] mouth."[32] In the split second before Alison slams the window shut on Absolon—"for wel he wiste a womman hath no berd" (3737)—the text offers the possibility that the clerk actually feels and tastes Jesus' iconically bearded face in Alison's "naked ers," a scandal further emphasized by Nicholas's gleeful "A berd! A berd!" (3742) and "By Goddes corpus, this goth faire and weel"(3743). The "bourde" is, in fact, God's body in "ernest," momentarily present in the fantasy stage of the window. The cruel humor of the situation lies precisely in the difference between the kiss that Absolon imagines he has experienced—with disgust at its indeterminate bodily nature—and the allegorical kiss of incarnation that he has produced textually.[33]

The shot-window's oscillation between presence and absence, as well as between "pryvetee" and publicity, is the essence of the imaginative faculty at work in both theater and mystical understanding. Pronounced by either Chaucer or the Miller himself after he describes John's falling for the Noah's Ark scheme, the emblematic lines of the tale are "Lo what a gret thing is affeccioun! / Men may dyen of ymaginacioun / So depe may impressioun be take" (3611–13). This warning, however ambiguous its tone, draws on the same idiom as the roughly contemporary *Cloud of Unknowing*'s warnings against "the curiousity of imagination" for contemplatives:

> And therefore beware that thou conceive not bodely that that is mente goostly, thof al it be spoken in bodely wordes, as ben thees: *up* or *doun, in* or *oute, behinde* or *before, on o side* or *on other.* For thof that a thing be never so goostly in itself, nevertheless yit yif it schal be spoken of, sithin it so is that speche is a bodely werk wrought with the tonge, the whiche is an instrument of the body, it behoveth alweis be spoken in bodely words. But what therof? Shal it therfor be taken and conceived bodely? Nay, but ghostly.[34]

The *Cloud*'s program of interior discipline to counter the tendencies of fantasy, "the which is not bot a bodely conceyte of a goostly thing, or elles a goostly con-ceyte of a bodely thing,"[35] provides a context for the theatricality and the humor of the *Miller's Tale* in the boundless dangers of all language to misrepresent the difference between letter and allegory. The carpenter's mimetic excess and the literalizing mystery plays in general are, in this light, only extreme examples of the spatial and spiritual errors with which the *Cloud* is concerned. With its focus on the Song of Songs, however, the *Miller's Tale* makes God's incarnation into the ultimate challenge to the stable representability of body and spirit.

Bernard of Clairvaux's hermeneutics in his *Sermons on the Song of Songs* rele-gates the text's carnal language to the pedagogical function of reminding readers of the distance between their own understanding and divine truth. In a passage that directly anticipates the *Cloud*'s cautionary tone, Bernard warns against the "fantasies" of literal reading: "Shall we imagine for ourselves a powerful man of great stature, captivated by the love of an absent girl-friend and hastening to her desired embraces . . . ? Surely it will not do to fabricate physical images of this kind, especially when treating of this spiritual song."[36] If this underlines the na-ture of Absolon's "rebellion" in playing the *Sponsus* with the same "lightnesse and maystrie" that he played the historical role of Herod, it also points to the *Ser-mons*' conception of Christ's incarnation as entirely different from this fatal imag-ining.[37] For Bernard, the "kiss of his mouth" that the feminized contemplative seeks is the sign of incarnation itself, Jesus' dual nature as mediator between God and humanity. In his sermon on Song of Songs 2.9, which the *Miller's Tale* echoes in its central architectural metaphor, Bernard further describes the work of Christ's body:

> Our flesh is the wall, and the Bridegroom's approach is the incarnation of the Word. The windows and lattices through which he is said to gaze can be un-derstood, I think, as the bodily senses and human feelings by which he began to experience our human needs. . . . On being made man, therefore, he has used our bodily feelings and senses as openings or windows, so that he would know by experience the miseries of men and might become merciful.[38]

The lesson of the window-as-stage in the *Miller's Tale* is a similar inextricable linking of visual pleasure and bodily "misery." Similarly, the "incarnation" that Absolon, as the *Sponsa*, experiences in his kiss points to a reading of God's "pry-vetee" that interestingly coincides with the common fabliau idea of the indeter-minately gendered body.[39]

The true novelty of the *Tale*'s insight into theater, then, is that God's body cannot be represented as male without doing violence to the same multivalent glossed Scripture that the *Tretise* so stridently opposes to the mimetic stage. In response to Leo Steinberg's *Sexuality of Christ in Renaissance Art and in Modern Oblivion,* Jean-Claude Schmitt and Jerome Baschet write that the work's sharp focus on Jesus' literal, physical masculinity ignores the multitude of symbolic sexualities, female and male, encompassed in the idea of incarnation.[40] Eluding any one stable symbolic meaning, Christ's "sexuality" is never fully representable by a human image; indeed, an attempt to represent divine "pryvetee" might actually yield an image as seemingly blasphemous as the reflection of Jesus' face in Alison's "nether yë." This bodily indeterminacy is, needless to say, especially apparent in the exegetical tradition of the Vulgate Song of Songs where, within the first line, "Let him kiss me with the kiss of his mouth / for your breasts are better than wine," glossators have interpreted the *Sponsus*'s breasts as signs of feminine or maternal plenty. Even the philologically minded Nicholas of Lyra leaves the reading of this line open to different levels of meaning:

> *For thy breasts are better than wine.* The Hebrew says, *for thy loves are better.* The Hebrew word used here means both "loves" and "breasts." The Hebrew interpreters follow the first meaning, and our translation follows the other. But in this case the Hebrew interpreters seem to be on better ground, because, according to the peculiar nature of the Hebrew language, what seems here to be directed to the bride is actually directed to the groom, and, in praising the groom, it does not seem proper to mention his breasts. On the other hand, it might be said that, by the breasts of the groom, the fullness of God's mercy is understood. So, according to the Hebrew interpreters the sense is this: For thy loves are better than wine, that is, your love is more delicious to a devout mind than any earthly flavor to the sense of taste. According to our translation the sense is: Thy breasts are better than wine, that is, the fullness of your mercy is sweeter to the human mind than wine to the sense of taste, wine being among the things that people consider very delicious.[41]

Despite the conflict of meanings at the level of language, the exegete reconciles the "impropriety" of the hermaphroditic or bisexual body generated by the Vulgate's (mis)translation of Hebrew with the traditional Latin allegorical interpretation of a maternal, nourishing God. The "improper" body of the *Sponsus* here becomes a sign of allegorical plenitude, an excess not just of God's mercy but of potential meanings and interpretations. As the Miller warns in his Prologue, "An housbonde shal nat been inquisitif / Of Goddes pryvetee, nor of his wyf. / So he may fynde Goddes foyson there, / Of the remenant need not enquere" (3163–66). The *Tale* bears out the intimate relation of Goddes "pryvetee" and his "foyson"— or fullness of mercy—in the Song of Songs as Absolon finds both by sticking his head through the carpenter's "wyf's" window; in his disastrous theatrical anti-exegesis, however, he feels only the monstrous impropriety of incarnation—"a thyng al rough and long yherd" (3738)—and tastes something apparently much less delicious than wine.

From the moment of Absolon's kiss, the *Miller's Tale* can only parody the mystical language of the Song of Songs' own play of body and spirit: the mystic's "wounding love, " derived from exegeses of "You have wounded my heart, my sister, my spouse, with one glance of your eyes" (4:9) is reduced to Alison's three lovers' various experiences of damage.[42] The contemplative reader's "ghostly eye" or "eye of the mind" becomes Alison's infinitely desiring "nether yë." If he punishes his three male characters' theatrical attempts to shed their social identities for greater degrees of lordship with a feminizing humiliation, the Miller, identifying with Alison's wounding "eye," much more successfully grounds his own rebellion in the same reversals of gender. For playing God to John's Noah, Nicholas gets the mark of a stronger hand ("an hand-brede aboute") (3811) on his ass; John, already characterized by his young rival as a duck swimming after her drake, loses the power of his arm for his hope to be "lordes . . . of al the world" (3581–82), and the brief King Herod-like assertion of "the effeminate dandy" Absolon to be "a lord at alle degrees" (3724) subjects him to the claims of Scripture itself as he turns from *Sponsus* to *Sponsa*.[43] Chaucer preserves the subversive force of this moment, beyond its punishment of errant clerics, by aligning it with Christ's own metaphoric reversals of gender. In their feminization, the men transcend "natural" gender to participate, like Alison and the Miller, in the "bisexuality" of the paradoxically incarnate but unrepresentable Christ.

In two very different registers, the *Tale*'s final scene of John's cutting the makeshift ark loose and Absolon's burning Nicholas's ass—the crashing fall of the exegetical stage—parodies not just the "wounding love" of contemplative discipline but the grandiose funeral pomp of the *Knight's Tale*. In the latter, the Miller's theatrical "bisexuality," his "goliardeys'" affinity for both Pilate's and Alison's desires, is clearly linked to his revolt against the Knight's naturalizing arena. If Noah's ark, especially in Hugh of St.-Victor's influential *De Arca Noe Moraliter,* could represent the most perfect totalizing allegory, in which each measurement corresponded to a tenet of Christian doctrine, then Theseus's correspondingly totalizing structure collapses along with it in the theatrical denouement of the *Miller's Tale*.[44] Like the *Tretise*'s warnings against the contemporary stage's counter-allegorical play of flesh and spirit, "bourde" and "ernest," the Miller grasps theater's potential to erase the "natural" distinctions between "churl" and "lord" as well as bodies and genders. Robin's "quiting" of the *Knight's Tale,* then, recalls the suppressed power of the "bisexual" Amazons from the previous narrative in its gesture toward the most radical goals of the Peasants' Revolt. Like the 1381 rebels themselves, as well as the monks who recorded their history and the Wycliffite author of the *Tretise of Miraclis Pleyinge,* the Miller, performing another "cherles tale" (3169), understands contemporary theater, with its representations of the unrepresentable body of Christ, as a challenge to all fixed social identities. Theater, along with the larger idea of "fantasye" that blurs the line between "ernest" and "game," is finally the golden-thumbed goliard's potentially deadly route to "Goddes foyson."

In the pages that follow, there are many more *jangelers* and *joculatores.* The "remnaunt" of this book explores the challenges of theatricality and exegesis posed by the *Tretise of Miraclis Pleyinge* and Chaucer's *Miller's Tale* as they play out in the fifteenth century. The plays I consider here take up a series of contests over who could legitimately interpret Scripture and stage such ideas for a wide audience: men or women, clerics or laypeople, rulers or subjects, Christians or non-Christians. These works, in text and especially in performance, translate the temporal ideas of biblical exegesis into a range of new spatial models, each with its own implications for the audience's self-definition. The following chapters examine this continual interplay of textual hermeneutics and spatial politics both in the large-scale urban mystery cycles and in later theatrical works that react against the ideologies of the civic stage.

Staged Interpretations

Civic Rhetoric and Lollard Politics
in the York Plays

In the Gospel sermon for Palm Sunday, the Wycliffite author of the long vernacular sermon cycle makes a curious gesture toward contemporary biblical
drama. Having recounted how the "princes of preestis and þe pharisees" asked
Pilate to guard Christ's sepulchre until the third day to prevent his disciples
from claiming that he had risen, the preacher adds, "And þis *pagyn* (pageant)
pleyen thei that huyden the trewþe of Godis lawe" (emphasis added). With
this sardonic remark, he launches into the sermon's polemic against the authorities of church and state who keep the English Bible away from the laity:
"And by such execucion of false prelatis and frerus is Godis lawe qwenchid
and anticristes arerud. But God wolde þat þese lordes passedon Pilate in þis
poynt and knewon þe trewþe of Godis lawe in þer modyr tonge."[1] The heterodox preacher's evocation of a Resurrection play is a revealing rhetorical strategy,
notable not least for its recognition of a kindred anticlericalism inherent in the
drama's characterizations of the persecuting priests as bishops and friars. While
interesting in itself as a rare trace of audience perception, the preacher's attack
likewise points to the common concern of Wycliffite social thought and the

York Corpus Christi plays with the "mother tongue." Both the Wycliffite polemicists and the plays' authors are deeply invested in the role of secular powers,
whether "lords" or municipal officials, in providing education in vernacular Scripture to laypeople.

This chapter argues that the York plays, written for the celebration of the
Eucharist itself and so usually taken as an epitome of late medieval conservative piety, in fact draw on heterodox ideas about translation, interpretation, and
secular authority over Scripture. This sort of polemical material, often exclud-
ing mention of Wyclif's eucharistic heresy and other radical theological positions, was disseminated widely in the early fifteenth century in the Wycliffite sermons and their various more or less "orthodox" expurgated derivatives. As Anne
Hudson makes clear in her sweeping appraisal of the heresy's impact in the decades following Wyclif's death in 1384, the Lollards' reformist ideas drew interest from thinkers representing a "spectrum of opinion," particularly in the growing body of Middle English literature.[2] Building on recent work on reformist
preaching, I will show the convergence of certain aspects of popular Lollardy,
as a readily available idiom of vernacular devotion and politics, with the civic
ideology that underwrites the plays' elaborate and idiosyncratic representations of
biblical narrative. The York plays articulate a program of urban self-legitimation
that emphasizes, like more familiar forms of European protohumanist political
discourse, the role of public rhetoric in civic rule. In the plays' stagings of biblical
history, York's concerns with political voice and citizenship become inextri-
cably bound up with issues of exegesis and lay authority central to the Wycliffite program.

In pursuing the connections between urban political consciousness and diffuse Wycliffite ecclesiological and exegetical discourses, I offer a new approach
as well to the York plays' own vexing politics, especially the "Trials of Christ" sequence's obsessive concern with images of bad government at the expense of more
directly sacramental or devotional themes.[3] My account focuses on the two plays
that most clearly show the emergence of a civic voice from dissenting notions of
language and interpretation: the *Entry into Jerusalem* imagines ideal city government as not only good speaking but good reading, according the eight leading
citizens who welcome Christ the responsibility for providing a coherent vernacular exegetical narrative; the *Judgement of Christ before Pilate,* in its dramatization
of the iconoclastic story from the apocryphal Gospel of Nicodemus of the banners falling before Christ, examines the rhetoric of misrule and the inability of
tyrannical rulers to construct a true narrative.

Lollardy and theater have usually been considered mutually exclusive both ideologically and aesthetically on the basis of the former's iconoclasm and strong disapproval of public entertainments. As I have discussed in the previous chapter and elsewhere, the early Wycliffite *Tretise of Miraclis Pleyinge* attacks the plays as failed exercises in figural hermeneutics produced by town economies themselves carnal and idolatrous.[4] As Ritchie Kendall and others have pointed out, however, sole critical attention to the *Tretise*'s ferocious polemic has tended to obscure other connections between these competing expressions of lay piety.[5] To situate my own reassessment within the context of urban spirituality and civic government in early-fifteenth-century York, I will begin with Hudson's account of the dissemination of what she terms "vernacular Wycliffism."

In *The Premature Reformation,* Hudson sets out a helpful periodization for the development of Wycliffite thought into heresy: a fourteenth-century window of opportunity for the relatively free exchange of reformist ideas, an early fifteenth-century hardening of divisions between orthodoxy and Lollardy, and a crackdown on heterodoxy after the promulgation of Arundel's *Constitutions* in 1409 and especially after John Oldcastle's abortive rebellion in 1414.[6] The *Constitutions,* besides theoretically forbidding open discussion of Wyclif's works, unlicensed preaching, and translation of Scripture, explicitly ordered in the third statute that preachers could no longer expose the sins of the clergy to the laity in sermons.[7] Hudson's primary interest in this framework is in establishing that the ideas about church reform and translation later associated with the Lollards were more mainstream at the turn of the century than had previously been accepted, and accordingly she considers the Wycliffite strains in Chaucer, Langland, and John Trevisa, the Oxford-trained translator of Higden's *Polychronicon.*[8] The radical Franciscan author of *Dives and Pauper* and the Longeat sermons (both c. 1410) provides a further illustration of a decidedly non-Lollard writer whose advocacy of preaching in English in opposition to the archbishop and adoption of Wycliffite vocabulary pushed his works into the realm of heterodoxy after the boundaries were fixed by the *Constitutions.*[9] Hudson also takes up the even more problematic issue of textual exchange, charting both Lollard revisions of orthodox English works such as Richard Rolle's *Psalter or Psalms of David* and the *Lay Folks' Catechism* — products of the explosion of lay piety in fourteenth-century Yorkshire — and orthodox revisions of the Wycliffite sermons into a body of hybrid vernacular texts. As witnesses to a move to preserve those tenets of Lollardy that advance less extreme forms of lay devotion, the latter are analogous in some respects to the York plays. Amid the shifts in intellectual climate and sliding definitions of orthodoxy in the fifteenth century, they above all demonstrate the mechanisms of transmission. Like the derivative sermons, the York plays testify to the long afterlife of Lollard thought, the reformulation of Wycliffite ideas in new polemical contexts after official condemnations forced the question of what it meant to appropriate vernacular theology.

The relation between sermons and medieval drama is, of course, hardly a new topic. G. R. Owst, most prominently, has argued that the mystery plays were "little more than a dramatized set of sermons" that depended for their satirical treatments of the corrupt lords, judges, and bishops embodied by Herod, Pilate, and other assorted tyrants on a long tradition of estates satire and anticlerical invective in the Latin preaching of such figures as Bishop Thomas Brinton, the Dominican John Bromyard, and Robert Rypon.[10] While Owst deals in passing with Wycliffite preaching, especially when he wishes to cite outspoken vernacular texts, he sees it as largely an extension of this clerical tradition: siding with Arundel, he explains that revolt loomed when the "secrets" of "the synodal sermon" hit the "streets," "either through the indiscreet zeal of the orthodox or the deliberate malice of Lollards."[11]

In her reevaluation of Owst's classic work, H. L. Spencer, focusing specifically on vernacular preaching, underscores the importance of "the radical tradition." In an analysis of the surviving manuscripts of vernacular sermons, she concludes that the long Wycliffite sermon cycle was the predominant influence on collections made before the repressive measures of the *Constitutions* took hold, whereas its ultraorthodox ideological opposite, Mirk's *Festial,* took over in the late fifteenth century. As Spencer argues, "[T]he conflict between the Lollards and their adversaries was a battle over education, specifically the education of the laity."[12] Although the sermon collections were primarily written for secular priests, they were likely used also as "pious lay reading."[13] Spencer's careful study of the dissemination of the Wycliffite sermons and their derivatives shows that Lollard ideas, and above all the Lollard defense of English preaching and reading, had a wide currency among both ostensibly "orthodox" preachers and laypeople in the fifteenth century. On the evidence of sermon collections put together by Lollard "sympathizers," like Bodley MS 806, Sidney Sussex MS 74, and the latter's derivative, Bodley 95, there was a serious effort on the part of reform-minded preachers to incorporate the Lollard Sunday gospel sermons' attacks on the abuses of prelates and friars and polemics in favor of lay access to Scripture into more moderate devotional discourses.[14]

Spencer's claims about the influence of the Lollard sermons accord well with Jonathan Hughes's account of the tensions caused by the growth of lay piety within the York diocese in the fourteenth and fifteenth centuries.[15] Concentrating on the eremitic movement inspired by Richard Rolle, Hughes traces the church leaders' efforts to contain the tendencies of mysticism to devalue the institutional church in favor of domestic and personal devotion. Lollardy, in Hughes's mapping of York's religious trends, is just a more extreme form of the rebellious spirituality that appealed to Rolle's lay followers with its emphasis on ascetic poverty and vernacular reading.[16] This interpretation is, moreover, borne out not only by the Lollard additions to Rolle's *Psalter or Psalms of David* but by manuscripts containing material from the Wycliffite sermon cycle that also include vernacular and Latin works by Rolle.[17]

The problem of directly tracing Wycliffite theology in Yorkshire's mainstream religious culture remains. While J. A. F. Thomson's definitive survey of Lollard activity based on archbishops' registers shows few signs of actual heresy in Yorkshire (beyond periodic though telling displays of episcopal concern), Hudson's analysis of one particular artifact of northern Lollardy provides us with an intriguing way to reconceptualize Wycliffite influence.[18] This text is the thoroughly expurgated version of the whole sermon cycle that Hudson attributes to a friar in northern Yorkshire c. 1400.[19] Although the redactor of this collection leaves in enough Lollard doctrine, especially on the Eucharist, to confirm him as a heretic, he removes almost all of the sermons' lengthy broadsides against the church hierarchy and the "newe sects" of friars.[20] What the remaining text—essentially translations with commentary—demonstrates, beyond the obvious point that the sermons were in circulation in York, is that northern Lollardy encompassed a range of beliefs. Wycliffite influence in Yorkshire could produce on the one hand the radical rejections of clerical authority and image worship in a text like the *Apology for Lollard Doctrines* and on the other the cautious emphasis in the sermons on the importance of vernacular Scripture apart from its more extreme political implications.

THE STRIFE OF INTERPRETATION

The advocacy of a common language to convey a literal and "open" sense of Scripture is the social ideology of the Wycliffite sermons that resurfaces most clearly in the York plays. The Sermon for the Sunday after Advent includes a full elaboration of Lollard hermeneutic principles, extrapolated from the interpretation of the dove as the Holy Spirit in John 1:32:

In þis mote men undirstonde diversite in wordis and to what entent þes wordis ben undirstondene. And þus by auctorite of þe lawe of God schulde men speke her wordis as Godis lawe spekiþ and straunge not in speche from the undirstondyng of þe peple, and algates be war that þe puple undirstonde wel, and so use comun speche in þer owne persone; and, ȝif thei spekon in Cristes person wordis of his lawe, loke þat þei declaren hem for drede of pryve errour. (*EWS*, 1:347–48)

In this lucid characterization of the preacher's own language, the defense of the Lollard idiom gives way to a politics of audience, aligning the true expression of God's law with a common understanding newly invested with legitimacy. As Rita Copeland argues, the Lollard ideal of the "open" text "takes on [a] political inflection of public rights and common accessibility."[21] The terms that determine the meaning of Scripture come, in this theory, from the people themselves rather than a clerical "tradition"; the vernacular has more authority than Latin for the very reason that it is a public rather than a "privy" language. As the sermon finishes: "And þus the comun undyrstondyng schulden we algatis holde, but ȝif Godes wordis tauȝten us his propre sence. And such *strif* in wordis is of no profiȝt, ne proveþ not that Goddis word is in ony wey false. In þis mater we han inow *stryven* in Latyn wiþ adversaries of Godis lawe, that seyn þat hit is the falsest of alle lawes in þis world þat evere God suffrede" (*EWS*, 1:348–49, emphasis added). Echoing Wyclif's position against subjecting scriptural language to the methods of scholastic logic, the preacher calls on the common understanding to uphold biblical meaning in much the same way as Wyclif had invoked the authority of secular lords to defend the Bible from clerical fictions.[22] Above all, the common understanding is here contrary to the "strife" of the Latin exegetes who would obscure Scripture, an image of language as fuel for a kind of interpretive faction. The preacher, renouncing even the Lollards' own part in such debates, speaks both from and to an imagined position of consensus in "common" English.

Other sermons, like the Palm Sunday text, inveigh against the conspiracy of prelates to hide the true sense of the Bible with glosses, a practice elsewhere in the cycle explicitly treated as the "tyranny" of the clergy: "And herfore þei seyn þat Godis lawe is false, but ȝif þei gloson it after þat þei wolen; and þus þer gloos schulde be trowed as byleve of cristen men, but þe tixt of Godis lawe is perelows to trowe" (*EWS*, 1:424–25). Denouncing the collusion of secular powers in this clerical outrage, the preacher continues: "and herfore þei make statutes stable as a stoon, and geton graunt of knytes to confermen hem, and þese þei marken wel wiþ witnesse of lordis, leste that trewþe of Godis lawe hid in þe sepulchre berste owt to knowyng of comun puple" (1:426). In another Sunday gospel sermon, the preacher condemns the "sects" of friars, monks, and canons in terms of a metaphor of psychological and social division:

> And þat þei seyn þat þei ben herberys bettur than comun pastur, for eerbys of vertew that growen in hem;— certes, makyng of eerberys in a comun pasture wolde destruye þe pasture and lyfe of the comunys boþe for dychyng and heggyng and delvyng of turuys. And, ȝif we marke alle syche eerberys in Englond þat be plantyd of newe in comune Cristis religioun, as þei spuylen þe remenaunt of temporal goodys, so (þat is more duyl) þei spuylen hem of vertewes: for alle cristen men schulden ben of o wille, and variaunce in syche sectis makyþ variaunce in wille, and gendreþ discensioun and envye among men. (*EWS,* 1:266)

The "life of the commons," both economic and ethical, is threatened by the friars' attempts to divide the common will and common "maner of lyvyng" into "arbors," in the interests of private property and private theological discourse. The Lollard sermons' efforts to define their own community or audience, an abstract body of the "people" possessing a single will or understanding of Scripture, depend on exposing the language of the institutional church, whether Latin exegesis or false metaphor, as the source of all conflict.[23]

In practical political terms, the Lollard preachers' work in establishing a common language ultimately rests on the support of the same secular powers who are otherwise helping prelates to imprison the Word. In the sermons, the lords assume a distinct religious identity by taking responsibility for lay devotion. As the Lollard version of the *Lay Folks' Catechism* declares, following Wyclif, "secler lordys schuld in defawte of prelatys lerne and preche þe lawe of god in here modyr tonge."[24] In a long passage on the church's persecution of Lollard translators in Sermon 66, in the *Commune Sanctorum,* the preacher emphasizes the role of "knights" in countering church authority:

> And herefore o greet buschop of Englond, as men seyn, is yvel payed þat Godis lawe is wryton in Englisch to lewede men; and he purseweþ a preest for he wrytuþ to men þis Englysch, and somneþ hym and traveyluþ hym, that it is hard to hym to rowte. And þus he pursewede anoþur preest by þe help of pharisees, for he prechede Cristus gospel frely wiþowte fables. . . .

> But o counfort is of knyʒtus, that þei saveron myche þe gospel, and han wylle
> to redon in Englisch the gospel of Cristus lyʒf.[25]

What the sermon most forcefully evokes is the *desire* of lay rulers for Scripture,
the "will" that leads them away from the bishop and his "pharisees" toward the
"lewd men" or commons and demands both the translation and interpretation
of the gospel.[26]

In the York plays, the issues of language and secular power raised by the Wycliffite sermons, as well as their anticlericalism, are translated into the very different political vocabulary of civic rule. In its most costly and significant cultural
production, the "oligarchic" or "magisterial" government of the city indirectly answers the Lollards' call for a secular defense of the Bible with a metamorphosis
of ideology. Lawrence Clopper has convincingly presented the case for the cycle
plays in northern cities as the province of civic government alone, arguing that
even the playwrights were not necessarily clerical, given the availability of English
devotional texts like the *Northern Passion* and the *Meditations on the Life of Christ*
for laypeople to use as models. For Clopper, "[T]he curious fact is not that these
plays were intended to instruct but that the providers of the instruction were
secular guildsmen and secular governments rather than the clergy."[27] The York
plays' authors and directors, working from Lollard-influenced English sermons
in the likely repertoire of lay reading still at their disposal in the 1420s and 1430s,
adapt Wycliffite concepts of secular exegetical authority and "common speech" to
the political desires of all participants. Both the city's mercantile governors and the
guild artisans or "commonality" act their parts in the invention of this new dramatic public discourse.[28]

STRIFE IN THE CITY

The secular urban ideology that encompasses the plays' understanding of the commons and the vernacular comes out of formulations that, following Susan Reynolds's terms, could loosely be called "republican" rhetorical thought in English
civic government. While a brief "custumal" detailing the duties of York's mayor
and municipal officials survives, records that might have provided a more extensive conceptual account of civic government, like the York *Liber Albus,* unfor-
tunately do not.[29] Since Reynolds, however, demonstrates that the vocabularies
cities used to define their governments were fairly uniform in thirteenth- and

fourteenth-century England, I rely on a document from London to theorize a broader municipal understanding of the politics of rhetoric, interpretation, and will.[30] The work that illuminates this cluster of political ideas is a version of part of Brunetto Latini's *Livres dou tresor* that the London chamberlain Andrew Horn included in the *Liber Legum Regum Antiquorum,* a collection from the 1320s of guild ordinances, charters, and trade regulations.[31] In a fascinating translation of theory directly into practice as recorded custom, London city officials, changing the original text's terminology only slightly, take up the Florentine encyclopedist's advice on how citizens should choose a city governor and how such a governor should behave in office. Beginning with the importance of counsel for burgesses electing a just, wise, and fiscally responsible mayor, the *Tresor,* adjusted to fit these offices, warns against basing the choice on money and connections rather than virtue: "[W]ar and hatred are multiplied here and elsewhere in cities and towns because of the division of the commons and the diversity of *will* (*volente*) of the two parties of citizens."[32] The London *Tresor* extracts, all from the final section of book 3 on rhetoric and politics, retain Latini's Ciceronian emphasis on proper language as the basis of civic rule. Public speech numbers among the twelve qualities of a good ruler: "[I]t is appropriate for a governor to speak better than other people because everyone considers the person who speaks wisely to be wise."[33] The *Tresor* extracts go on to warn the mayor to guard against excessive talking and the theatrical performances of "*janglers,*" among other forms of rhetorical discord:

> Also you ought to beware of laughing too much. For it is written that laughter is in the mouth of the fool. And you can still laugh and play sometimes, but not in the manner of a child or a woman and not in a way that seems false or haughty. He who is good in other things will be feared all the more when he shows a serious visage, especially when he is seated to hear pleas. Also you must not praise yourself, even though the good praise you; and do not get upset if the bad don't praise you. And beware of *gengleours,* who praise you to your face.[34]

Moreover, a good mayor must further settle pleas quickly without raising strife and mete out punishment or "deeds of cruelty" like a king, for the common good, rather than like a tyrant, for his own pleasure.[35]

As will become clear from looking at how the Passion sequence of the York plays envisions city rule, the ideas in Latini's hugely popular handbook were as prescriptive for York a century later as they were for London.[36] As many critics have pointed out, the Corpus Christi plays were not only a civic ceremony but also an integral part of York's corporate government.[37] The plays were perhaps the main concern of the guilds, with half the fines levied by the searchers, the guild officials who policed regulations of labor and product quality, typically going toward production of the play and the other half going to the city council. Moreover, the meetings of the city council that specifically dealt with the production of the plays appear to be virtually the only occasions on which the "forty-eight," the representative body of artisans, had even a minor role in civic decisions.[38] The "forty-eight," a shadowy collection of guildsmen who complemented the actual ruling structure of the mayor, twelve aldermen, and the "twenty-four" further representatives of the mercantile class, defined the theoretical authority of the commons, consenting formally to the decisions of the council or participating in the symbolic "election" of the mayor from one of three aldermen, without wielding any real power.[39] The voice of the commons, if always muted, is most clearly heard in documents like the 1399 petition to the mayor and aldermen to limit the number of stations where the plays would be acted to allow for a one-day show, reminding them that "the said pageants are maintained and supported by the commons and the craftsmen of the same city in honor and reverence of our Lord Jesus Christ and for the glory and benefit of the same city" and demanding that "these matters be performed or otherwise the said play shall not be performed by the aforesaid commons."[40]

The question of how the commons expressed themselves within the formal constraints of the plays is a matter of some debate. Sarah Beckwith has examined Heather Swanson's extensive historical research on York's artisan class for what the extant documents reveal about drama. Although the plays themselves served the government's agenda of regulating the workforce by maintaining the guilds' strict artificial divisions of labor, they also, she argues, advanced an "artisanal ideology" at odds with the cultural ideals of the mercantile elite.[41] While Beckwith concentrates on the plays' representations of acts of manufacturing or "making" as the artisans' code to voice their social and political identity, I focus instead on the plays' negotiations between the municipal government and the commons in their treatment of disparate civic and Lollard-derived ideas of collective will or intention. In the performance of political authority that initiated the production calendar for the plays, six sergeants-at-arms of the mayor delivered the *sedule paginarum,* or scripts, to the guilds during Lent.[42] While the city enacted its control over these biblical texts with such notable fanfare, however, the guilds' collaboration and theatrical interpretation remained the condition for not only a continuous sacred narrative but a coherent civic ideology.

READING CITIZENS: THE *ENTRY INTO JERUSALEM*

As Martin Stevens demonstrates in his consideration of the York plays in the ceremonial context provided by the city's two Memorandum Books, the skinners' pageant of the *Entry into Jerusalem* occupies the conceptual center of the cycle.[43] In Stevens's account, the play recapitulates the forms of both the liturgical procession of the Host through the city on Corpus Christi and the royal entry ceremony, defining the occasion as a symbolic connecting of sacred and secular histories. But what Stevens ignores by his focus on the *Entry* play's ceremonial and ritual evocation of York as Jerusalem, with Jesus as the "King of Kings," is the text's attention to the distinct vocabulary of civic government as the basis of its version of scriptural interpretation.[44] In fourteenth- and fifteenth-century civic triumphs, exegesis functions only to magnify the ruler's grandeur; indeed, as Gordon Kipling shows, pageants devised for royal entries emphasize the liturgical imagery of Christ's final advent to the Heavenly Jerusalem rather than the Palm Sunday advent.[45] The temporality of exegetical practice is already, in these displays, fulfilled; no possibility of further interpretation remains. Richard II's entry into London in 1392, for example, celebrated him as the heavenly *sponsus* of Song of Songs commentaries returning to his *sponsa*'s — London's — bridal chamber.[46] Similarly, when the prophets of Christ's advent appear in civic triumphs, they serve only to formally greet the ruler and confer their biblical authority, as exemplified by the entry of Margaret of Anjou and Prince Edward to Coventry in 1456.[47] In the York plays, by contrast, exegesis adheres to an entirely different concept of the political process.

    The skinners' pageant presents an idealized account of the principles of rule by ancient tradition and consensus recorded in the York custumal, the codification of the mayor's court, mayoral elections, and oaths to be taken by the various city officials.[48] Together with the guidelines for the sheriff's court created by the 1396 charter from Richard II that established York as a county (a transcript, actually, from the record of the London sheriff's court), this document provides the justification for an oligarchy theoretically grounded on the consent of "tut la commonealte" (the entire commons). The court held by the mayor and aldermen in the Guildhall to deal with violations of civic and guild ordinances gives orders (*treiter et ordiner*) for the "governance of the city for the maintenance of the peace of our lord the king [and] for the profit of those who live in the city."[49] The mayor's oath is to uphold justice (*comune droit*) for rich and poor alike; the oath for the thirty-six members of the city council is to "counsel, assist and support" the mayor "for love and profit (*lamour et prouffite*) for both the said mayor and the city." The commonality of the city, while raising their hands, are given the same oath of counsel.[50] Similar appeals to the "common profit" underwrite the guilds' written expressions of identity: the skinners' own ordinances begin with an appeal to the mayor to grant the recorded points "pur profit du dit artifice et pur comune profit du poeple."[51] These terms are, of course, simply York's version of a language of common liberties and common will that, as Reynolds shows, was much the same in the records of all late medieval western European cities.[52] The *Entry* play, produced with the fines paid by recalcitrant artisans to the searchers and pageant masters, demonstrates a recognition on the part of city and guild that the "republican" ideal of governance by counsel raises broader problems of interpretation and language that, like the Lollards' polemics, demand a theory of common understanding.

The shift from the description of the skinners' pageant in the 1415 *Ordo Paginarum,* calling for "six rich men and six poor men," to the play extant in the manuscript, which celebrates the rule of eight rich men or "citizens chief," doubtlessly reflects the "growing polarization of merchant and artisan" during the fifteenth century that Swanson finds characteristic of York's overall civic development.[53] Yet the *Ordo* leaves us with a tantalizing trace of a play that took all strata of the urban community into account as public figures, allowing for at least the rhetorical representation of poor artisans and possibly for even poorer unemployed or homeless people.[54] The surviving play, however, probably a product of a period of large-scale revision of the entire cycle that those critics who dare place roughly between 1420 and 1440, presents the mercantile class as fully in charge of public discourse. The one "Pauper" is duly relegated to a brief role in the section at the end of the play recounting Jesus' healing of the blind man and absolution of the tax collector Zacheus (Luke 18–19), transposed from Jericho to Jerusalem itself. Yet it is ultimately guildsmen, representing on stage the aldermen who—in theory—politically represent them, who are responsible for interpreting and conveying the play's sense of counsel. While Stevens comments that the skinners "flatter" their governors by reenacting their rhetorical and political skills, they also disconcertingly claim these skills for themselves, straining the play's implicit ideological division between imagined and practiced rule.[55]

The premise of the *Entry into Jerusalem* is that nothing less than the fulfill-ment of prophecy depends on the smooth working of civic government. As Jesus phrases the problem in his opening instructions to his disciples, they must find an ass for him to ride upon, "So þe prophicy *clere menyng* / May be fulfillid here in þis place" (24–25, emphasis added).[56] In "this place," York, the prophecy must be not only carried out, as in the historical Jerusalem, but rightly understood, that is, the allegorical sense of the Old Testament text translated and made plain to the people of the city. Throughout the play, the Lollard appeal to a common and open exegetical language reverberates as the basis of an authentic vernacular civic discourse. The initial problem of governance is to resolve a dispute over the ass as common property. The apostle Philip interprets *common* here according to its most general sense:

> The beestis are comen, wele I knawe.
> Therfore us nedis to aske lesse leve;
> And our maister kepis þe lawe
> We may þame take tyter, I preve.
> (57–60)

The gatekeeper—an actual municipal official described in the York custumal as a "prudhomme," a wise man chosen by the mayor and council—reinstates the civic meaning, demanding signs of citizenship:[57]

> Saie, what are ȝe that makis here maistrie
> To loose þes bestis withoute leverie?
> Yow semes to bolde sen noght þat ȝe
> Hase here to do.
> (64–67)

The idea of common property here provides an occasion for the ideal community to demonstrate its mechanisms for sound rule by negotiation: the gatekeeper weighs the apostles' lack of city livery against their "intente" (73), or account of Jesus as "God and man withouten blame" (83), and decides by "gode resoune" (75) to give them the ass. The gatekeeper then proposes to "declare playnly" (93) Jesus' coming to the chief citizens "þat þey may sone / Assemble same to his metyng" (95). He calls the council together, firmly stressing its main function as the sup-pression of discord:

For his comyng I will þam mete
To late þam witte, withoute debate
Lo, wher þei stande,
The citizens cheff withoute debate
Of all þis lande.

(108–12)

With this, the core of the play begins, the collective process by which the eight
"burgenses" or aldermen present their case for secular authority over Scripture
and, in the process, translate the vocabulary of urban government into a method
of exegesis. Scriptural interpretation here takes the form of civic dialogue "without debate." Two of the burgesses recount in turn Jesus' miracles, establishing
their rhetorical style in terms of the narrative coherence of Christ's life; a third
cuts to the chase by posing the crisis of the New Law:

In our tempill if he prechid
Agaynste þe pepull þat leved wrong
And also new lawes if he teched
Agaynste oure lawis we used so lang,
And saide pleynlye
The olde schall waste, þe new schall gang,
þat we schall see.

(141–47)

Legitimation by custom alone — by laws in use for a long time — is insufficient
and must give way to the priority of language and the counsel, argument, and persuasion of a wisely chosen representative body. The burgesses exemplify something like Latini's Ciceronian "bone parleure," the combination of eloquence and
good sense necessary for any civil association, but raise the stakes of good speaking considerably by making it also do the work of good reading.[58] In this exegetical formulation of civic discourse, however, the means by which the aldermen would rhetorically negotiate the traditions or history of the city becomes a
kind of allegoresis by committee, with the "pleyn" text of the Old Testament under
consideration. Punctuating their speeches with "ʒa's" of consensus, the burgesses
present "arguments" that are actually interpretations of scriptural passages foretelling Christ's coming. As one of them recalls Jesus' own accounts of "Moyses
lawe" and the prophets:

He telles þam so þat ilke a man may fele
And what þei say interly knowe
Yf þei were dyme.
What þe prophettis saide in þer sawe
All longis to hym.

(150–54)

The prophecies are all thus enunciated not only as the "plain," "clear," or "open"
sense of the text but as public knowledge, accessible to every man. Another burgess announces the prophecy of Isaiah, "þus saide *full clere:* / Loo, a maydyn þat
knew nevere ille / A childe schuld bere," and yet another affirms that "David
spake of hym I wene / And lefte witnesse *ȝe knowe ilkone*" (159–63, emphasis
added). In this city council, the secular "common understanding" of the Bible
prevails over any possible strife among the burgesses; in striking similarity to
the Lollard hermeneutic position taken in opposition to the divisions of clerical interpretation, the "clear" vernacular Scripture here supports a single secular communal will.

Jesus is duly "elected" king by the eight citizens, though the ceremony—
in the notable absence throughout the play of a magisterial figure—has as much
affinity with an ideally conceived mayoral election as with a royal entry. Having
reached narrative unity, the burgesses must still agree to act in the name of a civic
will, a process that carries them through one hundred or so lines of further delib-
erations. As the final burgess to speak summarizes the "exegetical" assembly:

Sirs, methynkyth ȝe saie right wele
And gud ensampelys furth ȝe bryng,
And sen we þus þis mater fele
Go we hym meete as oure owne kyng,
And kyng hym call.
What is youre counsaill in þis thyng?
Now say ȝe all.

(169–75)

The point of the next round of counsel is to translate textual "examples" into action. Before the burgesses can actually welcome Christ into the city, they must
voice not only their agreement on the meaning of Scripture according to "reason" but their common desire to have him as their ruler. As one burgess puts it:

"And hym to mete I am right bayne / On þe best maner þat I cane, / For I desire
to see hym fayne" (218–20). The burgesses' will is figured as a form of mutual
persuasion, a disavowal of any factions in favor of perfect hermeneutic clarity. The
citizens, moreover, freely attribute their consensus on interpretation to each other's
rhetorical abilities. One describes his experience as a devotional education by way
of civic argument: "Of your clene witte and your consayte / I am full gladde in
harte and þought" (246–47). The next echoes him, meshing, to an even greater de-
gree, the idioms of urban counsel and devotion, expressions of both collective
and inner desire for Christ:

> 3oure argumentis þai are so clere
> I can no3t saie but graunte you till,
> For whanne I of þat counsaille here
> I coveyte hym with fervent wille
> Onys for to see,
> I trowe fro þens I schall
> Bettir man be.
>
> (253–59)

With the final decision of the burgesses to meet Christ in a procession, singing in
"unysoune" (262), or perfect harmony, the *Entry* play completes its double work
of legitimating the vernacular language of civic governance and of extolling a lay
exegesis performed in the same language, wholly under the control of secular authorities. While as Stevens points out, Jesus' grim words foretelling the destruction
of the city, ending with "agayne þi king þou hast trespast, / Have þis in mynde"
(480–81), look ahead to the Passion plays and a less optimistic view of worldly
rule, the pageant's final ceremony in which the burgesses formally hail Christ fully
expresses the idea of political accord. Their civic agreement is stable enough to
sustain biblical interpretation through the voices of representatives. Reiterating
the theme of reading by common will, the seventh of the eight aldermen speaks
to and for York in a new governing vernacular:

> Hayll texte of trewthe þe trew to taste
> Hayll king and sire,
> Hayll maydens chylde þat menskid hir most,
> We þe desire.
>
> (534–37)

As in the Wycliffite sermons, vernacularity is here defined as a sign of communal spiritual desire. The threat of civic strife, which is suggested in order to be quelled in the skinners' pageant, nonetheless keeps its edge in light of the play's own theatrical challenge of letting the guild's representative moment so thoroughly take over the city council's self-definition. Early incarnations of the play may well have answered to an immediate instance of faction — either between merchants and artisans or within the mercantile oligarchy itself — such as took hold in the revolts of 1380–81, during which the commonality expelled the mayor, John de Gisburne, from office. As R. B. Dobson has written of how artisans conducted the fourteenth-century uprisings in York, Beverley, and Scarborough through the channels of municipal government, "[T]he evidence available bears witness to a remarkably self-confident and articulate commons, almost obsessively litigious and incapable of forgetting some private or public wrong."[59] The skinners' pageant in its surviving post-*Ordo* form denies its artisan actors a political voice, yet the ideological means that it advances to suppress strife — the institution of a common idiom figured as lay exegesis — could easily be taken as a good argument for the inclusion of the commons in actual as well as symbolic governance. While the play bears the influence of a Lollard-inflected politics of interpretation, however, it is no surprise that it fails to follow through on the full antihierarchical implications of an "open" exegesis. If the *Entry* play, as it emerges in the fifteenth century, as an ongoing collaboration between oligarchy and guild, stages its republican ideal of consensus only to reveal a more pervasive strife, the Passion plays that follow it directly take on the representation of misrule.

FALLING STANDARDS: THE *JUDGEMENT OF CHRIST BEFORE PILATE*

The logic of authority in the *Entry* play, which identifies civic rule with allegoresis, sets the stage for the Passion plays, in which consensus disintegrates into political and hermeneutic tyranny. Where the *Entry* play celebrates language and rhetorical negotiation as the basis of an intelligibility of both sacred and secular narratives necessary for any rule, the so-called "tyrant" plays present a devastating attack on political rhetoric as practiced by both secular and ecclesiastical powers. As Stevens puts it, the atmosphere of the York Passion sequence is "an urban nightmare of treachery, abuse, injustice, torture, and utter disorder."[60] It is, in short, an inversion of the public space rhetorically created by the *Entry* play.

A specifically republican dynamic of power is at work in the York Passion plays. According to Randolph Starn and Loren Partridge's interpretation of the social psychology behind the diabolical image of tyranny in Lorinzetti's "Allegory of Bad Government" in Siena's Palazzo Pubblico, the legitimacy of the city-republic depends on the citizens' displacing anxieties about their own tyrannical proclivities at all levels of authority onto an all-powerful, arbitrary central figure.[61] Similarly, York's collective civic identity, defined against the competing jurisdictions of the royal government and the church, is constructed primarily against its own mirror image of failed rule. The "tyrant" plays could thus be read to reflect especially traumatic periods in York's political history — the suspension of the city's liberties by Henry IV after the Scrope Rebellion in 1405–6, for instance — or the ongoing feuds between urban authorities and various church establishments that occupy the Memorandum Books. Above all, they serve to depict the conceptual collapse of the governance by common interpretation and will carried out by the *Entry* play's citizen-rulers.[62]

All of the plays involving the trials of Christ open with a speech by the tyrant of the hour, staking a rhetorical claim to absolute powers of judgment. In the cases of Pilate and Herod, the basis of the pronouncement is force; in the case of Cayphas in the bowers' and fletchers' play, it is clerical learning. As the high priest boasts:

> By connyng of clergy and castyng of witte
> Full wisely my wordis I welde at my will,
> So semely in seete me semys for to sitte
> And þe lawe for to lerne you and lede it by skill,
> Right sone.
>
> (5–9)

This is a prelude to the series of willful "misreadings" by various authorities of Jesus' life and words that ends with the crucifixion. The idea of tyrannical misinterpretation, reading without the benefit of counsel, is especially pronounced in Pilate's repeated "ranting" public decrees of his authority. In the *Remorse of Judas,* he warns his court to "stynte with your stevenyng so stowte / or with þis brande þat dere is to doute / All to dede I schall dryve you þis day" (6–8); he then exhibits a grotesque self-involvement parodic of the moderate ruler's love for his community:

> My forhed both brente is and brade
> And myne eyne þei glittir like the gleme in þe glasse.

And þe hore þat hillis my heed
Is even like to þe gold wyre
My chekis are bothe ruddy and reede
And my coloure as cristall is cleere.

(20–25)

Pilate is his own best court-poet and indeed courtly object of desire; his "clarity" is the political opposite of the clear language of the citizen-exegetes, with his power grounded only in the "text" of his person in its various blazoned, fragmented parts. His "clarity" and his "color," in the sense of rhetorical amplification, are literally identical in these speeches, as the catalog of formal praise that institutes tyranny and demands obedience in the form of stylistic imitation. In the York plays' projection of courtly discourse, then, the exegetical arguments of the *Entry* play are replaced by an arbitrary method of interpretation entirely subject to political power. Counsel, ungrounded in any textual form, becomes a transparent repetition of the tyrant's desire and style.

In the York tilemakers' pageant of the *Judgement,* Jesus speaks only once, to distill the play's theme of silence and language:

Every man has a mouthe þat is made on molde
In wele and in woo to welde at his will.
If he governe it gudly like as God wolde
For his spirituale speche hym thar not to spill.
And what gome so governe it ill,
Full unhendly and ill sall he happe;
Of ilk tale þou talkis us untill
þou accounte sall, þou cannot escappe.

(300–307)

A distinctive extension of Christ's words of defense to Pilate in the play's source, the Middle English *Gospel of Nicodemus,* the climactic lines drive home the overall emphasis of the York Corpus Christi cycle on issues of political rhetoric.[63] The governance of "spiritual speech," as Jesus puts it here, grounds the government of the city.

From Pilate's opening speech in the *Judgement,* echoing several earlier colorful alliterative tirades, we are in a morass of rhetorical misrule, vacillating between praise of the court and wild threats:

Lordyngis that are lymett to þe lare of my liaunce,
3e schappely schalkes and schene for to schawe,
I charge 3ou as 3our chiftan that 3e chatt for no chaunce,
But loke to your lord here and lere at my lawe—
As a duke I may dampne 3ou and drawe.
Many bernys bold are aboute me,
And what knyght or knave I may knawe
Þat list no3t as a lord for to lowte me
I sall lere hym
In the develes name, þat dastard, to doubt me—
3a, who werkis any werkes without me
I sall charge hym in chynes to chere him.
Tharfore 3e lusty ledes within þis lenght lapped,
Do stynt of 3oure stalkyng and of stoutnes be stalland
What traytoure his tong with tales has trapped,
That fende for his flateryng full foull sal be falland.
What broll overe-brathely is bralland
Or unsoftely will sege in þer sales
Þat caysteffe þus carpand and calland
As a boy sall be brought unto bales.
Þerefore
Talkes not nor trete not of tales,
For þat gome þat gyrnes or gales
I myself sall hym hurt ful sore.

(1–24)

Pilate's announcement of his intention to violently suppress all "tales"—abuses of language—is itself an exercise in self-reflexive rhetorical excess: he establishes his political power over his subjects with bludgeoning repetitiveness but gives no indication of how, either legally or logically, he intends to distinguish false claims or "tales" (or, in Lollard terms, "fables") from truth.[64] In this "republican" projection of tyranny, Pilate bases his rule on the strife he himself invokes, with no governing apparatus to negotiate or resolve it. Within the framework of the York plays' overall effort to stage an account of biblical narrative as a form of public political discourse, Pilate's self-indicting lack of any interpretive scheme becomes a problem of secular exegesis.

In the *Judgement* pageant, only unspeaking objects, the imperial banners that fall at Christ's feet, act in consensus, a gesture that is at best politically ambivalent, especially since the play emphasizes the slapstick incomprehension of two sets of burly standard bearers over the submission and reverence of these images. Banners, however, are historically central to the conception and governance of the York plays as a whole and the tilemakers' play in particular. In both 1399 and 1417, the council decreed "by common consent" that the stations where the plays were going to be put on would be marked by banners bearing the arms of the city, delivered by the mayor to the citizens who were responsible for the scaffolds and then promptly returned to the "hands" (*manus*) of the mayor and chamberlains after the play on penalty of a fine of 6s. 8d. to go toward the "work of the commons."[65] Moreover, in the final agreement of 1432 that assigned responsibility for the play to the tilemakers (with the saucemakers, hayresters, and millers contributing financially), the city claimed a symbolic priority over the guilds: "[N]one of the aforesaid four crafts may place any signs, arms or insignia upon the foresaid pageant, except the arms of this honorable city."[66] The *real* banners, representing the integrity and power of York's government by delimiting the route of the play via the houses of its wealthier citizens, would have presented, in the staging of the *Judgement,* a problematic visual identification of the city arms with the bowing play-banners. The dramatic moment, moreover, would have begged the question of a unified interpretation of this apparent division of will between the performing guild and the city government, theater and rule, devotional iconoclasm and power always in danger of becoming an object of idolatry.[67]

In the play, both the tyrannical rulers and their subjects are entirely unable to "read" the banners, failing in their rhetorical inventions to align words and intentions. As one of the standard bearers formally addresses Pilate and the priests:

> We beseke you and tho senioures beside ʒou sir sitte
> With none of oure governaunce to be grevous and gryll,
> For it lay not in our lott þer launces to lett,
> And þis werke þat we have wrought *it was not oure will.*
> (180–84, emphasis added)

Pilate compounds this essentially nonsensical disclaiming of agency ("we worked without meaning to") while still claiming "governance" by finding new and bigger standard bearers who boast in vain that they will hold the banners up, echoing their governor's own excesses:

> I, certayne I saie as for myne,
> Whan it sattles or sadly discendis

Whare I stand —
When it wryngis or wronge it wendis,
Outher bristis, barkis, or bendes —
Hardly let hakke of myn hande.

(246–51)

The confusion over language created by the silent solidarity of the banners with the silent Christ reflects the play's overall concern with misinterpretation. In contrast to the *Entry* play's hermeneutic ideal, Scripture — in the narrative form of the things that Jesus has supposedly said and done — is subjected to systematic misreading by the "prelates" Annas and Cayphas. Most of the interminable squabbling between the priests and Pilate, however, concerns the understanding of speech itself. Pilate at first encourages the priests' obsequious words:

ʒoure praysing is prophetable ʒe prelates of pees
Gramercy ʒoure goode word, and ungayne sall it noʒt you.
That ʒe will say the sothe and for no sege cese.

(37–39)

But when Cayphas offers to provide a list of witnesses to Jesus' teachings, claiming "þer tales for trewe can they telle" (117), Pilate questions their motives: "ʒa, tussch for your tales, þai touche not entente" (120). Or, in another exchange, Pilate threatens, "For me likis noght youre langage so large" (130), to which Cayphas protests that he should bring Jesus to trial:

Oure langage is to large, but ʒoure lordshipp releve us.
ʒitt we both beseke you late bryng hym to barre;
What poyntes þat we put forth latt your presence appreve us.

(131–34)

Despite his discernment that the priests' narratives of Jesus are false — in the sense at least that their "tales" don't match their intentions — Pilate cannot construct a coherent narrative out of his own will, especially since, as his soldiers inform him, Jesus remained stubbornly silent before Herod in the previous play: "For all þe lordis langage his lipps, ser, wer lame; / For any spirringes in þat space no speche walde he spell" (63–64). Pilate's tyrannical rhetoric, limited to reiterations of his own power, is entirely resistant to the secular exegetical discourse of the idealized York burgesses, the "truth" he claims to be seeking in the so-called trial. His argument with the priests ultimately ends in an explosion of violence as he orders Jesus' scourging. As the soldiers in this protracted scene lovingly describe each blow with "brasshis," "lasshes," "swappes," "rappes," and "flappes," words and will are finally identical, but only in a brutal inversion of the interpretive act. The torturers' hermeneutic is imagined as a tyrannical desire for cruelty in response to the logic of the Incarnation itself; when the soldiers finish beating Jesus, they present his "*corpus*" (429) to Pilate.

Ultimately, Jesus' one pronouncement warns of the fragility of "spiritual speech," that is, Scripture itself, under secular authority; only a government founded on sound rhetorical principles can carry out York's civic ambitions of lay exegesis. The tilemakers' Christ, commenting on the good and bad governance of language, sounds more than a little like Brunetto Latini on the ideal city governor: "Above all else he should be careful not to speak too much because excessive speaking cannot be without error. Just as one string untunes (*une corde descorde*) a whole zither (*cytole*), one bad word destroys the honor of all one's reason."[68] Civic discord, the demon haunting the York plays' uneasy collaboration between mercantile leaders and guildsmen, becomes in Christ's voice the unintelligibility of sacred narrative, the loss of biblical meaning itself threatened in the Lollard sermons' pleas for a common language. For the citizen-players as much as for Pilate, the unstrung tyrant, there is no escape from the bad word of politics or, for that matter, from the dangers of raucous theatricality.

The York *Entry into Jerusalem* and *Judgement* demonstrate the city's absorption of Lollard hermeneutic ideas, filtered through English sermons, into a wider conceptual matrix of rhetoric and government. The common interpretive "will" that the Lollard sermons set forth as the basis of authentic Christian exegesis becomes, in the vernacular plays, the political will that can either unite the burgesses in their civic and theological purposes or dissolve under the interpretive chaos of tyrannical rule. As the Wycliffite Palm Sunday text admonishes, the guildsmen and their rulers must strive, when the play is over, to surpass Pilate and know the truth of God's law in English.

Naked Visions

*Sometyme Satanas his aungel desgisiþ him as þeyჳ he were an
angel of liჳt and makeþ siche images to begile and deceyve men to his
purpos, whanne me trowiþ him in doinges that beþ opunlich goode.*

—Bartholomaeus Anglicus,
On the Properties of Things, Liber VI, Cap. 27

In the York *Nativity* play, a dramatization of St. Bridget of Sweden's vision of
the scene in her voluminous *Revelations,* Mary experiences the birth of Jesus
as a moment of the highest contemplative ecstasy:

> Nowe in my sawle grete joie have I
> I am cladde in comforte clere,
> Now will be borne of my body
> Both God and Man togedir in feere,
> Blist mott he be.
> Jesu my son þat is so dere,
> Nowe borne is he.
>
> (50–56)[1]

St. Bridget describes the Virgin's prayer, itself identical with the process of birth in gesture and language, in terms at once concrete and beyond words. As the Middle English translation, the *Liber Celestis,* renders it:

> And when sho had made all redi, sho knelide downe with grete reverens and praied, and sett hir bake againe þe cribe, and turned hir visage to þe este and helde up hir handes and her een up into þe heven, and sho was raised in contemplacion with so gret a swetnes þat hard it is to tell. (486)[2]

The themes of this prayer, in which Mary's soul and body together produce the clear vision of Christ, are explored further in the rest of the play: Jesus appears both in his humanity, as the "sweet thing" that Joseph sees on Mary's knee, and in his divinity, as a bright light that suffuses the stage. Mary's intimate devotional praise of Jesus after the delivery—"Hayle my lord God, hayle prince of pees, / Hayle my fadir, and hayle my sone" (57–58)—echoes through the rest of the York plays in the more public declarations of Symeon and Anna the Prophetess in the temple in the *Purification* and finally of the Burgesses in the *Entry into Jerusalem.*

I begin with this inaugural moment of contemplation and meditation in the York plays to raise the problem of publicly staging visionary narratives, especially those authored by women. St. Bridget's vision of the Nativity exemplifies her specular identification with Mary as a contemplative who knows and enjoys Christ through her body and spirit.[3] It became one of her most authoritative additions to the Gospels, accounting for the physical appearances of both mother and child right down to the divinely glowing afterbirth, "liand all white" on the ground beside the Virgin (*Liber Celestis,* 486).[4] By reenacting the vision on stage, the York *Nativity* fully embodies images that are understood to mediate between body and spirit, subjecting the very idea of "contemplative" drama to a set of concerns over representation, imagination, and "discretion" that emerge in late-fourteenth-century English mystical writing.

That the Middle English cycle plays are heavily indebted to the Franciscan devotional tradition, with its affective emphasis on Jesus' humanity, is a commonplace of criticism.[5] At one of its levels, the drama functions as a communal vernacular version of the Pseudo-Bonaventuran *Meditations on the Life of Christ,* projecting actors and audience into the directed "visualizations" of the Poor Clare on Christ's physical experiences, inviting them, like her, to read with desire, "to contemplate, explain and understand the Holy Scriptures in as many ways as we consider necessary." [6] Like the *Meditations*' "incarnational stylistics," the plays fictively create or remember the historical setting of biblical narrative from "the varying interpretations of the mind" and a wealth of imaginative detail.[7]

While the mystery plays demonstrate the influence of any number of meditative devotional works, the York cycle also includes a strange and dazzling play, the *Dream of Pilate's Wife,* that presents a deeply ambivalent assessment of the relationship between contemplative practices and theatricality. More specifically, the play considers women's visionary authority as a potential threat to scriptural interpretation, a dangerously excessive form of knowledge and writing that is always beyond the grasp of its lay audience. In the previous chapter, I examined the York cycle's ideal of hermeneutic clarity in the skinners' pageant of the *Entry into Jerusalem,* in which eight citizens interpret Jesus' arrival in the city through allegorical readings of Old Testament prophecies. The Burgesses' civic voice, by which they direct their political "counsel" to the fulfillment of Scripture, celebrates the common end of lay devotion and good urban rule as vernacular exegesis. As long as the representative oligarchy can read the "pleyn," "open," and "clear" sense of English Scripture with a single rhetorical and political will, their laws will be just.

Needless to say, accounts of visionary experience, especially those set forth by women, pose a formidable challenge to this kind of restrictive and patriarchal hermeneutic when the desire or will of the mystical subject demands different theories of interpretation. Not only does the visionary supplement the "plain" historical sense of Scripture by receiving new words directly from God, Jesus, or the saints, but she calls the authority of her interpreters into question depending on how they "read" her visions. The revelatory text, which always has the potential to interrogate its interrogators, presents a particular danger to the concept of a civic exegesis, as it threatens to divide the larger scope of political judgment along with doctrinal enquiry. Yet the visionary can bestow political legitimacy as well as undermine it. As I will argue in this chapter, St. Bridget of Sweden, whose *Revelations* are marked by numerous unambiguous political directives, presents an especially destabilizing spiritual model. In the 1430s, as the influence of Bridgettine spirituality was growing with the translation of the saint's works into English and their circulation among lay readers, the York playwright-reviser who worked on the series of Passion plays transformed one of Christ's trials into a timely examination of the political vision. For a prophecy that represents many of the problems raised by women's visionary authority, he turns to the skeletal accounts in Matthew 27 and especially in the apocryphal *Gesta Pilati* of the mysterious dream of Pilate's wife Procula warning her to prevent the crucifixion.[8]

The 1415 *Ordo* in the *York Memorandum Book* describes the pageant put on by the tapiters' and couchers' guild as "Pilate, Anna, Caiphas, two councilors, and four Jews accusing Jesus."[9] In the later text, the York reviser uses this juridical frame to dramatize the interpretive problems associated with the "discernment of spirits," the testing of visionary experiences. Perhaps the most striking aspect of the *Dream of Pilate's Wife* is that it demands a split stage of some kind, a division of the space between Pilate's court, where the "trial" of Christ takes place, and Procula's bedroom—a conceptual barrier between the realm of government and the realm of dreams. Appropriately for the guild concerned with the production, which made coverlets and tapestries—as well as for us post-Freudian readers of how repressions, laws, and dreams generate each other and are put into words—the main prop for either side is a lavishly ornamental draped couch.[10]

The play opens immediately into a flood of unstable definitions. Pilate threatens his audience to be quiet "or ellis þis brande in your braynens sone brestis and brekis" (4) and with this violence proclaims his power and his illegitimate descent from the emperor to his court: "sir Sesar was my sier and I sothely his sonne" (10). Altering the playwright's immediate source, Jacobus de Voragine's *Legenda Aurea*, he then expounds the meaning of his name, a jumble of claims that darkly hints at incest between his mother and her father, a miller. Even as the play winks at its own theatrical "tyranny" of a craftsman pretending to be a prince, Pilate undermines his own original assertion:

> And my modir hight Pila þat proude was o plight
> O Pila þat prowde, Atus hir father he hight
> This 'Pila' was hadde into 'Atus'—
> Nowe renkis, rede yhe it right?
>
> (14–18)[11]

In the York playwright's wholly original treatment of the relationship between Pilate and his wife, the tyrant interrupts his ranting account of authority to greet Procula, "A luffe, here, lady?" (25). She in turn affirms his power to kill anyone who disobeys his "precepts" and asserts her own status as his trophy wife: "Consayve nowe my countenaunce so comly and clere / The coloure of my corse is full clere" (40–41). As quickly becomes evident, Procula's bodily "clarity" is of a different order than either the virgin's ecstatic "comforte clear" or the "clear meaning" of vernacular language valorized by the *Entry into Jerusalem*. When Procula declares that "no lorde . . . hath a frendlyar feere / Than yhe my lorde, myselffe þof I saye itt" (44–45), Pilate gives her words legal authority, the clarity of power: "Nowe saye itt may ye saffely, for I will certefie þe same." As the couple's legalistic joking turns to Procula's charms "in bed," the judgment seat threatens to become a loveseat where "all ladise we coveyte þan to be kyssid and clappid" (54). Pilate's Beadle, who throughout the play steadfastly represents the voice of civic rule established by the Burgesses in the *Entry* play, interrupts just in time to chase out the unruly woman in accordance with "oure lawes" (68). After a brief squabble with Procula, in which she berates him as a "horosonne [whoreson] boy" (60), the Beadle explains to Pilate that his duty is to keep the realm of legal authority and the realm of dreams and female bodies as far apart as possible. Interestingly, he suggests that Procula is already predisposed to visions:

> Yhe may deem aftir no dremys,
> But late my lady here, with all hir light lemys,
> Wightely go wende till her wone;
> For ye muste sitte sir þis same nyght, of lyfe and of lyme.
> It is noȝt leefull for my lady by the lawe of this lande
> In dome for to dwelle fro þe day waxe ought dymme.
>
> (79–84)

Pilate's "doom" or judgment, in other words, must be sober, removed from his apparently uncontrollable sexual desire for his wife but also from "dreams" in the sense of allegorical narratives that present interpretive difficulties.

The initial hostility between Procula and the Beadle foreshadows the play's central conflict between two hermeneutic principles, the discernment of visionary authority and civic order. Having had a quick glass of wine with the affectionate Pilate, whose judgment seat inauspiciously doubles as his bed, Procula retires to her own bed, "arayed of þe beste" (153), to be met by the Devil.[12] The vision he sends her as a last-ditch effort to halt Jesus' crucifixion is paradoxically both a demonic hallucination designed to prevent salvation and an accurate political prophecy:

> O Woman, be wise and ware, and wonne in þi witte,
> There schall a gentilman, Jesu, unjustely be juged
> Byfore thy husband in haste, and with harlottis be hytte.

And þat doughty today to deth þus be dyghted,
Sir Pilate, for his prechyng, and þou
With nede schalle ye namely be noyed
Your striffe and your strenghe schal be stroyed,
Your richesse shall be refte you þat is rude,
With vengeaunce, and þat dare I avowe.

(167–75)

Immediately believing the dream to be the "true" vision of Pilate's and her own political ruin that it is, Procula calls her son to deliver her message to the court:

Saie to my sovereyne þis same is soth þat I send hym:
All nakid þis night as I napped
With teen and with trayne was I trapped,
With a swevene þat swifely me swapped
Of one Jesu, þe just man þe Jews will undoo.
She prayes tente to þat trewe man, with tyne be noȝt trapped,
But als a domesman dewly to be dressand,
And lelye delyvere þat lede.

(186–92)

The play's crisis of meaning ensues when Procula's dream reaches the other side of the stage, as a third-person narrative repeated by her hapless messenger: "al nakid þis nyght as sche napped." At this moment, Procula's interior experience, which interrupts the "prelates" Annas's and Cayphas's accusations of Jesus, becomes a public text subject to different interpretations and interests. The stage literally divides the dream itself, the words of the devil in Procula's bedroom, from the "textual" account that Pilate receives; it likewise divides her body from her voice as distinct sites of meaning. Procula's "nakedness" here signals the doubleness of her visionary status, both her fundamental carnality and the ironic transparency of the dream itself. In the sense that it means exactly what it says, despite its demonic origin, the vision is a "naked text" or "pleyn text" in much the way Chaucer in the Prologue of the *Legend of Good Women* uses these terms: it is, as Jesse Gellrich puts it, "self-disclosed," a text that in ideal formal isolation would need no gloss.[13] It is, indeed, almost indistinguishable from a "true" vision: as Jesus instructs Bridget in reading his language in the *Liber Celestis,* "Sometim I understand mi wordes on gosteli maner, sometime as þe lettir soundes, and þan

I will mi wordes be undirstandin *nakedli* as þai are spokine, for þare mai nevere man reprove me of lie" (36). The rest of the play problematizes how ambiguous "meaning" is generated from such a text by the work of political power through the terms of exegesis and contemplative imagination.[14]

Procula's vision is technically a *visum* or *phantasma*, considered the most deceptive form of dream in Macrobius's classifications and subsequent medieval theories, as it occurs between wakefulness and sleep.[15] In his equations of dreams with literary forms, for example, Pascalis Romanus compares the *visum* to the *fabula*, as a fictional product of disordered imaginings.[16] The play hence uses the resources of this singular *visum*, at once the *locus classicus* of bad dreams and bad judgment, to probe the uncertainties that attend even the divine visions granted to canonized saints.[17] In the writings on the discretion of spirits that it draws on, as well as in theories of dreams, the emblematic image of delusion is the Pauline devil who transfigures himself into an angel of light.[18] Making Pilate's wife, a sexy cipher who disappears from the play after voicing her dream, into a representative female visionary, the York reviser draws on a problem given great attention in mystical writing: the translation of inner experience into the language of visual and spatial terms, and indeed into text itself. This strand of caution over the "transfiguration" involved in all expression, associated in particular with the apophatic mysticism of the late-fourteenth-century *Cloud of Unknowing*, in turn challenges the "meditative" basis of the cycle plays.

THE *CLOUD* AND THE JANGLERS

The *Cloud*-author, whose other works include a Middle English abridgement of Richard of St. Victor's *Benjamin Minor* and treatises on the "Discretion of Spirits" and "Discretion of Stirrings," writes to a circle of contemplatives while considering with grave concern the wider lay audience who would read his vernacular texts.[19] The Prologue of the *Cloud* speaks to a fear of incomplete textual reception and worse, reception by "fleschely janglers, opyn preisers and blamers of hemself or of any other, tithing tellers, rouners and tutilers of tales, and alle maner of pinchers: kept I never that thei sawe this book" (22).[20] The *Cloud* thus anticipates a devotional culture like mid-fifteenth-century York's, in which anthologies of mystical works were produced for pastoral care and the terms of inner understanding were translated into public discourses.[21] The *Cloud* emphasizes Richard of St. Victor's warnings about the snares of imagination and sensuality at the

expense of his visualizing scheme of contemplative ascension through the faculties of the mind, from imagination to reason to the ecstasy that lies beyond reason.
In the *Benjamin Minor,* Richard characterizes imagination as the handmaid of reason and associates it with the vivid imagery in Scripture directed toward "human
infirmity": "it describes invisible things through the forms of visible things and
impresses the memory of them upon our minds through the beauty of very de-
sirable appearances."[22] The *Cloud*-author, who omits such passages from his version of this work, instead associates imagination with all of the dangers that as-
sail the contemplative. In the *Cloud,* the contemplative is told to approach God
with a "nakid entent"(31), a pure will free from images.[23] In the later chapters of
the work, the author focuses at great length on the consequences of "fantasie" or
"curiousté of witte," which leads the novice as well as "greet clerkis . . . and men
and wommen of other degrees" (73) to misapprehend spiritual words and things
as carnal:

> And be wel ware that thou conseyve not bodily that is seyde goostly. For
> trewly I telle thee that bodely and fleschely conseytes of hem that han corious
> and ymaginatyve wittys ben cause of moche errour. . . . And thus me thin-
> keth that it nedith greatly to have much warnes in understonding of wordes
> that ben spokyn to goostly entent, so that thou conceive hem not bodily but
> goostly, as thei ben mente. And namely it is good to be ware with this worde
> *in* and this worde *up,* for in mysconceyvyng of these two wordes hangeth
> moche errour and moche disseite in hem that puposen hem to ben goostly
> worchers, as me thinketh. (78)[24]

The very carnality of language itself, as well as the double sense of these kinds of
spatial terms, allows the devil to claim his own "contemplatives" through bodily
sensations taken as spiritual:

> For thei turne theire bodily wittes inwardes to theire body agens the cours
> of kynde; and streynyn hem, as thei wolde see inwards with theire bodily
> ighen, and heren inwards with theire eren, and so forth of alle theire wittes,
> smellen, tasten, and felyn inwards. And thus thei reverse hem agens the cours
> of kynde, and with this coriousté thei travalyle theire ymaginacion so undis-
> creetly, that at the last thei turne here brayne in here hedes. And than as fast
> the devil hath power for to feyne sum fals light or sounes, swete smelles in
> theire noses, wonderful taastes in theire mowthes, and many queynte hetes

and brennynges in theire bodily brestes or in theire bowelles, in theire backs and in theire reynes, and in theire privé membres. (79)[25]

The *Cloud*-author further attributes the "venemos disseites" (82) of spiritual hypocrisy to the inherently deceptive nature of both language and behavior; in the *Cloud,* he describes theatrical devotions which falsely connote holiness through bodily signs, like a "pipyng" voice (82). In his *Pistle of Discrecioun of Stirings,* he warns the novice against the potential hypocrisy of "sodein steringes of singulere doynges" that set him apart from "comoun custom," since these can be performed mimetically "fro wiþouten on ape maner" rather than coming "fro wiþinne of habundaunce of love."[26] In his scheme of the twelve patriarchs, Richard of St. Victor allegorizes Joseph in his role as dream interpreter as Discretion, the hermeneutic power of reason necessary for the final end of contemplative ecstasy.[27] For the *Cloud*-author, however, discretion becomes a radical distrust of all forms of representation rather than a way to order mental imagery. In his deconstruction of the Victorine's visual and spatial categories, he rejects as essentially hypocritical the very possibility of a contemplative theatricality.

DISCRETION

The theory of discretion set out in the *Cloud*-author's texts feeds into the more specific and more public concern over women's visions that emerges at the end of the fourteenth century in response to the overtly political mysticism of figures like St. Catherine of Siena and St. Bridget. After 1415, when the newly crowned Henry V, on the advice of his Yorkshire courtier Henry Fitzhugh, founded the double Bridgettine monastery at Syon, St. Bridget, who had herself lent prophetic support to the English claim to the French throne in the Hundred Years' War, became a central figure in Lancastrian state devotion.[28] Syon, along with the Charterhouse at Sheen, served as a chantry for the new dynasty, a monument to Henry V's desire "to place the monarchy at the spiritual centre of English life."[29] Bridget's *Revelations* were translated into English at around the same time as the foundation of the Abbey and became a widely circulated and excerpted text of the "Northern spirituality" of both the clergy and lay patrons of Yorkshire, along with the works of Rolle and Hilton.[30]

Yet even the enthusiastic reception of Bridget's *Revelations* in England was marked by continual controversies raised by the text's political implications during the process of her canonization, proclaimed in 1391, and in the further attacks on her sanctity by pro-French clerics at the Council of Constance.[31] Besides her famous prophecy in which Christ warns the French king to submit to a peace with England through a marriage that would produce a rightful English heir, while condemning both kings' "intollerabill taxis and takyng of þer sogettes gudes" (*Liber Celestis,* 344), Bridget's principal political visions include numerous attacks on corrupt priests, friars, and bishops as well as advice couched in harsh terms for both popes and princes. For example, St. Ambrose "þe bishope" appears to Bridget to warn that any bishop who lives for "worldi profite" will be "smetin as sore as, be likenes, he were smetin þe whilke from the crown of þe heved to þe sole of his fote, in all his parties of his fleshe" (206); and in book 6, Christ instructs her to write to Pope Clement VI to make peace between the kings of France and England, " þat are two perelows bestis, traitoures of menes saules" (450), and to return the papacy from Avignon to Rome. In book 7, toward the end of Bridget's life, Christ delivers the harshest of these orders through her, warning the king and "evill lifers" of Cyprus to adhere to the Roman papacy or face annihilation: "I sall distroi thi kinde . . . and I sall never spare riche ne pore, and that in short time, als thou had never been" (483).

This last prophecy in turn served for Bridget's main editor and spiritual director, Alfonso of Jaén (1329/30–1389), to confirm the truth of her visions in his treatise on discretion, the "Letter of the Hermit to the Kings, " also tellingly the preface to an additional book of the *Revelations* in which he rearranges the passages involving secular politics into a "mirror for princes." Opening with a general defense of female visionaries based on Old and New Testament exemplars— Miriam and Esther, Anna the Prophetess, and the Virgin Mary's cousin Elizabeth, as well as the Tyburtine and Ericthean Sybils—Alfonso ominously reminds his audience of "most serene kings" and their counselors that Cyprus, whose prince would not believe Bridget's warnings to reform, has just fallen into destruction.[32] Alfonso's text, a set of methods drawn from patristic, scholastic, and contemplative sources for, as the Middle English version puts it, "discernyng godly visions fro the cursid illusions of sathan the devle," aligns Bridget's revelations with the higher, noncorporeal forms of visionary knowledge established by St. Augustine.[33] Although her experiences almost always involve bodily images and are hence "spiritual," he collapses the categories and describes them as "intellectual," infused directly by God as absolute knowledge. While Alfonso refutes Bridget's detractors by presenting her as a contemplative who has herself been instructed in discernment by Christ and the Virgin Mary—an acute reader of spirits—he also, as Rosalynn Voaden argues, maps the outer contours of female spirituality, providing a handbook of discretion for visionaries seeking to satisfy, or to elude, the authorities.[34]

It is this very possibility of imitation that the *Epistola*'s translators into the vernacular sought to curtail; as Voaden notes of the version that accompanies one of the full translations of the *Revelations,* it suppresses most of the specific descriptions of Bridget's ecstatic behavior that Alfonso uses to prove her divine inspiration.[35] The body of the *Epistola* is similarly translated in the widely circulated devotional work *The Chastising of God's Children* (c. 1400), which also includes translations from John Ruusbroec's polemics against the so-called "heresy of the Free Spirit " from his *Spiritual Espousals.*[36] The author, retaining only Alfonso's celebration of Bridget as "þat hooli ladi, seint and princesse [who] as longe as she lyvede, ȝonge and oold, she lyvede ever under obedience and techyng of hooli clerkis and vertuouse and discreet elder men" (178), suggests an ever-greater need for "discernment." The examiner must take into account both the character of the visionary — her or his "virtuous living," humility, and obedience to the church — and the content of the visions, to see if they accord with Scripture and doctrine. The *Chastising,* despite its professed faith in the clergy, is a stunningly anxious text that at once warns that almost all visions are potentially demonic and, citing Thomas Aquinas, acknowledges the difficulty of assessing "intellectual" mystical experiences like the "inward knowynge and goostli liȝt of triewe shewyng" that the devil cannot mimic through "sensible speche" or "sum oþer vision imagynatif " (179). As the *Chastising* cautions the reader about the limits of judgment:

> For if [visions] be demed sodeynli and undiscretli, þanne shal sooþ be taken for fals, and fals sumtyme for sooþ, into gret perel; and so goode visions and sooþ shuld be forsake, and men shuld not obeie unto the privy speche of god, ne ȝeve no credence to hem, but rather take errour for triewþ, as oft tyme haþ it falle, and falliþ all day, for defaute of discreet and triew examynacion. (177)

In 1415, Jean Gerson again reworked Alfonso's methods of discernment to redefine the authority of spiritual advisors in his attack on St. Bridget's *Revelations* for the Council of Constance, *De Probatione Spirituum.*[37] Seeking to discredit the influence of Bridget's political positions on France and the papacy, Gerson became the most acute critic of the epistemological assumptions underlying the idea of discernment.[38] Gerson readily admits that the "testing of spirits" can never be based on a knowledge of Scripture alone and that the examiner, to hold "official" ecclesiastical authority, must himself also have had mystical experiences. Although Gerson refrains from direct condemnation of Bridget's visions, he suggests that confirming them, if they were "illusory," might be a disgrace to the council. Given the problems he finds in assessing the contemplative experience of another person, Gerson relies on long-standing antifeminist allegory to make his polemical point. "If the visionary is a woman," he writes,

> it is necessary to consider how she interacts with her confessors and instructors, whether she incites protracted conversations under the pretext of frequent confession, or with long narrations of her visions, or with other kinds of discussions. Believe the experts, St Augustine and St. Bonaventure; there is no plague more harmful or incurable. . . . [Women] have an insatiable urge to look around and talk — not to mention touch. According to Virgil, this happened to Dido: "*His face, his words hold fast her breast. / Care strips her limbs of calm and rest.*"[39]

By conflating St. Bridget with "Infelix Dido," Gerson reinfuses the discourse of discernment with the carnal desires of female visionaries, discounting women's interiority altogether. While men's visions must be subjected to examination, women can be condemned as improperly "curious" and sensual simply for publicly, or even privately, articulating their experiences.[40] The evidence that Alfonso and earlier writers subject to discretion — the visionary's narrative or text — is itself here the source of peril to stable doctrine; in their prolixity, Bridget's *Revelations* are "insatiable." As Marilynn Desmond shows, Dido is allegorized in a series of medieval commentaries on the *Aeneid* as the figure for *luxuria* or libido that Aeneas, as Wisdom, rejects as error.[41] Perhaps more significantly for a type of the false contemplative, Dido in these Augustinian glosses also represents the body as a site of interpretation, the dangerously sensual classical text that always needs a Christian reading to reveal the naked truth beneath the poetic *integumentum*.[42] Gerson's theologian and contemplative must be precisely this kind of reader of visions, one who through his own spirit can discern the truth hidden in bodily images.

These treatises' conflicting interpretations of Bridget's *Revelations* all speak to the dangers for clerical and secular authorities alike of both affirming and disregarding women's visions. St. Bridget's political visions proved useful to Lancastrian propagandists like Hoccleve, who, advocating the marriage of the future Henry V to Princess Katherine in the *Regiment of Princes,* emphasized their near-scriptural status:

The book of Revelaciouns of Bryde
Expressith how Cryst thus seide hir unto:
"I am pees verray; there I wole abyde.
Whereas pees is, noon othir wole I do;
Of France and Engeland the kynges two,
If they will have pees, pees perpetuel
Thei shul han." Thus hir book seith, woot I wel.
$$(5384-90)^{43}$$

More locally, in 1422–23, the York anchoress Emma Rawghton, through a prophecy, influenced the Earl of Warwick, Richard Beauchamp, who wanted a male heir, to found a chantry at "Gibcliff"; moreover, she foretold his influence over the child king Henry VI as a member of his council.[44] Yet clearly, this kind of vision of political legitimacy could in theory just as easily provide a different interpretation, especially when loosed from the bonds of patronage. From this ruling perspective, the worst-case scenario of uncloistered, unanchored Bridgettine spirituality would look a lot like *The Book of Margery Kempe.* In Chapter 20, Christ tells Kempe that "rygth as I spak to Seynt Bryde, ryte so I speke to þe, dowtyr, & I telle þe trewly it is trewe every word þat is wretyn in Brides boke, & be the it xal be knowyn for very trewth."[45] The truth of Kempe's visions is proved by Bridget's example, and again affirms the canonization of the still-controversial saint. "Discernment" of Kempe's narratives turns to deadlock, with clerics like her Carmelite confessor Aleyn of Lynn, who had composed an index to Bridget's *Revelations,* affirming her visions and others, like Henry Bowet, the Archbishop of York, remaining less than convinced. With the *Revelations* as her license, however, Kempe goes on to recount visions that challenge church and political authorities, from Archbishop Bowet himself to the mayor of Leicester to the king's brother John, duke of Bedford.[46]

WISER MEN THAN I?

The *Dream of Pilate's Wife,* in its futile trial of Christ, stages interpretive problems much like those raised by Kempe's traveling *Imitatio Bridgettiae.* As a commentary on both the vernacular "naked text" of the *Nativity's* luminous revelation and the *Entry's* "pleyn" biblical exegesis, the play interrogates the authority of the body in contemplative practice and the hermeneutic stability of the entire civic dramatic production. As a foil to the *Nativity's* Mary—the ideal of Bridgettine contemplation—the couchers' and tapiters' Dido-like Procula presents a demonic, pagan vision that can only be read by its audience as seductive and ornately deceptive. In its actual indeterminacy, however, the dream-as-text mirrors the unresponsive figure of Christ himself, stripped of the metaphysical staging of his divinity in the *Nativity* and reduced here to the narrative of his humanity.

In his adaptation of the Middle English version of the *Gesta Pilati,* the York reviser erases Pilate's most crucial question to Jesus: What is truth? ["what thing es sothfastnes?"] (46–47). In place of his direct attempt to find "truth" in scriptural accounts, the play's Pilate focuses instead on determining truth through the "entent" in the evidence before him; as he rebukes Cayphas when he claims his story is "true": "youre tales wolde I trow but þei touche none entente" (416). This multivalent term covers both a subject's will or desire—as in the *Cloud of Unknowing*'s "nakid entent" of the contemplative—and the meaning of a text or a dream. Legally, *entent* carries the sense of a claim as well as an intention; however, the legal context of the play above all gives form to its spiritual politics and serves to put the flawed language of interpretation itself on trial.[47] As Richard Firth Green has shown, the word *truth* changed meanings at the end of the fourteenth century, absorbing the ethical and theological senses of *soth* while retaining the sense of fidelity, the legal opposite of *treason*.[48] As Jesus is hauled before him precisely for "treason" as a crime of language, Pilate is unable to find truth in the "intent" of either his wife or the Beadle.[49]

The *Dream*'s opening, "a ludicrously amorous little scene," in Rosemary Woolf's words, sets the stage for the worst possibilities of visionary experience.[50] The nightcap of wine, a signature of the York reviser's tyrannical rulers throughout the Passion sequence, here takes on connotations beyond a kind of profane Eucharist. With their carousing at court, Pilate and Procula exemplify the *Benjamin Minor*'s allegory of the "handmaids" Sensuality and Imagination ungoverned by Affection and Reason, figured respectively as unquenchable thirst and "foul" chatter.[51] Perhaps most interesting in the York reviser's conception of the couple with their separate rooms, however, is that they never fall into the traditional gendered division of spirit and body, central, for example, in the *Meditations'* discussion of contemplative practice as the rule of man over woman.[52] Rather, as they retire to sleep, both judge and visionary are pointedly carnal, surrounded by "rich array": Pilate, indeed, warns his Beadle to be gentle when he touches him, in terms that sound not unlike a sexual invitation: "Have in thy hands hendly and heave me from hyne / But loke þat þou tene me not with þi tast-

ing, but tendirly me touche" (133–34). The devil likewise describes his noctur-
nal visit to Procula, like all demonic apparitions, as a type of seduction or rape:
"I will on stiffely in þis stound / Unto ser Pilate wiffe, pertely, and putte me in
prese" (165–66).[53] The boundary between Procula's realm and Pilate's, then, is no
sooner established than collapsed; the distinction between dream and interpretation remains fluid, the two emblematic couches mirror images of desire.

The morning after this murky if eventful night, the play returns to the judgment of Christ, which in his near-silence becomes the judgment, in turn, of vision
and Scripture. Procula's dream is immediately subject to the clerical "discernment
of spirits" by the priests Annas and Cayphas, who falsely attribute it to Jesus' own
"fantome and falshed" (298):

> With wicchecrafte þis wile has he wrought.
> Some feende of his sand he has sente
> And warned your wiffe or he went.
>   (293–95)

The Beadle counters this official interpretive act with his own interior experience, which amounts to having seen and correctly understood the earlier *Entry*
play: "this forward to fulfillle I am fayne moved in myn herte" (307). When Pilate orders him to produce Jesus, the Beadle worships him "with witte and with
will," reason and affection in control:

> This reverrence I do þe forthy,
> For wytes þat were wyser than I,
> They worshipped þe ful holy on hy
> And with solempnité sange Osanna till.
>   (311–15)

The Beadle's "eyewitness" account of Jesus, parallel in content if not in style to
Procula's vision, evokes the same sense of political danger from the prelate Annas:
"such a lourdayne unlele (disloyal wretch), dare I laye, / Many lordis of oure lan-
dis might lede fro oure lawes" (332–33). Under this pressure, the Beadle expands
his conversion narrative into a meditative memory:

> And þan þis semely on an asse was sette
> And many men myldely hym mette,

Als a God in þat grounde þai hym grette,
Wele semand [psalming] hym in waye with worschippe lele.
"Osanna" þei sange, "þe sone of David,"
Riche men with þare robes þei ran to his fete,
And poure folke fecchid floures of þe frith
And made myrthe and melody þis man for to mete.

(339–46)

The Beadle's "stirring" in his heart transforms both the gospel accounts of Christ's entry in Jerusalem itself and the *Entry* play into a contemplative text. His devotional memory, however little embellished from the Gospels, is a version of the *Meditations'* spiritual exercise that privileges the visual, sensual experience of Christ's presence in gesture, song, or flowers over the *Entry* play's exegetical process. The York reviser expands the Beadle's role from the *Gesta* to have him, rather than the Jews, translate for Pilate when he asks: "What is 'Osanna' to saie?"

Sir, constrew it we may by langage of þis land as I leve,
It is als moche to me for to meve—
Youre prelatis in þis place can it preve—
Als, "our saviour and soverayne þou save us we praye."

(349–51)

While the Beadle here rehearses the *Entry's* textual basis, translating the "prelates'" Hebrew—a substitute for clerical Latin—into the "pleyn" English of the York plays' political idiom, his narrative is severed from the hermeneutic work of the earlier play. In its other "translation," from the Wycliffite-influenced lay exegesis of the *Entry* to Pilate's "tyrannical" law, the Beadle's recollection of "men wiser than him" reflects the loss of the civic authority that confirmed the burgesses' readings. In the *Dream,* the Beadle's visual and spatial memory of Jerusalem transforms the scriptural historical event, also just represented on stage, into a text from the *Meditations* uneasily close not only to St. Bridget's "canonical" vision of the Nativity but to Procula's demonic *visum.* The dream at the play's core, at once naked and opaque, true and false, exposes the shaky ground of these other "imaginative" representations and visions, including the orthodox devotional program of the *Meditations,* when subjected to the methods of discernment.

NAKED INTENTIONS

In the *Dream,* the devil embodies the principle of theater itself, as he does in Robert Hanning's classic account of his "false mimesis" of God in the *Fall of Lucifer* plays.[54] Satan is "disguised" as an angel of light, making "images" to deceive, as Bartholomaeus Anglicus describes the workings of false dreams. In terms of Alfonso's tenets of discernment, rehearsed in the *Chastising,* Procula's theatrical *visum* sets off every alarm of falsehood: she is a woman of querulous character and given to carnal imaginings; she has no wise spiritual advisor; she is asleep rather than awake; and the devil addresses her "bi sensible speech" (179). Yet her vision is also the most difficult kind to discern, since it is all true and, as far as it goes, accords with doctrine: as the devil correctly informs her, Jesus will be unjustly judged, and she and Pilate will be destroyed. "Naked as she napped," however, stripped of the ornaments of her and Pilate's power, the York tapiters' coverings by which she could be "read," Procula's dream closely resembles Bridget's most extreme political prophecy, her fulfilled warning to the king of Cyprus. As such, it is the kind of vision most significant for a city like York governed by "wise men," a feminine, spectral supplement to the textual economy established in the *Entry.* The woman's voice, excluded from the public vernacular exegesis of the earlier play, could nevertheless be the "privy speech of God" always in danger of being ignored by those in political power. Unlike Pilate, the lay exegetes should be able to "discern" the truth of a dream, yet this would seem to require them to possess a contemplative knowledge beyond Scripture. In its treatment of Procula's "naked text," the *Dream* stages the proximity between the authority of a demoniac woman and a saint; as in Bridget's case, the play suggests, the difference is perhaps simply a matter of political forces and their readings.[55]

    In the problems it raises and never solves, the *Dream* enacts not only the *Chastising*'s fears about the consequences of misjudgment but, as Nicholas Watson has called it, the "self-deconstructing" polemic of the *Cloud* against its own language of representation. As a series of images never correctly interpreted, the play literalizes the *Cloud*'s fear of confusing body and spirit, words and reality. In the ultimate throwaway line of one of Pilate's boorish soldiers, "for wordis are as þe wynde" (236). Procula's dream and the Beadle's meditation on the *Entry* remain equivalent under the pressure of the mystics' radical doubt, products of interior "imagination" unreadable by political authorities. In the play's greatest irony, both texts, originally based on scriptural passages, become "phantasmatic," or unreal in the play's legal context. As the *Dream* plays out, Pilate hears the priests

charge Jesus with "treason," itself, as Green points out, a contested term in medieval English law and political discourse: it here functions in the sense of a crime
against "truth" as well as an attack on royal authority or law.[56] Jesus' terse self-
defense in answer to Pilate's question as to whether or not he is Christ not only
throws responsibility back on the interpreter and his language but finally confirms the truth of Procula's dream-as-text of the "just man" and her own ruin,
retranslating the demonic *visum* as divine *visio:*

> þou saiste so þiselve. I am sothly þe same
> Here wonnyng in world to wirke all þi will.
> My fadir is faithfull to felle all þi fame;
> Withouten trespas or tene am I taken þe till.
> (477–80)

As unable to discern the truth in Christ's own words as in his wife's, Pilate
finally orders his soldiers "that warlowe ye warrok and wraste / And
loke þat he brymly be braste" (528–29); the last resort of his law is to torture Jesus in an attempt to wring "truth" from the naked body.[57] As Jody Enders writes of Passion
plays in which Christ is subjected to both the theological *quaestio* and the legal
"question" of scourging, "Like torture itself, the scourging scenes undermine
the stability of the so-called truths extracted from suffering bodies — including
the truth so near and dear to the mystery play of how to lead a good Christian
life."[58] The scourging of Christ is, of course, also one of the central scenes in the
Meditations' program of empathic identity with his humanity; the *Dream,* like the
plays Enders considers, calls attention here to its own theatrical illusion of pain, as-
sociating the political breakdown of legal and textual interpretation with a "hypocritical" contemplation marked by false bodily and spatial sensations. Reminiscent
of the *Cloud*'s dire warnings, Pilate's call for torture is akin to the dangerous
imagination or "curiosity" of false contemplatives in its demand for the Incarnation to announce itself by means other than "pleyn" language.

If the aim of judicial torture in the York reviser's subsequent passion plays,
Christ before Herod and Jesus' second appearance before Pilate, *The Judgement,* is to
make Christ's body — the *Corpus Christi* — speak some form of truth to both the
judges and the audience, in the vertiginous *Dream* torture reflects, above all, the
impossible logic of the discernment of spirits. Just as Christ presents Pilate with
an unreadable text, a body that without his "intent," the evidence of his reported
signs and wonders, becomes simply the mirror of his self-reflexive "thou sayest

so thyself," so too the body of the visionary proves resistant to interpretation. As Dyan Elliott has shown, works on discernment, in their relentless concern with distinguishing spiritual from corporeal experiences, end up dwelling upon the female body as an "unreliable witness" that mimics true rapture in melancholia, madness, and brain injury.[59] In the *Dream,* Procula's theatrical body exemplifies the problem Elliott addresses as "the body's penetration of the soul through the senses, the imagination, the passions and physical illness"; as a text apart from her vision itself, naked yet wrapped in ever more layers of interpretation, it never yields the truth about Christ.[60] In her unreadability, Procula remains the spectral double of Mary as she appears in the *Nativity,* the exemplar for the saint's contemplative manifestation of her spirit through bodily rapture. So, through this figure, the York reviser obliquely acknowledges the ongoing ambiguity of St. Bridget's *Revelations* as a devotional source. The records of Bridget's canonization provide an eloquent testimony to the necessary role of the body in sanctity in pages of posthumous healing miracles; the evidence of the sick and injured, whom the saint returns to wholeness, verify the authenticity of her visions.[61] Yet even after her canonization, Bridget's own body, as Gerson's *Probatio Spirituum* demonstrates, was open to reinterpretation as a site of hypocrisy and delusion. As a reflection of these pressures, the *Dream* ends on a note of terrible pessimism about the hermeneutic capacities of political and legal authorities as Jesus is led off in pain to reappear in the *Christ before Herod* play as an absolutely silent body subject to an unstable and incoherent judge.

THE MARIAN MOMENT

Middle English theater, however, includes a unique text that, outside the civic ideology of a Corpus Christi cycle, bespeaks an entirely different assessment of Bridgettine spirituality and the powers of contemplative women. Like the York *Nativity,* the East Anglian *Mary Play* represents a version of Bridgettine devotion on stage, portraying the Virgin herself as the exemplary prophetic author. By focusing on the bounded historical moment between Mary's birth and Christ's, a narrative drawn almost entirely from the *Legenda Aurea* and devotional texts, the play casts Mary as the prophet, a "new David" in her own right, who mediates between Old and New Laws as well as between Latinity and vernacularity. The entire play is in essence an interpretation of the *Meditations'* description of Mary before the Annunciation as, in the translation of Nicholas Love's *Mirror of the*

Blessed Life of Jesus Christ, "In þe wisdome of goddus lawe most kunnyng. In mekenes most lowe. In þe song & þe salmes of david most convenyent and semelich" (20). The *Mary Play*, which was incorporated into the civic N-Town Cycle of Bury St. Edmunds by the manuscript's scribe/compiler, is an anomaly in the body of surviving drama. A self-contained series of plays on Mary's early life with the female allegorical figure of "Contemplacio" presiding as expositor, the work celebrates women's devotion and visionary authority within the frame of salvation history. With its complicated manuscript record of composition and revision, and with no outside documentation of its performance, the *Mary Play* is notably difficult to contextualize; much speculation, however, suggests that it may have been produced for a guild of St. Anne or for performance on St. Anne's Day.[62] In this setting, it may have included female as well as male performers.[63] As restored to its "original" form by Peter Meredith in his edition, the *Mary Play* comprises the plays of the *Conception,* the *Presentation in the Temple,* the *Betrothal,* the *Parliament in Heaven and Annunciation,* and the *Visit to Elizabeth.*[64] Probably the work of a single author, the play also underwent various revisions, especially to the speeches made by Contemplacio, before being worked into the N-Town cycle in the 1460s.[65]

Considered as a work independent of the cycle, the most puzzling thing about the *Mary Play* is that its unifying figure, Contemplacio, despite her Latin feminine-gendered name, has been hitherto universally imagined as *male.* This is partly the work of the N-Town scribe, who, apparently as an afterthought, also attributed the unrelated prologue of "an exposytor in doctorys wede" in *Passion Play II* to Contemplacio.[66] Aside from a possible anticipation of the aged holy hermit Contemplation of Spenser's *Faerie Queene,* the identification otherwise seems to be based on critics' ideas that Contemplacio assumes too many signs of clerical authority to be female.[67] The trajectory of the *Mary Play,* however, which moves from an ambiguous view of the Jewish priests' authority — conceived of as Christian and Latin — in the temple, to Mary's and Elizabeth's perfect revelatory authority in Zacharias's house, only confirms Contemplacio's status as the principle of female lay devotion.[68] Contemplacio is the concept that licenses the female desiring reader of the *Meditations'* prologue to reinvent the details of the Gospels' prehistory. As Love's translation renders the pertinent passage:

And þouh hit so be that the bigynnyng of þe matire of þis boke, þat is þe blessede lif of Jesu crist, be at his Incarnation. nevereles we mowen first devoutly ymagine & þenk sume þinges done before, touchyng god & his angeles in hevene, & also as anentes þe blessed virgyne oure lady seynt Marie in erþe, of þe whech is to bygynne. (13)

Undocumented by Scripture, Mary's life is especially open to a kind of contemplative fictional license that, looking back to the original audience of the *Meditations,* becomes a feminine theatricality.

Contemplacio, whose first speech in the *Mary Play* is concerned with making sure that the audience clearly understands "þe personys here pleyand" and that "non oblocucyon make þis matere obscure" (3–5), represents the theatrical process that connects the "lernyd" and "lewd" (15) alike to Mary as she emerges as an intercessor and exegete.[69] She is, then, neither a priest onstage nor, as Gail Gibson has proposed, a monk, but rather a stylized allegorical female prophet who mirrors Mary herself as well as the allegorical daughters of God (Misericordia, Pax, Justicia, and Veritas), who later debate human salvation. Contemplacio in this context is best seen as the ascending series of spiritual understandings that Richard of St. Victor describes as ranging from the apprehension of "corporeal things" to the "divine light." To describe the objects of contemplation, Richard uses the explicitly theatrical term *spectaculum* — a play or spectacle as well as a mystical "showing." At its lowest level, the imagination of visible things, Richard says of contemplation:

> Marveling we venerate and venerating we marvel at the power, wisdom, and generosity of that superessential creatrix [God, here female]. However our contemplation is engaged in imagination and is formed according to imagination only when we seek nothing by means of argumentation and investigate nothing by means of reasoning, but rather our mind runs freely here and there, wherever wonder carries it away in this kind of manifestation (*spectaculum*).[70]

In this *spectaculum,* the contemplative theater of the *Mary Play,* the audience ascends to reason through the example of the Virgin as she undergoes her own education in Scripture. In this regard, the *Mary Play* imitates the Bridgettine spiritual model of prayers to the Virgin based on the *Revelations* and the study of devotional texts that appears in St. Bridget's *Sermo Angelicus* and later in the long Syon vernacular commentary on the Office of the Virgin, the *Myroure of Oure Ladye.*[71]

As Nicholas Watson has written of kenosis in late-fourteenth-century texts such as the *Pore Caitif* and the *Pricking of Love,* "Christ's extravagant gift of his divinity in humility and love is seen as a revelation of God's essential nature, which is more fully understood through Christ's incarnation than by any other means."[72] In its symbolic alignment with Christ's flesh and humility, the vernacular "mother tongue" surpasses Latin as a language of contemplation and revelation.[73] This is exemplified by the *Sermo Angelicus;* as the *Myroure* describes its composition:

> In the chambre saint Birgit eche day after she had saide her houres & her prayers, she made her redy to wryte with pen & yncke & paper or parchmyn so abydyng the angell of god. . . . And so stondynge he endyted the sayde legende dystynctely and in order in the moderly tongue of saynte Brygytte. (19)[74]

The *Myroure* continues to explain how then Bridget's spiritual father, Master Peter, translated the text into Latin "governyd of one spyryte" (20) with the angel. In contrast to this double revelation, the *Myroure*'s author, not without a certain irony, frames his own translation from Latin to English in terms of the demands of ecclesiastical authority.[75] In these narratives of translation, Mary, the subject of the *Sermo* and *Myroure,* encompasses both vernacular and Latin writing, mediating between them. In the *Mary Play,* which ends before the Nativity, the authority of divine kenosis remains within Mary's body, harnessing the authority of the Incarnation to the Virgin's role as a female learned and "lewd" author.

As in the *Myroure*'s description of Mary as "desyred and lovyd of holy faders" (15), the Virgin in the play likewise represents the culmination of Old Testament history, the fulfillment of the patriarchs and prophets at the end of the sixth age of the world and the Incarnation at the advent of the seventh.[76] Mary emerges as an allegorizing exegete of the Old Law in the second play, in which her parents Anne and Joachim present her, "as a child of thre 3ere age" (262), in the temple. This follows as a commentary on the opening play, in which the Jewish "prynce of prestys" (30) Ysakar, curiously depicted as a Christian priest celebrating a version of the Mass of the Trinity in Latin, rejects Joachim's offering of "tweyn turtelys" (75) and orders him away from the temple.[77] When Anne and Joachim return with Mary as their new "offering," she ascends the fifteen steps of the temple while reciting the fifteen gradual psalms; she begins in English with a spiritual commentary, then quotes the opening of the psalm in a loose English translation and finally quotes in the "original" Latin—for example:

> The fyrst degré gostly applyed
> It is holy desyre with God to be:
> In trobyl to God I have cryed,
> And in sped that Lord hath herde me
> *Ad dominum cum tribularer clamavi; et exaudivit me.*
>
> (355–60)

As Mary allegorizes the temple itself in this scene, transforming the steps into degrees of interior contemplative experience, she also, in her role as exegete and translator, begins her engagement with the psalms as both prophecies and literary devotional works.[78] In the thirteenth step, she conflates her identity with David's as both the author and subject of the psalms:

> The threttene is feyth þerwith,
> With holy dedys don expresse:
> Have mende, Lorde, of Davyth
> And of all his swettnes.
> *Memento domine David; et omnis mansuetudinis eius.*
>
> (427–32)

In the tradition of commentary on the Psalms, David, "who composed the psalms, or at any rate most of them, is called not only a prophet but the most outstanding among the prophets."[79] His prophecies exemplify Augustine's highest "intellectual" level, performed "solely through the inspiration of the Holy Spirit without any external aids."[80] In his Aristotelian *Prologue to the Commentary on the Psalter,* Nicholas of Lyra theorizes David's role as author: "[T]he principal cause is God Himself, who reveals the mysteries described in this book. The instrumental cause is David."[81] As Alastair Minnis characterizes this new fourteenth-century view of authorship, "[D]ivine inspiration works on and through the human *mens.* The man [sic] who sees visions or dreams dreams is now much more than a mere 'sleeping partner' of God."[82] In the *Mary Play,* Mary takes on the role of human authorship in the same way she takes on the Incarnation; in the moment prior to Jesus' birth, Mary herself allegorically fulfills David's prophecies in her study of the psalms and, finally, in her composition of her own psalm, the *Magnificat*.[83]

In the *Betrothal* play, Joseph's descent from David by blood contrasts with Mary's descent by spirit and prophecy, a reversal of the usual gendering of body and spirit, literal and allegorical meaning.[84] An angel summons Joseph to the temple as a candidate for marriage to the Virgin:

> This is Goddys own byddyng:
> þat all the kynsmen of Dauyd þe kyng
> To þe temple xul brynge here du offryng,
> With whyte ȝardys in þer honde.
>
> (718–21)

In this account drawn from the *Legenda Aurea,* when the aged Joseph's rod miraculously blossoms, he is chosen from the other descendants of David. In the original treatment of the *Mary Play,* the scene of Mary's marriage to Joseph is followed by her immediately returning to her studies in "þe holy psalms of Davyth / wheche book is clepyd þe sawtere" (1003–4). Mary's exposition in this passage establishes the continuum of her "monastic" practice in the temple with her "lay" devotion as "bothe mayde and wyff" (1002). It is, as Meredith notes, similar to the "praysyng of these psalmes" in the *Myroure of Oure Ladye* (37), which includes Augustine's standard interpretation that all of Scripture — Old Law, prophets, and New Law — is contained in the psalter in the form of praise.[85] The *Myroure* also stresses that besides David, "many other bothe men & wymen fylled with the spiryte of god made songes, & psalmes" (36). The scene is also reminiscent of Richard Rolle's prologue to his *Psalter or Psalms of David,* which, together with the versions of the psalms "out of Englysshe bibles" (3), the *Myroure*'s author recommends to his readers. As Rolle explains:

> This book of al haly wri is mast oysed in halykyrke servys, forthi that in it is perfeccioun of dyvyne pagyne. for it contenys all that other books draghes langly. That is, the lare of the ald testament & of the new. Thare in is discryved . . . the lyf of actyf men. the meditacioun of contemplatifs. & the joy of contemplacioun, the hegest that may be in man lifand in body & feland.[86]

In the *Mary Play,* the psalms become the Virgin's direct vehicle of intercession with God:

Wyth these halwyd psalmys, Lord, I pray the specyaly,
For al þe creatures qwyke and dede,
þat þu wylt shewe to hem þi mercy,
And to me specyaly þat do it rede.
I have seyd sum of my sawtere and here I am
At þis holy psalme indede:
Benedixisti domine terram tuam;
In this holy labore, Lord me spede!

(1022–29)

By reading Psalm 84, Mary ushers in the next play, the *Parliament in Heaven,* which presents the allegorical sense of the lines "Misericordia et Veritas obviaverunt sibi, / Justicia et Pax osculate sunt." Closely following the "debate of the daughters of God" in the fourteenth-century devotional text *The Charter of the Abbey of the Holy Ghost,* the play stages the rhetorical triumph, conducted largely through quotations of the psalms, of Mercy and Peace over Truth and Justice, which in turn justifies Jesus' redemption of humanity.[87] Through her understanding of reading as "holy labor," Mary takes an active and prophetic role in the Incarnation. Invoking the psalm, she performs the role of a contemplative exegete, speaking in David's voice as a prophet of Christ. "Christ in his totality," according to Cassiodorus and subsequent exegetes, is the subject of the psalter; by her work of interpretation, Mary intercedes for the "mercy" of the Incarnation even before the Annunciation.[88]

In the *Parliament of Heaven,* Contemplacio likewise mirrors Mary's prophetic exegesis, speaking in the voices of Isaiah and Jeremiah in order to plead for redemption.[89] Like the psalms in this play, the Old Testament prophets are "fulfilled," or given allegorical meaning, by being spoken in a female voice. Contemplacio, the idea of female devotion, also literally gives a body to Isaiah's words, performing a textual "incarnation" as exegesis:

Have mende of þe prayour seyd by Ysaie;
Let mercy make þin hyest magesté
Wolde God þu woldyst breke þin hefne myghtye
And com down here into erth
And levyn ȝerys thre and threttye,
Thyn famyt folke with þi fode to fede;
To staunch þi thrysté lete þi syde blede.

(1066–72)[90]

This "contemplative" reading of Isaiah 64:1 is a version of the "double intercession" of Jesus and Mary, which symbolically links Mary's breast with Christ's wounded side.[91] As Carolyn Walker Bynum describes this account of the Incarnation: "[Medieval writers] often went so far as to treat Christ's flesh as female, at least in certain of its salvific functions, especially its bleeding and nurturing."[92] In the logic of incarnation in the *Mary Play,* Mary embodies prophetic language through reading, giving Christ her female flesh or matter in the process.[93] The play underlines Mary's learning and agency, as she essentially interprets the Incarnation into being textually even before the three persons of the Trinity enter her body.

After the Incarnation, Mary fully emerges as a prophet and author, composing her psalm, the *Magnificat,* in Latin, while her cousin Elizabeth simultaneously translates it into English. As the commentary on the *Magnificat* in the Bridgettine *Myroure* recounts Mary's visit to Elizabeth:

> And at her comynge thyder saynte John joyed in hys mothers wombe & hys mother was fylled with the spyryte of prophesy and blyssed oure lady and sayde. Blyssed be thow amongest all women and blyssed be the fruyte of thy wombe. Then oure lady as she tellyth to saynte Birgytte was sturred in her harte wyth unspecable & unknowen gladnesse so much that her sowle mighte skante holde yt selfe for joye. But her holy tongue brake out with wordes in praysynge of god wythoute studye or thynkeynge before and seyd *Magnificat anima mea dominum,* My sowle prayseth the lorde.
>
> (157–58)

If this recently revealed version of the story from Luke 1 connects St. Bridget to both Mary and Elizabeth as a female prophetic author, the play's representation, by contrast, emphasizes "study" and authorship itself in the composition of the psalm. As Contemplacio explains in her prologue, Elizabeth's husband, the old high priest Zacharias, has been punished for his disbelief in his wife's conception of John the Baptist by being struck dumb. Elizabeth herself tells the Virgin by way of explanation, "sethe for his mystrost he hath be dowm alway" (1490). With this emblem of clerical silence on stage, Mary and Elizabeth together enact a new kind of female Davidic authorship, pronouncing a divine text in human form. Like David, the two women receive the prophecy as a direct "intellectual" experience, without images; the *Magnificat* itself is nonetheless the verbal expression of the Incarnation, continuous in some sense with Mary's and Christ's as yet undifferentiated body. Mary, by this point in the play, appears as an author consciously imitating the style of the psalter she has studied so intently. The human authorship of the *Magnificat* is more pointedly signified by Elizabeth's production of a vernacular version at the time of composition:

MARIA: For þis holy psalme I begynne here þis day:
           Magnificat: anima mea dominum
           Et exultavit spiritus meus: in deo salutari meo
ELIZABETH: Be þe Holy Gost with joye Goddys son is in þe cum.
           þat þi spyryte so injouyid þe helth of þi God so.
                                           (1492–96)

As Meredith notes, Elizabeth's English *Magnificat* is more a free "adaptation" than a translation: she not only changes Mary's first-person pronouns into the second person but provides extra commentary, as in the first line. In this opening, Elizabeth specifically uses the resources of the vernacular to describe the Incarnation in terms of body as well as spirit, the "son" literally within Mary's womb. Elizabeth's version is, in the play's terms, not an inferior text but an inherent part of the prophecy. As Mary declares at the end of the recitation: "This psalme of prophesye seyd betwen us tweyn, / In hefne it is wretyn with aungellys hond" (1538–39). The vernacular, as well as the Latin, is the divine text, with the "mother tongue" performing the work of kenosis by announcing Christ's humanity to the "lewd" theatrical audience. English, as Watson says, is a mark of the "universality" of the prophetic text.

    The *Mary Play* concludes with two alternative endings, an acknowledgment by the author, in the voice of Contemplacio, of the narrative fluidity of Mary's life, even as it appears in the Gospels. Taking advantage of the Gospel of Luke's silence, the contemplative reader or playwright could imagine Mary and Joseph leaving just before John's birth or staying around to help out Elizabeth. As in its reimagination of the *Magnificat*'s two versions as one essential text, the *Mary Play* ends by celebrating its own contemplative and theatrical license. The first ending has Elizabeth and Zacharias preparing to return to the temple, a gesture perhaps towards the neglected institutional church. The second ending, however, includes a further extension of Elizabeth's authorial role that implies a radically new understanding of language and the Incarnation. Contemplacio narrates the scene immediately after Elizabeth gives birth to John:

And þan Zacharye spak iwus,
þat had been dowm and his spech lorn.

He and Elizabeth prophesyed as þus,
They mad *Benedictus* them beforn;
And so *Magnificat* and *Benedictus*
First in þat place þer made worn.

                    (1579–84)

By reattributing the *Benedictus,* the psalm in praise of John, to the joint authorship of Elizabeth and Zacharias, the *Mary Play* advances the idea that after the
Incarnation, all writing must involve a female element. Elizabeth's presence in
this prophecy, as in the *Magnificat,* elevates female vernacular authorship to a
sign of Christianity itself. In this play, which makes the most of the virgin's early
history as a liminal period, a transition between the Old Law in the temple and
the New Law in Elizabeth's home, prophecy becomes an essentially female language, perceived and fulfilled through the body.

In its staging of Mary's engagement with the psalms as exegete, author, and
prophet, the *Mary Play* offers a Bridgettine-influenced account of the possibilities
of female visionary and contemplative authorship. If the play does little to address
the specific contemporary anxieties about women visionaries that emerge in the
treatises on the "discretion of spirits" and in the York *Dream of Pilate's Wife,* it
nevertheless represents a rejoinder to these works' distrust of the female body as a
site of revelatory knowledge. Framed by Contemplacio herself, the power of female devotional experience *and* exegetical desire, the *Mary Play* reconceives the
Virgin's brief historical moment as the birth of the lay woman author.

Labor's End

The Wakefield Master's Poor Theater

In the Towneley *Crucifixion* play, Jesus' torturers make an extraordinary admission. Following a rendering of his plea for God's forgiveness from Luke 23, "They wot not what they doyn / Nor whom they have thus spilt," one of the torturers insists, "*Yis, what we do full well we knaw,*" and another menacingly echoes, "Yee, that he shall fynde within a thraw" (298–99, emphasis added).[1] An interpretive swerve from earlier Passion plays, where the moment provides an ethical reprieve for the actors and audience imaginatively rehearsing the crucifixion, the Towneley version implicates its players in a newly self-aware, intellectual labor.[2] At this point in the York *Crucifixion,* a likely precursor of the Towneley text, Jesus absolves the pinners' guild of both deicide and the botched workmanship with their own nails that gives the play its agonizing dramatic force: "Forgiffis þes men þat dois me pyne [pin, pain] / what þei wirke wotte þai noght" (260–61).[3] Even the pinner-soldiers' labor is, along with the other York artisans' "makings," ultimately redeemable in this quintessential play about the place of work in the sacred narrative.[4] But the Towneley *Crucifixion*'s torturers themselves refuse the role of "mere" artisans, identifying themselves with, in the terms of Nicholas of Lyra's exegesis, the knowing "literati" who recognize Jesus but, "blinded by hatred and envy," murder him, rather than identifying with the "simplices et illiterati" led astray by the priests.[5] The significance of their literacy fully emerges later in the play when the torturers' discussion of Pilate's "boke" labeling Jesus the "kyng of Jues" becomes a full-blown critical panel on this irresolvably ambiguous "fiction," with one claiming, "I am the best Latyn wright of this company" and translating the text, while another objects, "yonder is a fals tabyll / theron is writyn noght but fabyll. . . . It is falsly writen iwis" (603–6). I begin this chapter with a play almost surely revised by the so-called "Wakefield Master," if not generally counted among his real works, in order to underscore the playwright's translation of the theme of labor into terms of writing and exegesis. In the plays attributed to the Master, as in the *Crucifixion,* the "wright" or maker has become the "Latin wright" or author.

In most critical assessments of the surviving mystery plays, the Wakefield Master himself represents the claims of literary genius. He is the poet who stands out from the urban collectives who produced the York and Chester cycles, the author who reflects upon his art and the potential of language itself—at God's expense. As Martin Stevens most forcefully articulates this view: "Many great artists have endowed their least hallowed characters with their own versatility and their own highest verbal gifts. It is in this sense that Mak and Herod and Tutivillus are precursors of Falstaff, Satan, Mr. Macawber, and even Humbert Humbert."[6] In a different vein from this idea of a brilliant psychologist pondering "my sin, my soul," Robert Weimann characterizes the pre-Shakespearean Master's innovation as a secularization of his craft in the interest of social justice:

> Here the function of the theater itself is utopian, bringing regeneration to the spirit and solidarity to the community. It is a theater old and new but consistently original in its incipient awareness of the spatial, temporal, verbal, and emotional correlatives of dramatic action. It is a religious theater that developed a new type of secular drama, interrelating the message of Christianity, the representation of society, and the self-expression of ordinary people.[7]

As emerges in both Stevens's and Weimann's accounts, the Wakefield Master is a transitional figure in the history of English theater, a writer who reflected critically on the existing Corpus Christi drama and produced a different, more problematically "modern" kind of play. Whether we regard this elusive medieval playwright as having primarily aestheticized or politicized an earlier form of drama, it is clear that he fulfills our need for at least one "author" among the fragments of text that constitute early drama.

As I will argue, the Wakefield Master's plays thematize ideas of authorship not to advance a newly secular and individualistic "literary" understanding of the stage but to use an emerging idea of literature to offer a critical gloss on the civic theater cycles of York and other towns. If the York Corpus Christi plays' narrative unity lies in their alignment of vernacular biblical exegesis with the rhetoric of good civic government, the Wakefield Master's plays wrench the work of exegesis from its urban context in order to recast an earlier version of lay spirituality with a radically different idea of mimesis. In the works on which I will focus my discussion, the *First Shepherds' Play* and its brutal dramatic inversion, the *Buffeting,* the Wakefield Master borrows from the literary culture of *Piers Plowman* in order to reimagine the terms of labor, poverty, and prophecy in an alliterative biblical theater.

Given that so little is known about the composition, production, staging, or even provenance of the plays in Huntington Library MS HM1, it is particularly difficult to assess the context of the Wakefield Master's work. Much of the critical discussion of the Towneley plays, moreover, has involved misguided attempts to interpret the "luxury volume" manuscript, based on scraps of external evidence, as some form of a Wakefield Corpus Christi cycle, analogous to the York or Chester plays, or even to the N-Town plays taken as the compiled cycle of Bury St. Edmunds. The same problem vexes all such arguments: most critics date the composition of the Wakefield Master's plays to the mid–to late fifteenth century, a time when the manorial center of Wakefield had not yet become a city with the population to support a full mystery cycle.[8] Barbara Palmer, in an exposé of sorts of the nineteenth-century ideological stakes in an urban "merry olde Wakefield" with its traditional mystery cycle, advanced the commonsensical idea of regarding the plays as a West Riding production of indeterminate origins, "a 'cycle' of parish, manor, hamlet and town . . . parts of which were acquired from York, parts of which already existed as independent plays . . . and parts of which were newly-written."[9] While this thesis leads to no further conclusions about either the venue of the plays or the identity of the Master, it does suggest a range of possibilities for the composition of nonurban theater, including the patronage of monasteries, town religious confraternities, and even the great Manor of Wakefield itself. And, as I believe the internal evidence shows, the Wakefield Master, taking the York plays as his primary exemplar, wrote his contributions in polemical contrast to the urban form of the Corpus Christi cycle.[10]

Even as they appear in the manuscript, the Towneley plays constitute a lopsided "cycle" at best, punctuated throughout by the Wakefield Master's characteristic amplification of episodes treated cursorily in other plays. Nothing suggests that any of the plays, with the possible exception of the Passion sequence, were ever performed together.[11] In place of the York *Entry into Jerusalem* that establishes the identity of the city with Jerusalem and lauds the vernacular hermeneutics of its citizens, the Wakefield Master locates his central consideration of exegesis in two plays on a *locus classicus* for theological discussions of Jesus' absolute poverty, his appearance to the shepherds.[12] In contrast to the York *Entry's* urban ideal of a prophetic exegesis based on the consensus of enfranchised burgesses, the Wakefield plays attribute prophetic insight exclusively to the dispossessed. Far from being "constructed as outsiders" for the amusement of an urban audience, as P. J. P. Goldberg has argued, the rural shepherds are at the very core of the "outsider" playwright's polemic.[13] Likewise, instead of the series of elaborate York plays on Jesus' trials in various tyrants' households, the Wakefield Master produces the stark *Buffeting,* which focuses on the violent desires of Cayphas and the four *tortores* rather than the biblical narrative sequence.[14]

The Wakefield Master's transformation of urban theatrical space, whether to the rural setting of the Shepherds' Plays or the "interior landscape" of the *Buffeting,* effectively decontextualizes and dehistoricizes the concept of theater exemplified in the York Corpus Christi celebration. Removed from the production of the city government and craft guilds, the Wakefield Master's plays reject the ideological claims that equate the annual display of worldly, civic tradition with the performance of sacred history. As Sarah Beckwith has demonstrated, the York cycle articulates the entire ritual field of Corpus Christi, Christ's sacramental body made and unmade, in terms of the definition and regulation of labor.[15] Whether primarily the expression of the political ideals of the city's mercantile governors, as I have argued, or, in Beckwith's reading, the space for an emergent "artisanal" voice, the York plays stage vernacular exegesis and spirituality as products of urban labor.[16] Players and audience alike interpret and imaginatively participate in the biblical narrative mapped onto the spaces of the city through the work of skinners, pinners, couchmakers, and weavers advertising their commodities as stage props that function as collective mnemonic devices. In this ultimately redemptive idea of human work as a creative act mimetic of divinity, labor and its made objects become spiritually "legible, " signs in a narrative that links worldly and salvific time.[17] In direct opposition to this entire urban ideology, however, the Wakefield Master's few odd works and revisions put the *form* of the Corpus Christi play to the new polemical end of dismantling the theater of labor in favor of a theater of prophetic vision.

By focusing in the two Shepherds' Plays on the oppressive conditions of rural labor, the Wakefield Master introduces a new kind of peasant to the late medieval stage. Although entirely unlike the snarling, greedy Cain, who was previously the representative rural figure in mystery plays, the Wakefield shepherds are themselves displaced plowmen, symbolically identifiable with neither the primal killer nor his sacrificed brother.[18] They are instead typically voiceless small land-holders given voice, like Piers Plowman and his heirs, through a privileged access to truth in exegetical reading. While in the York *Shepherd* play, which survives only in fragmentary form, Pastor 2 is sure to defer to scriptural interpretation "by witty lerned men" (18), in the Wakefield versions, the Shepherds themselves have become the "learned men." Yet their collective voice, in its frank condemnation of the injustices of lords and hypocrisies of friars, also, as Weimann stresses, carries an undertone of revolt.[19] If the memory of Corpus Christi 1381 was revived with each subsequent English political rebellion, including Jack Cade's abortive uprising of 1450, the Shepherds' Plays, however quietly, share that uneasy legacy. Although representative of a rebellion of artisans and lower gentry rather than peasants, the surviving "Bills of Complaint" of 1450, with their outrage at legal corruption, find resonance in the shepherds' laments.[20] The bills, like the documents of earlier revolts as well as a long history of social complaint, single out for condemnation the practices of *maintenance,* the magnates' support of lawless bands of liveried retainers, and *purveyance,* these retainers' pillaging of food and property. Particularly if a manorial audience took in the *First Shepherds' Play* rather than its funnier and safer alternate piece, those in positions of power might well catch the warning encoded in the peasants' learned and lewd spiritual discourses.

Rosemary Woolf recognizes Virgil's *Eclogues* as an intertext of the Wakefield Shepherds' Plays that "provided for the poet at least a literary context in which the shepherd as a man of learning would not be out of place."[21] The *Eclogues* also provide a model for a politicized poetics in Virgil's criticisms of Octavian's land confiscations and a vocabulary with which to explore, in Annabel Patterson's words, "the responsibility of the intellectual for telling the whole truth" even while in the service of power.[22] As the *First Shepherd's Play*'s idiosyncratic quotation of the "messianic" lines from the *Fourth Eclogue* shows, in a passage I will discuss later, the Wakefield Master draws attention to the similarities between Virgil's rustics and his own. The English shepherds are dispossessed like Meliboeus, the exiled farmer of the *First Eclogue,* and left with an enforced *otium* that becomes the occasion for not only political allegory but poetic inspiration, and, finally, prophecy.[23] Moreover, the shepherds' theatrical idea of their own *otium* as "play" likewise signals their authorial status, following Servius's definitive equation of Virgil's musical *ludere* with *scribere* or poetic composition.[24] Above all, the

Wakefield shepherds, by analogy to the *Eclogues'*, are players open to interpretation, exemplary *literary* figures—not unlike Langland's Will the Dreamer and Piers the Plowman—understood to encompass multiple social identities according to exegesis.[25] Heirs to a tradition of readings, beginning with Servius's widely circulated commentaries, they are at once rural and urban, peasants and poets.

If, as Claire Sponsler has argued, the York plays themselves encompass a "locus for antilabor sentiment" in the images of the broken, and hence economically unproductive, bodies of Christ and the slaughtered innocents, the Wakefield Master takes this implicit concept of resistance to a new level.[26] In the *First Shepherds' Play,* the characters' loss of work allows them to reclaim their bodies intact for the privileged acts of prophecy and interpretation. The Wakefield Master here and elsewhere shows a concern with the metaphysics as well as the politics of theater. By staging various themes of creation, he offers a critique of urban mystery cycles similar in one respect to that of the *Tretise of Miraclis Pleyinge;* his plays all reject the material reproduction of biblical history and instead work to convey a sense of exegetical or allegorical understanding.

THE EMPTY BAG

In the long social laments that open both the Shepherds' Plays, the shepherds interestingly reveal that they aren't even really shepherds but rather farmers, agricultural laborers forced out of work by the oppressions of the local gentry. As Coll (1 Pastor) puts it in the more detailed version of the *Second Shepherds' Play,*

> No wonder, as it standys, / If we be poore,
> For the tylthe of our landys / Lyys fallow as the floore,
> As ye ken . . .
> These men that are lord-fest / Thay cause the ploghe tary;
> That, men say, is for the best— / We find it contrary.
>
> (18–32)

He goes on to describe the "swane" liveried with a "paynt-slefe or a broche":

> He can make purveyance / With boste and bragance,
> And all is thrugh mantenance / Of men that are gretter.
> Ther shall com a swane / As prowde as a po;

He must borrow my wane, / My ploghe also;
Then I am ful fane / To graunt or he go.
Thus lyf we in payne, / Anger and wo
By nyght and day.

(49–61)

Coll's solitary "mone" provides the elements that set both Shepherds' Plays in motion: the plowmen's actual inability to perform their labor and their rebellious interiority that articulates the "contrary" to a dominant political and literary voice, as these peasants actively resist their redefinition into "shepherds." Coll here also reveals the theatrical limits of maintenance itself, the social insubstantiality of the retainer/robber identifiable only by his sign of livery, much as the play's stolen sheep is finally known from its earmark. Coll's "swane" in turn foreshadows Mak's brief unsuccessful attempt to impersonate such a figure, "sond from a greatt lordyng," by speaking in his "Sothren tothe."

Gyb (Pastor 1) in the *First Shepherds' Play* gives much the same account of the loss of his livelihood at the hands of "bosters and bragers": "Both ploghe and wane / Amendys will not make." While in the more celebrated second play, the shepherds' laments set them up to deal, as rather inept "readers," with the metatheatrical, falsely emotional complaints of Mak and Gyll, as well as the duo's attempted "purveyance" of a sheep, Gyb's speech introduces the first play's theme of absolute "poverté."[27] As Gyb goes on to explain, he actually has neither plow nor sheep:

All my shepe are gone, / I am not left oone
The rott has theym slone; / Now beg I and borrow. . . .
I have nerehand nothyng / To pay nor to take.

(36–47)

Reduced to the bottom of the social order, where he is no longer of any use to potential "purveyors," the beggar turns inward, to the resources of "mynde" and "wytt" to invent new livestock. As Jak rebukes Gyb when he claims he's going to buy some new sheep, "What, dreme ye or slepe?" (148). From this point, the shepherds' begging reveals itself as a kind of imaginary economics, a demand for words and mental images more than for things.

Critics have long commented that the Wakefield Master's "shepherds" speak to a social realism concerning contemporary tensions over land enclosure.[28] The shepherds' description of themselves as former plowmen or small freeholders does suggest the playwright's awareness of those who were losing their land through a combination of a bad rural economy and oppressive political conditions. In their range of social identities beyond the strained exegetical role of biblical shepherds, however, the peasants also articulate resonances with a constellation of Franciscan, Langlandian, and even Wycliffite ideas about poverty.[29] In this regard, the two Shepherds' Plays are a brief exception to Nicholas Watson's observation that there are "no clearly orthodox works after *Piers Plowman* in which a *rusticus* acts as a teacher"; indeed, the Wakefield Master's *rustici,* by expounding a vernacular prophetic authority, actually foreclose the Corpus Christi play's potential simple allegorical identification of them with more orthodox clerical *pastores.*[30]

Piers Plowman, in its three versions, the A, B, and C-Texts, enjoyed an extraordinarily wide circulation throughout England by the fifteenth century. Although no manuscripts of the poem appear to have been copied in Yorkshire, two of the earliest references to *Piers*'s readership, in 1396 and 1431, are from the wills of secular clergy in York.[31] The poem's initial diverse audience of ecclesiastics and laymen, as Anne Middleton has shown in a study of Piers manuscripts and their owners, were drawn to the poem not by regional or class affiliations but by a "common social location" and a set of intellectual interests. The poem's readers, concerned with their own practices of rule, counsel, and education, were deeply invested in the "foundations of Christian authority" and the ideas of how best to live and work within an authentically spiritual community.[32] The Wakefield Master surely came from a background similar to that of these readers, given his own clear intellectual interests in these very questions of spirituality and politics. The traces of *Piers Plowman* in his work mirror the poem's immediate reception and transmission and the adoption of Piers himself as the embodiment of an ideal spiritual community. The *First Shepherds' Play,* as a drama of literary production, recapitulates the genesis of Langland's plowman as an "author," from the enigmatic reference in "Jak Carter"'s 1381 Letter to "Peres the Plowman my brothur" to Chaucer's pregnantly silent Plowman, the virtuous Parson's brother in the *Canterbury Tales,* to the desperately poor farmer of the Wycliffite *Piers Plowman's Crede.*[33]

The Wakefield Master likewise follows Langland's spiritual map, moving from the city to the world of rural labor to his protagonists' exegetical dreamscape. The city, in this scheme, is, however, not the London of *Piers Plowman*'s satire on Mede and the court but instead the exemplar of the York plays, the most elaborate performance of urban identities as defined by labor guilds. The York *Entry into Jerusalem* play, as we have seen, erases the truly poor in its vision of burghal community. The Wakefield Master explodes the city's equation of social identity with work by evoking, in the agrarian setting of the Shepherds' Plays, an inherent theatricality of poverty.[34] The "teacher" who emerges in the *First Shepherds' Play* is the ironically named Slawpase (3 Pastor), who, when he finds his two fellow-shepherds arguing over where Gyb can pasture his imaginary sheep, makes his own empty grain sack into the play's central heuristic emblem. The bag, emptied of visible material, becomes a multivalent site for a performance of both poverty and fictional representation. In the absence of the plow, the peasants' labor turns into the work of mimesis. As Slawpase admonishes the shepherds:

> This sek thou thrawe / on my bak,
> Whylst I, with my hand, / Lawse the sek-band
> Com ner and by-stand, / Both Gyg and Jak.
> Is not all shaken owte, / And no meyll is therin
>
> . . . .
>
> So is youre wittys thyn, / And ye look well abowte
> Nawther more nor myn; / So gose your wyttys owte,
> Even as it com in. / Geder up and seke it again!
>
> (237–54)

The shepherds take Slawpase's abusive lesson at its most profound level: that is, in its use of the bag as a spatial and economic metaphor for the mind as well as the much-contested social mark of the beggar. Jak responds, " He has told us full plane / Wysdom to sup" (255–56), which leads immediately into the play's center-piece of a meal literally of "wisdom," the shepherds' communal feast on imaginary food and drink. When Jak claims: "I have here in my mayll / Southen and rost / Even of an ox-tayll / That wold not be lost" (322–25), his bag is the well-established Chaucerian figure for the generation of narrative—most familiar from Harry Bailly's response to the *Knight's Tale,* "unbokled is the male. / Let se now who shal telle another tale" (3115–16)—yet, in a mordant pun, the "mayll" is also his stomach, as empty as the shepherds' bags.[35]

The icon of the bag in the context of this episode also recalls the discourse of Franciscan debates over apostolic poverty and *Piers Plowman*'s translation of these terms into the registers of lay spirituality and labor. While in Francis's own Earlier Rule of 1221 Judas's bag represents the treachery of all property, later Franciscan polemics necessarily return to the more traditional view of the "common reserves" of goods held by Christ and the apostles.[36] In Bonaventure's *Apologia Pauperum,* written to defend the Franciscan doctrine of absolute poverty against the objections of the secular masters, Judas's bag becomes central to the question of whether Jesus and the apostles held common dominion over money.[37] For Bonaventure, interestingly, the bag is an outward sign of imperfection, used by the absolutely poor Christ as an example, "an act of condescension" to his less perfect followers.[38] As a material sign, the bag is, in effect, Jesus' version of a theatrical prop, an unnecessary sign for the Franciscans themselves, who seek to follow the naked Christ's example to the perfect. In the *Legenda Maior,* his life of Francis, Bonaventure likewise reports the saint as advancing a spiritual metaphor of the bag as any mark of the self or the "proper."[39]

For Langland, as for the later Spiritual Franciscans, the bag once again becomes the sign of the false disciple's attachment to property, and hence the means by which to distinguish truly apostolic from false beggars.[40] In his own highly ambiguous *apologia* in Passus V of the C-Text, the Dreamer / Will describes himself as wandering between London and "upland," laboring with his primer and psalter and begging only for food: "on this wyse I begge / withoute bagge or bottel but my wombe one." (51–52)[41] In Passus IX, he elaborates on the "lunatyk lollares and lepares about" (107) who "bereth none bagges ne boteles under clokes" (139), those who, together with the working poor, "oure neyhebores . . . pore folk in cotes, / Charged with childrene and chief lordes rente" (71–73), will be included in Truth's pardon to Piers Plowman. As opposed to the false beggars, these are "munstrels of heaven, / And godes boys, bourdeyors" (127–28). Rather than the friars, "beggares with bagges" (98), it is the truly poor who are given prophetic knowledge: "Right as Peter dede and poul, save þat þey preche nat / Ne none muracles maken; Ac hem many tymes hem happeth to profecye of the peple, pleinge, as hit were" (112–14). The Wakefield Master's Langlandian touch is to directly relate "playing," in the senses of vernacular fiction making and theater, to prophecy, and to both a literal and spiritual poverty.[42]

THE SHEPHERD'S PLOW AS UNMADE OBJECT

The Wakefield Master transforms his Langlandian laborers not only into holy "minstrels" or prophets but into exegetes and writers. In this line of representation, he comes close to the Wycliffite gloss *Piers Plowman's Crede,* in which Langland's elusive allegorical figure becomes "Peres . . . *the pore man,* the plowe-man"

(473, emphasis added), the teacher of the vernacular *Credo* and implacable foe of the four orders of friars.[43] As Anne Middleton has argued, Langland defines his literary project through the breakdown of fixed social identities evidenced by the labor and vagrancy acts of the Cambridge Parliament of 1388: the "permutability" of identities among laborers, beggars, and gentry enables the work of the "maker" of social representations.[44] While the *Second Shepherds' Play* demonstrates the limits of one kind of social "making" as the endlessly permutable Mak and his partner Gyll utterly fail to convince the shepherds of their invented identities, including the "false wark" (887) of sacramental parody in "making" a sheep into their child, the *First Shepherds' Play* suggests more radical possibilities.

In this play the empty bag, an emblem of apostolic poverty, occupies the place of the made object, the commodity that functions as the guild's collective signature in each of the York Corpus Christi plays. By replacing a sign of redemptive labor with a sign of its absence, the Wakefield Master subverts the urban form of the play in order to recall invisible acts, the fictive and then prophetic work of the unemployed plowmen-shepherds.[45] As Beckwith argues of the "sacramental culture" of the York plays, the stage reveals "the tension between the seen and unseen at its most impossible and contradictory."[46] The plays produce the visible body of Christ over and over while undermining simultaneously both his disciples' and the audience's need for ocular proof; in Beckwith's reading, "[W]e encounter Christ's body in the confused vision of the others who continually fail to see."[47] The Wakefield Master pushes these contradictions of the Corpus Christi play to their limits by harnessing invisibility to material poverty and finding the possibility of privileged spiritual "vision" in the shepherds' unstable social identities. In the Wakefield Master's polemical stagecraft, the audience is forced to confront what it *doesn't* see. The *First Shepherds' Play*'s drama of absence and presence ultimately demonstrates the gulf between the materially mimetic Corpus Christi stage and its own exegetical theater.

Much has been made by critics of the "incongruities" of the feast that the three shepherds imagine, with its combinations of "aristocratic" recipes like "a calf-liver scored with the veryose" (341–42) and peasants' fare like "two swynegronys" (330).[48] The Wakefield Master, however, uses the social valences of these imaginary dishes to emphasize that the shepherds' "store," as they call it, is actually a "storehouse of forms," a term in late medieval faculty psychology for imagination, the power that enables the mind's division and recombination of images in the absence of objects.[49] The shepherds' *phantasia* in this case is pointedly political; by means of their imaginative powers, they "lay forth" a meal that points to a dissolution of the very social boundaries between shepherds and "prowde" thieves that set the play in motion. If, as seems more than likely, the Wakefield Master wrote the *First Shepherds' Play* in response to an exemplar resembling an earlier version of the Chester play, in which the shepherds draw from their bags and eat a plentiful if rough feast on stage, the politics of his "incongruities" are indeed striking.[50] The shepherds' plenitude in the Wakefield play is instead an imaginative "poaching"—or, in reverse social terms, "purveying"—of aristocratic culture that, in its intimations of political unrest, evokes the theatricality of the events of Corpus Christi during the 1381 Peasants' Revolt.[51]

As a response to the stolen plow and dead sheep that explain the emptiness of the stage, the shepherds' production of food becomes a literary exercise, a eucharistic parody with a rebellious edge. If the peasants' agricultural labor provided them with a real and symbolic link to the bread of the Eucharist, the visible and edible Corpus Christi, the trio of shepherds work instead to represent the invisible Christ. As Gyb reacts to Slawpase's mouth-watering catalog of gourmet meats:

> Yee speke all by clergé / I here by youre clause
> Cowth ye by youre gramery / Reche us a drynk,
> I shuld be more mery—Ye wote what I think.
>
>   (346–51)

Contrary to the assertions of various of the play's readers, most recently Lois Roney and Lauren Lepow, that the imaginary feast is somehow an "unwitting" parody of the eucharistic bread and wine enacted by mindless "fools," the shepherds' vocabulary is self-consciously literary, a product of their "incongruous" Virgilian and Langlandian learning.[52] Indeed, Gyb later uses almost the same terms to characterize the *Eclogues,* conflating the sacramental and the poetic, the miraculous and the fictional: "Virgill in his poetré / Sayde in his verse, / Even thus be gameré" (556–58). Like the clergy whose role they perform here, the shepherds make their food and wine by "grammar," the learned use of language. The obvious anachronism of the Corpus Christi parody only lends further weight to the play's central idea that radical poverty is the true basis of prophetic insight.

The shepherds' simultaneously utopian and ironic *memoria* of food— another "dish" they share is "moton / Of a ewe that was roton" (318–19)—recalls the historical "memory" of the Peasants' Revolt and the "forgotten" or suppressed meanings of Corpus Christi. As both Margaret Aston and Steven Justice have demonstrated, the idiom of the feast, its rituals and festivities, shaped the rebels' sense of communal identity as well as the specific terms of their protests against restrictions of labor, landholding, and milling.[53] Aston in particular emphasizes the theatricality of the revolt in her account of how certain rebels adopted new identities:

> Other recruiters for the rising, who resorted to false pretences and intimidation, were busy on the days leading up to Corpus Christi. In Northamptonshire about Trinity Sunday, John Seynt-Pere was said to have pretended that he was Sir John Philpot of London on a wool-purchasing mission, in order to incite people to rise in the villages of Church Brampton and Harlestone. In Cambridgeshire, Thomas Roo (Wroo or Roode) of Wood Ditton was accused of acting as a summoner, claiming royal authority for issuing threats of loss of life and burning of houses against those who did not join the rebel commons. He had been on his rounds on Corpus Christi Day and from six days before and after the feast.[54]

For the duration of the revolt, Corpus Christi became a license for the social fluidity that occasioned these "performances" in the first place. As opposed to urban artisans' impersonations of aristocratic or clerical figures like Herod or Cayphas in the mystery plays, or Mak's failed "southern gentleman" act, the rural rebels' new identities were apparently convincing to their audiences. And their audiences wanted to believe in these particular fictions. In these episodes, as Aston suggests, the rebels translated the miraculous eucharistic change of the substance of bread and wine into a diffuse social transformation. By enacting a kind of Corpus Christi play-within-a-play as a consequence of their own oppressions, the Wakefield Master's plowmen-shepherds reinscribe the social disruptiveness of the feast. The shepherds' imagined "consumption," rather than assumption, of aristocratic culture, however, actually does invest them with a new status, an authority of poverty.

ANOTHER VERSION OF PASTORAL

In the play's most radical valorization of poverty, the shepherds' imaginative play leads directly into their reception of divine prophecy. Following the path of Bonaventure's *Itinerarium Mentis in Deum* (*The Journey of the Soul into God*), the shepherds ascend to a perfect contemplation of divinity through the faculties of mind, including imagination and reason.[55] In the *Itinerarium*'s sacramental logic, the "vestiges, images, and displays" (*vestigia, simulacra et spectacula*) of sensible things ultimately lead the mind to spiritual vision; the contemplative moves "from external things to those that are within, and from the temporal to the eternal" (*ab exterioribus ad intima, a temporalibus conscendimus ad aeterna*).[56] Just as Bonaventure describes his imitation of the perfectly poor St. Francis as the beginning of his own illumination, the shepherds' apostolic poverty is the basis of their mystical ascent, from their memory of "sensible" food to the prophecies of Christ's birth, from the invisible signs of imagination to the invisible truth. In an antifraternal jab particularly close to the spirit of *Piers Plowman,* the shepherds conclude their feast by suggesting that they give the leftovers to the friars:

> 1 PASTOR: Then wold I we fest, / This mete who shall
> Into panyere kest.
> 3 PASTOR: Syrs, herys! / For oure saules lett us do /
> Poore men gyf it to.
> 1 PASTOR: Geder up, lo, lo, / Ye hungré begers frerys!
>   (405–12)

This exchange, which immediately precedes the shepherds' visionary experience, distinguishes their poverty from that of the falsely poor Franciscans. A distant echo of the thirteenth-century *Sacrum Commercium,* in which St. Francis's true disciples treat Lady Poverty to a *convivium* of stale barley bread, cold water, and bitter herbs, the shepherds' feast marks their own claim on the mendicant ideal.[57] While the debased friars receive scraps of nothing—empty signs from an empty bag—from these workers who have themselves become beggars, the laymen receive St Francis's real legacy of privileged vision. The friars' desire remains as the physical hunger staged in the play, while the shepherds' desire becomes an allegory of contemplation. As the "teacher" Slawpase describes the angelic visit that awakens them from their sleep:

> It was mervell to se, / So bright as it shone;
> I wold have trowyd, veraly, / It had bene thoner-flone,
> Bot I sagh with myn ee / As I lenyd to this stone.
>   (465–70)

The shepherds' "vision" in turn is revealed as the *Ordo Prophetarum,* the exegetical reading of the Old Testament and other prophecies that is the exclusive domain of either clerical commentators, royal entries, or, in the York cycle,
the urban elite. In one of the Wakefield Master's strangest passages, Gyb immediately perceives the revolutionary potential of the angel's thundering voice
but is worried at first that it is the sound of a new oppressor or perhaps, given
that it immediately follows the shepherds' antifraternal commentary, the noise of
a popular revolt:

> I am ferd, by Jesus, / Somwhat be wrang
> Me thought / Oone scremyd on lowde.
> I suppose it was a cloude; In my erys it sowde,
> By hym that me boght!
> $$(445-51)$$

Jak explains the socially leveling implications of prophecy in his interpretation
of the story of Nebuchadnezzar and the three young men thrown into the fur-
nace from Daniel 1–3. Of the fourth man who appears in the fire, he explains:

> That fygure / was gyffen by revalacyon
> That God wold have a son;
> This is a good lesson / Us to consydure.
> $$(512-16)$$

The nature of the shepherds' insight is presented here and elsewhere as textual; in their poverty, they become privileged readers of the bare "plain text" of
Scripture.

The relationship between the shepherds and the friars in their roles as exegetes becomes clearer at the end of the *Ordo Prophetarum,* with Gyb's backwards
rehearsal of the "messianic" lines of the Fourth Eclogue:

> *Iam nova progenies celo demittitur alto*
> *Iam rediet Virgo, redeunt Saturnia regna.*
> $$(558-59)$$

> [Now a new generation descends from heaven on high
> Now the Virgin returns, the reign of Saturn returns.][58]

Virgil's words, taken as those of the Cumaean Sybil, appear in the *Ordo*'s ultimate source, the Pseudo-Augustine *Sermo contra Judaeos,* and had been accepted as genuinely prophetic of Christ's birth since Lactantius's fourth-century interpretation.[59] St. Jerome, however, in contrast to other patristic thinkers, had early on expressed doubts about the pagan Latin poet's place in Christian biblical exegesis.[60] The Wakefield Master, to astonishing polemical effect, momentarily returns some of Jerome's anxiety about the pagan author to this text. In contrast to the trio's calm recitation of Isaiah, Jeremiah, and the minor Hebrew prophets, Jak explodes into obscenity at the mention of Virgil:

> Weme! Tord!
> What speke ye / here in my eres?
> Tell us no clergé! / I hold you of the freres; / Ye preche.
> It seems by youre Laton / Ye have lerd youre Caton.
>
> (560–66)

The shepherd here repeats a charge that the Wycliffites had frequently leveled against the friars: that their preaching was "ungrounded" in Scripture and relied instead on entertaining secular literature. In the words of the Lollard treatise *The Lanterne of Light:* "þei prechen cronyclis wiþ poyses & dremyngis & manye oþir helples talis þat riȝt nouȝt availen."[61] By applying these terms to the Fourth Eclogue, however, the playwright, again following the spirit of *Piers Plowman,* forces a reevaluation of the place of literary work in the sacred narrative. Not only does the eclogue's quotation of the Cumaean Sybil necessarily remain a prophetic text, as St. Augustine and subsequent tradition had established, but the shepherds' identity with Virgil's shepherd-poets becomes explicit. As readers and authors of fictions, they occupy an entirely different ethical position from the "turd" friars.

In the Wakefield Master's *Herod,* the spluttering tyrant himself demands an absolute distinction between sacred and secular texts as he orders his counselors to tell him the prophecies of Christ:

> Syrs, I pray you inquere / in all wrytyng,
> In Vyrgyll, in Homere,
> And all other thyng / Bot legende.
> Sekys poecé-tayllys, / Lefe pystyls and grales;
> Mes, matyns noght avalys — / All these I defende.
>
> (291–99)

With this topsy-turvy version of the Wycliffite position against combining Scripture and ungrounded "legend," the playwright downplays the distinction itself in favor of a sharp focus on the motives and powers of the canon-forming exegete. When his counselors reply that "prophecy . . . is not blynd" and disobediently recite the words of Isaiah, Herod orders the "dottypols" to cast their books "into the brookys" (335–36); he then immediately commands "all the flower of knighthede" (393) to massacre the children of the kingdom. For the Wakefield Master, the danger of prophetic texts lies with the interpreter; hence Virgil, ambiguously pagan and Christian, can represent both the tyrant's tool and the shepherds' model. In the *First Shepherds Play,* the citation of the *Fourth Eclogue* and the brief argument surrounding it functions as a trace of the shepherds' specifically *literary* work, a link between their imaginative play and their final prophetic insight. The eclogue's ambiguity is further underlined by the shepherds' reading of it, rather than the Hebrew prophets, as the answer to their poverty and oppression. Gyb translates Virgil's lines into idiosyncratic English poetry:

> He sayde from heven /A new kynde is send,
> Whom a vyrgyn to neven / Oure mys to amend,
> Shall conceyve full even / Thus make I an end.
> $$(569–74)$$

After pointedly finishing the christological interpretation of the text, Gyb adds:

> And yit more to neven,
> That Saturne shall bend / Unto us,
> With peasse and plenté / Wyth ryches and menee
> Good luf and charyté / Blendyd amanges us.
> $$(575–81)$$

"Saturn," the sign of Virgil's pagan text, the element that remains unabsorbed into the Christian narrative, becomes the very principle of theatrical social revolt. While medieval commentators on the *Eclogues* generally identify Saturn with peace and stability, the playwright's shepherds hint at the other Saturn, the melancholic god who, in Chaucer's *Knight's Tale,* announces: "Myn is the stranglyng and hanging by the throte, / the murmure and the cherles rebelling" (2458–59).[62] Like the rebels who adopted new identities on Corpus Christi in 1381, the shepherds foresee turning into the lords whom they accused of having stolen their property at the opening of the play. Instead of being at the mercy of a lord's "bosters and bragers," they themselves will be at the head of a "menee" or retinue. Virgil's line, a surplus to the *Ordo Prophetarum,* and like the empty bag, a sign wrested away from the friars' exegetical control, lingers as a reminder of the peasants' protest.

Hence even as the shepherds end the play teaching their ideology of poverty to the baby Jesus, they reiterate the material, political conditions of their lives with the hope of exchanging their enforced *otium* for a utopian plenitude. The three shepherds' gifts to Jesus are emblems of poverty and play analogous to the empty bag: an empty box, an empty bottle, and a ball.[63] As Gyb gives Jesus the box, also iconographically a pyx, a container for the Corpus Christi itself, his pun on the verb meaning at once "to play" and "to lack" again underlines the poor shepherds' imaginative work:

> I pray the to take, / If thou wold, for my sake —
> With this thou may *lake* [emphasis added]— / This lytyll spruce cofer.
> (669–72)

With considerable dramatic irony, the shepherds set the standard of apostolic poverty for Jesus himself, the newly born *joculator dei,* the Franciscan "player of God."[64] Moreover, in the final lines of the play, they reveal themselves not just as visionaries but as authors:

> 2 PASTOR (JAK):   We shall this *recorde* [emphasis added] /
>   Wheras we go
> 3 PASTOR (SLAWPASE):   We mon all be restorde — / God grant it so!
> (714–17)

Even with the advent of Christ, these lines leave the audience not far from where they began, as witnesses to the new record of these incipiently literary plowmen's complaint against the gentry. To the last, the shepherds' work has the double end of "restoring" their lost plows and sheep and the salvation promised by their exegesis.

As they describe their visionary experience, following Isaiah 29, the shepherds apparently collapse their singular understanding of prophecy and the visual event they are about to share with the audience:

1 PASTOR:	Wold God that we myght / This yong bab see!
2 PASTOR:	Many prophets that syght / Desyred veralee,
	To have seen that bright.
3 PASTOR:	And God so hee / Wold show us that wyght
	We myght say, perdé, / We had sene
	That many sant desyryd, / With prophetys inspyryd;
	If thay hym requyryd, / Yet closyd ar thare eene.

(634–46)

The appeal to vision, however, serves mainly to raise the question of what the audience actually does see. Given the Wakefield Master's rejection of the visible throughout the play in favor of the shepherds' inward senses, the audience ultimately has no material signs of identity with the actors. These lines epitomize the playwright's polemical response to the Corpus Christi cycles' focus on labor as the bond between the audience of guildsmen-actors and the mimetic stage. In contrast to the York plays' performance of exegesis as a form of obedience to urban political structures, the *First Shepherds' Play* demands social and psychological identity with its trio of empty-handed beggars as the precondition for allegorical and contemplative understanding. In his stagecraft of poverty, the Wakefield Master suggests that most of the audience's eyes remain closed to the shepherds' insights, whether they *see* the "yong babe" representing Jesus or not.

By drawing on the most radical political consequences of the Franciscan linking of poverty and prophecy, the Wakefield Master produces shepherds who sound like another Langlandian figure, the Wycliffite self-designated *agricola* Walter Brut, who cites the same passage of Isaiah 29 as the basis for his persona of the "laicus litteratus," the literate layman.[65] Writing in 1391 to the issue of why God would reveal prophecies of Antichrist to him rather than to Bishop John Trefnant and his other learned examiners, Brut writes, "But if you should find any goodness in my writings, ascribe it to God only, who, according to the multitude of his mercy, doth sometimes reveal those things to idiots and sinners, which are hidden from the holy and wise."[66] He continues, aligning himself with the Hebrew prophets:

> Also in Isaiah it is written . . . "*He shall shut your eyes, he shall cover your prophets and princes that see visions. And a vision shall be to you altogether like the words of a sealed book, which when he shall give it to one that is learned he shall say, Read here, and he shall answer, I cannot, for it is sealed. And

the book shall be given to one to one that is unlearned, and knoweth not his letters and it shall be said unto him, Read, and he shall answer, I know not the letters, I am unlearned."[67]

"Wat Brut," who was later celebrated by "Piers" himself in *Pierce the Plowman's Crede,* "for he seyde hem the sothe" (667–68) is no more "unlettered," despite his claims, than Virgil's poet-shepherd Tityrus. Nevertheless, he draws on the figure of the visionary plowman to remove exegesis from all clerical control. Indeed, in Brut's apocalyptic logic, extreme even for a Wycliffite, all legitimate reading practice becomes a form of visionary experience. The Wakefield shepherds, although neither explicitly apocalyptic nor heterodox, nevertheless follow the *Piers Plowman* tradition in their protest against urban culture and the exegetical assumptions that underwrite its version of lay spirituality. These new incarnations of the poor plowman reappear in the Wakefield plays specifically to renounce the mimetic experience of the Corpus Christi play, the sacrament made visible, in favor of the intellectual work of the "players." Even as he revives an earlier spiritual model, the Wakefield Master's metatheatrical "modernity" is manifest in his lesson to the audience: the illusion of theater—or even the sight of Christ's body—is blindness without the illumination of apostolic poverty.

"TO USE MY HAND"

If the *First Shepherd's Play* argues against the visual agenda of the mystery cycles with its staging of poverty and prophecy, the Wakefield Master's unique treatment of the *Buffeting* inverts his earlier politics of visibility as the three torturers concentrate at near-absurd length on the act of blindfolding Jesus. The playwright previews his conception of the *tortores* in the play of the *Murder of Abel,* when Cain beats his servant and then replies to the boy's complaints about the "boffetys," "Peas, man! I did it bot to use my hand" (395). For Jesus' torturers, buffeting is a similar type of compulsive labor. In the playwright's decontextualized treatment of the Passion narrative, Christ's antagonists are no longer the blaspheming "Jews" of N-Town or Chester or the Nuremburg Defense–ready "Soldiers" of York; they are defined solely by their work, as "tortores"—literally, those who bend and twist, here with their bare hands.[68] In their travesty of labor, the torturers "create" or fashion Jesus' body in response to an interiority that identifies them as the knowing, literate counterparts to the shepherds. The *Buffeting,* however, is a drama of interiority misdirected toward visible things rather than contemplative ascent. As Tortor 2 warns Jesus at the beginning of the play:

It is wonder to dre, / Thus to be gangyng.
We have had for the / Mekill hart-stangyng
But at last shall we be / Out of hart-langyng
(14–19)

Contrary to Kolve's argument that the *tortores'* self-focus reflects a lack of understanding that absolves them of full responsibility, the Wakefield Master's goal is to indict their emotional response *as* a flawed form of interpretation. Their joy in making is intimately related to their joy in seeing what they've made of Jesus' body, the precise pleasure at the intersection of work, interpretation, and theater.[69] Here the plot is driven not by corrupt legal or political forces but by a pure desire for violence; similarly, Cayphas, the main figure in the play, is torn between his priestly office and his own longing to wreak mayhem on Jesus. While the other priest, Anna, suggests that Jesus is "inwardly flayed" (263)—already damaged inside, too scared to answer their questions—Cayphas appeals to his own inner condition: "Bot I give him a blaw / My hart will brist" (276–77).

Jody Enders has written of the "ludic violence" of the Passion plays that "it was the province of some medieval dramas to invent and reinvent the spectacular, persuasive powers of torture as a great dramatic game with all of the ambiguous pleasures that derived from all the ambiguous pain."[70] In the *Buffeting,* the playwright himself stages the origins of visual pleasure in the theatrical desire for control over vision itself. Much in line with the *First Shepherds' Play's* theme of vision, Jesus' one speech in the *Buffeting* is the prophetic utterance of the gospel accounts:

For after this shall thou se / When that [I] come downe
In brightnes on he, / In clowdes from abone.
(365–68)

While this is what will happen, both literally onstage and allegorically, the torturers spend the rest of the play trying to deny the prophecy by blinding Jesus. While Cayphas threatens that "I shal out-thrist / Both his een on a raw" (279–80), the *tortores* come up with the "ludic" alternative of the blindfold. In a particularly convoluted version of the torturer's search for concealed "truth" in the victim's body, the *tortores* announce that they will use Christ's body to disprove his prophecy: "We shall preve on his crowne / The wordys he has sayde."[71] They next devote an inordinate number of lines to the act of blindfolding itself, as follows:

> 1 TORTOR: But his een must be hid
>
> 2 TORTOR: Yei but thei be wel spard, / We lost that we did. (535–37)
>
> . . . .
>
> 2 TORTOR: Thou must get us a vayll. (544)
>
> . . . .
>
> FROWARD: Here a vayll have I fon; / I trow it will last.
>
> 1 TORTOR: Bryng it hyder good son. / That is it that I ast.
>
> FROWARD: How shuld it be bon?
>
> 2 TORTOR: Abowte his heade cast.
>
> 1 TORTOR: Yei, and when it is well won, / Knyt a knot fast . . .
>
> 1 TORTOR: Now sen he is blynfeld, I fall to begyn.
>
> (560–74)

Just like the empty bags of the First Shepherds' Play, the blindfold — an otherwise useless and worthless piece of cloth — functions as a parodic version of the mystery cycles' commodity-props. As these torturers' sole instrument, the veil's only purpose is to disrupt Christ's narrative by obscuring his "vision." While this scene captures an irony already in the accounts of the buffeting in the Gospels — a reversal of the blindnesses of beater and beaten — the Wakefield Master charges it with a specifically theatrical meaning.[72]

In a striking similarity to the *Tretise of Miraclis Pleyinge,* the playwright zeros in on the *Buffeting* as the moment in the mystery plays where the actors most threaten to blur the distinction between representation and reality — the torturers' blasphemous pleasures and the audience's. If the *Tretise*'s Wycliffite-influenced author makes "the Jewis that bobbiden Crist" into his emblem for the "miraclis pleyers" who scorn God and, by extension, a mimesis that fails to convey allegorical meaning, the Wakefield Master, perhaps responding to this line of antitheatrical rhetoric, uses this play to explore theater's resistance to exegetical method. When the *tortores* put their sturdy "vayll" over Christ's eyes, it is they who remain in the "veiled" realm of Old Testament figures, refusing to heed the prophecy.[73] And Cayphas, like the Wakefield Herod, focuses his rage on Scripture and the unbearable responsibilities of the interpreter:

He that first made me clerk / And taught me my lare
On bookys for to barke — / The dwill gyf hym care!

$$(443-46)$$

As we have seen, Herod orders his counselors to throw their prophetic texts in the river right before he summons his soldiers to go massacre all children in order to nullify the prophecy of Christ. Cayphas's similar violence, both inspired and barely restrained by his learning, is also essentially a desire to be free of the script of an inexorable narrative.

In the *Tretise*'s terms, the theatrical audience's emotions are the main obstacle to a correct reception of Scripture. Of the viewers' tears for the suffering Christ, the *Tretise* draws a strict distinction between inner and outer stimuli:

> siche miraclis pleyinge giveth noon occasioun of werrey wepinge and medeful, but the weping that fallith to men and wymmen by the sighte of siche miraclis pleyinge, as they ben not principaly for theire oune sinnes ne of theire gode feith withinneforth, but more of theire sight withouteforth is not alowable byfore God but more reprowable.[74]

Cayphas, like this audience of mimetic theater, settles for visual pleasure to cure his heartache:

> But certys, or he hence yode, / It wold do me som good
> *To se* knghtys knok his hoode / With knokys two or thre.

$$(452-54, \text{emphasis added})$$

The torturers also take pleasure in their visible effect on Jesus' body even though he remains silent:

> FROWARD: Yei, that was well gone to; / Ther start up a cowll [bump].
> I TORTOR: Thus shall we hym refe / All his fond talys.

$$(584-87)$$

Caught in the paradox of torture that Enders considers, the *tortores* look only to the body for the truth, imagining that by wounding Jesus' flesh they will also change his "talys," the prophetic narrative that they themselves are in the process of fulfilling.

As in the conclusion of the *First Shepherds' Play,* the playwright challenges the audience to consider the invisible truth beyond the sight of the Corpus Christi, whether in the "real" form of the elevated Eucharist or the theatrical representations onstage. If the *Tretise of Miraclis Pleyinge* argues that theater, like torture, can never find the allegorical truth concealed by Christ's body, the Wakefield Master's stagecraft attempts to direct the audience's vision away from the stage and into an interior condition, a "heart" more akin to the idle shepherds' than the busily working *tortores'.* The playwright's own misgivings, however, perhaps explain the gratuitous and shocking final scene of the *Buffeting,* in which Cayphas, unsatisfied by the beating he's just witnessed, draws a dagger and once again laments that he cannot personally attack Jesus:

> I had mayde him ful tame — / Yei stykyd hym, I weyn,
> To the hart full wan / With this dagger so keyn.
>
> (640–43)

Strangely echoing the *Tretise,* Cayphas acknowledges that the "buffeting" has failed miserably as both torture and theater, resulting in nothing but fleeting visual thrills and a badly bruised Jesus. His crazy solution, which suggests that Christ's flesh must actually be cut open and his "heart" somehow exposed to sight, only takes us further into the impasse of carnal misunderstanding. In a bizarre ironic turn on the mystical image of Christ's sacred heart, a popular devotional icon revealed to visionaries, the "heart" that Cayphas longs to penetrate through Christ's body is his interior condition, his silence.[75]

Seth Lerer has argued that Cayphas is a "figure for the playwright" in the way he scripts and directs Christ's torture in this play.[76] Yet Cayphas perhaps also stands in for the playwright in his desire to defy the restrictions of theater and pierce the audience's metaphorical heart as well as Christ's. The tyrannical priest, his dagger a kind of writing instrument, desperately imagines that he could represent the invisible interior with this unscripted violent act — an alternate Passion in which his fictional theater would triumph over any scriptural or inner truths. The Wakefield Master acknowledges an uncomfortable proximity to these ideas but instead pens a theatrical art that succeeds in its representations only when the visible finally disappears inward and the stage, like the beggar's bag, is perfectly empty.

Into Exiled Hands

Jewish Exegesis and Urban Identity in the Croxton *Play of the Sacrament*

At the opening of the Croxton *Play of the Sacrament,* as a group of five Jews in "the city of Heraclea" in Aragon are discussing their plans to buy and torture a consecrated Eucharist wafer, one of them, called Malchus, interestingly says, "Onys out of ther handys and yt myght be exyled, / To helpe castyn yt in care wold I counsent" (219–20).[1] By suffering "exile" from Christian hands, the host becomes identified with the Jews, themselves exiles on many levels. It falls into a theatrical space that recalls the Fall of Jerusalem and, in David Nirenberg's phrase to describe the "ludic violence" of Passion plays in fourteenth-century Aragon, "sacrifice, vengeance, and the foundation of Judeo-Christian history in the diaspora."[2] As I will argue in this chapter, the sacrament in the Croxton Play's imaginary city becomes subject to a postexilic Jewish line of interpretation that presents a formidable challenge to Christian tenets of belief. The crisis that the play creates, mediated through Christian exegesis, can finally be resolved only by revelation and miracle. The Croxton Play's "Banns" announces the moment of the Jews' conversion at the end of the play as literally a fiery explosion of the "Old Law":

SECUNDUS [VEXILLATOR]:   And than thay putt hym to a new turmentry,
                             In a hoote ovyn speryd hym fast.
                             There he appryed with woundys blody;
                             The ovyn rofe asondre and all tobrast
PRIMUS: Thus in our lawe they wer made stedfast;
                             The Holy Sacrement sheuyed them grette
                             favour.

(45–50)

The stubborn Jews, usually "stedfast" in their own beliefs, will be shown to undergo an immutable conversion.

The Croxton Play or, as it is called in the manuscript, *The Play of the Conversion of Ser Jonathas the Jew by Myracle of the Blyssed Sacrament,* is a unique and elusive cultural document, one that confounds the traditions that it supposedly continues and refines.[3] It is the sole surviving play on the theme of Jewish host desecration from medieval England, but from a time long after the Jews had been expelled by Edward I in 1290 for, above all, their refusal to stop practicing usury in defiance of the Statute of Jewry.[4] The most persistent questions, then, that this oddly anachronistic text raises are: Who exactly are the Croxton Play's Jews, and what social and political ends did they serve on the East Anglian stage of the 1460s? In Miri Rubin's analysis, Christian accounts of Jews who purchase and then torture the Eucharist wafer with daggers, pins, and boiling oil until it turns into Christ, from the copiously reported Parisian miracle of Easter 1290 on, became "blueprints for action." Narratives of host desecration legitimated the massacres or expulsions of Jews from communities in France, the Rhineland, Austria, and Aragon—the imaginary setting of the Croxton Play.[5] The European host desecration stories usually involve a Jewish moneylender who convinces a desperately indebted Christian to bring him a consecrated wafer; as he tortures the host, a vision of Jesus miraculously appears, and the Jew is discovered, tried, and executed, while his wife and children in some versions convert to Christianity. In one account of the Parisian miracle, the unrepentant Jew claims that he could never be burned as long as he had a certain book with him; however, after both he and the book are "reduced to ashes," many Jews convert.[6] This version apparently conflates the host desecration narrative with the earlier condemnation and burning of the Talmud on papal orders in Paris in the 1240s and, more generally, thematizes a connection between the refutation and destruction of rabbinic texts, sacramental miracle, and conversion.[7] The enduring problem of Jewish exegesis in this narrative can be definitively answered by a miracle not only of blood but of fire.

The extant contemporary theatrical analogues to the Croxton Play—from late-fifteenth-century Paris and Italy, respectively—follow the basic plot of the 1290 Parisian miracle closely. The *Mistere de la Sainte-Hostie* interestingly includes the detail of the Jew Jacob's book; the *Miracolo de Corpo di Christo,* Marilyn Lavin has argued, was likely performed in order to stir up anti-Jewish violence in one of the cities in Tuscany or Umbria where, in the mid–fifteenth century, Franciscans were preaching against Jewish bankers who had emigrated from Spain and Portugal.[8] In the Croxton Play, as many critics have pointed out, there are several crucial differences from any other account of host desecration. Both Jonathas, the Jew who buys the host, and Aristorius, the Christian who sells it, are fabulously rich merchants. The Jew suffers dismemberment in the process of torturing the host, but in the end he and his fellow Jews happily become Christians without further bodily punishment. And, perhaps most puzzling, there is an odd interlude during which a local Brabantine physician tries to help Jonathas with his "crucified" hand, severed in the process of trying to nail the wafer to a post of wood.

The most common, yet still entirely unsatisfying, explanation for these changes is that the Croxton Play's villains are "not really" Jews but rather East Anglian Lollard heretics, who believed, following Wyclif, that the substance of bread remained in the host after consecration. In this reading, the Lollards, by doubting the doctrine of transubstantiation, present the church with the same kind of threat of unbelief represented by Jews in earlier eucharistic miracle literature.[9] As however, both Stephen Spector and, in a coauthored article, Robert Clark and Claire Sponsler have recently forcefully argued, the Croxton Play goes out of its way to emphasize a long tradition of stereotypical doctrinal and ethnic characteristics of the Jews.[10] In short, if these figures are supposed to be Lollards, they're curiously *Jewish* Lollards, and they give voice to positions that certainly defy Wycliffite belief, including questioning the christological interpretation of the Hebrew Bible. Structurally, the play's narrative recalls the episode in 1 Kings 13 of the rebel king Jeroboam's encounter with a "man of God" at his idolatrous altar in Bethel. When the man prophesies the destruction of the altar, Jeroboam stretches out his hand to order him seized, but his hand withers and the altar collapses, pouring out its ashes; the king's hand is finally restored by the man's prayer. For patristic and medieval Christian exegetes, the story is both a warning against idolatry and a figure of the division of the Jews into true believers who follow Christ—like King Rehoboam, from the line of David—and those who follow

Antichrist/Jeroboam.[11] In the Croxton Play's reworking of these elements, the Jews' belief in the idolatrous nature of Christian practice defines them as the actual idolators.

The Croxton Play's wandering Jews, transplanted from the Eastern "cyté of Surrey" (18) west to England, are, then, certainly Jews in regard to the exegetical work they perform. Recalled from a distant past and a faraway urban place, they are represented on stage in order to undo what the text imagines as the theological — as opposed to the economic and political — background of the 1290 expulsion: the refusal of the Jews to convert and their subsequent exile from the English cities.[12] The play urgently, if temporarily, brings the diasporic Jews back to East Anglia in order to negotiate this fragmented historical record and its dramatic mirrors from an apocalyptic perspective. Claudia Rattazzi Papka defines the apocalyptic dynamic as a paradoxical "fiction of judgment," a mode of exegesis that imagines the limits of postlapsarian language: "[T]hat which apocalypse reveals is a reality whose essential characteristic is precisely the transcendence of temporality, death, language, mediation . . . and the exchange of all these for certainty, justice, and eternity. Apocalypse, then, seeks to represent the unrepresentable."[13] The apocalypticism of the Croxton Play is a vision that performs the conversion of the Jews as a doctrinal necessity for the culmination of history, as spelled out in programmatic accounts of the defeat of Antichrist and the Last Judgment from Bede and Adso on.[14] As Suzanne Lewis has argued in a reading of English illustrated apocalypses from the 1260s, the period right before the expulsion saw, especially with the influence of the Franciscans, a new theological emphasis on both the conversion of contemporary Jews and the final battle of Christians with a Jewish Antichrist and his disciples.[15] The force of these polemical illustrations, commentaries on Berengaudus's commentary on Revelation, was to draw a sharp distinction between the Old Testament Jews of fulfilled biblical typologies and the Jews who remained, rejecting Christian exegesis, in England.[16]

After 1290, representations of apocalypse still had to account for these unconverted Jews, now expelled into a much more diffuse realm of memory and abstraction. The immensely popular Middle English poem *The Prick of Conscience* (c. 1350), in a particularly fire-and-brimstone-laden version of the Last Judgment, recounts how the prophets Enoch and Elijah will return to preach to the Jews:

þan sal Jewes þe sam lawe halde
þat thai haf, þat er cristen men calde
And als cristen men dus swa sal þai do

Als þe glose says þat acords þar-to:
Percipient fidem quam ipsi habuerunt.
"þe Jewes sal tak þan with hert glade
þe trouth þat cristen men byfor hadde."
Wharfor þe Jewes and cristen men,
Als þa twa prophetes sal þam ken,
Sal þan thurgh even entencion
Assent in Crist als a religion.

$$(4511-22)^{17}$$

In a fashion similar to this eschatological resolution, the Croxton Play's apoca-lypticism seeks to refute the counternarrative of medieval Jewish exegesis that con-tinues to vex the Christian narrative. Apocalypse can be understood in this scheme as a culmination of typology: at the moment of the Jews' conversion, the histori-cal or literal sense of Scripture will be understood only in terms of pure spirit or allegory. The apologetic rhetoric of typology will no longer be necessary in order to counter Jewish "carnal" interpretation. Paradoxically, however, such apoca-lyptic accounts also disturb the very idea of typology by emphasizing the conti-nuity of Jewish reading until the end of history and the Jews' final conversion. In its ultimate reliance on Jesus' spectacular "miracle" rather than an exegetical argu-ment to convert the Jews, the play offers a critique of the predominant English urban dramatic model, the typological play cycle in which the spiritual or alle-gorical senses attempt to neatly resolve history and the carnal, literal Jews ulti-mately disappear.

CITIES AND JEWS IN EAST ANGLIA

The Croxton *Play of the Sacrament,* set entirely in a city, is ultimately a profoundly antiurban play. The performance begins in a dizzying, superabundant market-place where Christian and Jewish merchants do business but ends with a bishop presiding over an absolute emptying or nullification of this same urban space. The Croxton Play, on the evidence of its Banns, a "traveling" production of some kind, was most likely performed moving from village to village, beyond city walls, in the greater urban area formed by Bury St. Edmunds and Norwich.[18] The one local geographical reference in the play is to "Babwell Mill," the northern border of Bury's banleuca and the site of the famous leper hospital of St. Savior's.[19] As

Gail McMurray Gibson has described at length in *Theater of Devotion,* late medieval East Anglia was a center both for monastic and anchoritic piety and for
growing mercantile power built on international trade.[20] According to Robert
Gottfried, the fifteenth century in Bury itself was marked by a shift in urban social and political power from the absolute authority of the Abbey of Bury St. Edmunds to the increasingly influential municipal rule of a wealthy mercantile
class or "burghal elite."[21] This group of great merchants and financiers, who made
their fortunes through the lucrative trade in raw wool and cloth with the Low
Countries and northern Italy and aspired to convert their wealth into land, attempted to represent their economic interests semi-independently of the abbey
through the corporate bodies of religious guilds.[22] Although there is very little
surviving evidence of these organizations' public ceremonies, the guilds almost
certainly participated in Corpus Christi processions, and, as Gibson has argued,
one or more of them probably collaborated with the abbey to produce a cycle of
mystery plays.[23]

   Both the city of Norwich and the Abbey of Bury St. Edmunds had, in their
earlier histories, played substantial roles in the worsening cultural imagination
of the Jews that preceded the 1290 expulsion. In the early thirteenth century, Jocelin of Brakelond, who also penned an account of the ritual slaughter of the
child martyr Robert of Bury at the hands of the Jews, celebrated Abbot Samson's
two great achievements: the expulsion of all Jews who refused conversion from
Bury in 1197 and the founding of the hospital at Babwell.[24] The subsequent
monastic chronicler of Bury, John de Taxter, and his revisers continued to show
a fascination with the Jews elsewhere in England: in 1375 the chronicle reports
that in London one Robert of Reading, a Dominican friar "very learned in the
Hebrew language, apostatized and embraced the Jewish faith; he even married
a Jewess, had himself circumcised, and changed his name to Haggai." When the
king sent for him, "he held forth brazenly in public against Christianity."[25] This
episode is positioned in the text right before Edward I's Statute of Jewry, by which
"the Jews throughout England were forbidden henceforth to lend money at interest to anyone, but were to live by trade, buying and selling according to the
laws of the Christian merchants."[26] This anecdote is particularly striking for its
focus on the dangers of language and exegesis. By learning to read like a Jew, the
missionary friar actually becomes Jewish; the would-be converter is himself converted. The chronicler's anxieties are confirmed by the 1286 Bull sent by Pope
Honorius IV to John Pecham, the archbishop of Canterbury, which warns that
the Jews, with the "abominations, falsifications, and faithless and abusive matter"

of the Talmud "to which they devote themselves with depraved solicitude," not only will not convert to Christianity but will attempt to convert "faithful Christians" to Judaism and lure converted Jews into apostasy.[27]

In Norwich, the deteriorating situation of the Jewish community between the Statute of Jewry and the expulsion was marked by the execution of at least sixteen Jews for coin clipping and one, the prominent moneylender Abraham fils Deulecresse, for blasphemy.[28] The notorious ritual murder accusation of 1144, which held that a group of Norwich Jews had subjected a boy, William, to martyrdom, led to the establishment of a miracle-working shrine at Norwich Cathedral.[29] The Norwich guild of the pelters founded in 1376 styled itself the "bretherhood of Seynt Willyam ye holy Innocent and marter in Norwyche" and provided for an annual procession to the saint's tomb in which a "knave chyld, innocent," theatrically played the role of little William, bearing a candle between two "good men" in "tokenynge of ye gloryous marter."[30] In East Anglia, then, including in Bury St. Edmunds, where they were exiled early on, the Jews were no sooner gone than they were remembered—and reimagined—with a vengeance.

EXEGESIS AND DRAMA

Bury in the 1460s, the date of the Croxton Play according to internal evidence, is also the most likely site for the compilation of the so-called N-Town plays.[31] This text of forty-one Old and New Testament plays represents a self-conscious attempt by a civic body to piece together a grand urban drama cycle with the thematic scope of the York or Chester plays, as a mark of urban wealth and prestige. As Alan Fletcher describes the N-Town production, the "scribe-compiler" copied the plays from earlier exemplars, including a "major play collection."[32] If, as Gail Gibson proposes, the Abbey of Bury St. Edmunds collaborated with a civic fraternity like the aldermen's or Candlemas guild—the most prominent political bodies of the city's mercantile elite—to sponsor and produce the plays, the texts that we have clearly survive in some form from an earlier era of East Anglian urban religious theater.[33] The N-Town "scribe-compiler" possibly even borrowed parts of the plays from the now-lost Norwich Corpus Christi cycle.[34] Hence, the N-Town *Passion Play I,* with its explicit interpretations of the relation between Scripture and sacrament, is a likely example of the kind of large-scale urban theater that both the Croxton Play's author and audience would have seen.

The N-Town opening "Proclamation," while not perfectly matching the sequence of pageants, provides a guide to the plays' emphasis on reproducing a style of literal, historical exegesis advocated earlier by Nicholas of Lyra and the translators of the Wycliffite Bible. As the final Vexillator announces, distantly echoing the idiom of earlier Lollard polemics against allegorical, extrascriptural excesses, "Of Holy Wrytte þis game xal bene, / And of no fablys be no way" (520–21).[35] The play that will connect the Old and New Testaments details the fulfillments of the prophetic books: "Off the gentyl Jesse rote / þe sefynt pagent, forsothe, xal ben, / Out of which doth sprynge our bote, / As in prophecye we redyn and sen" (105–8). Another play shows how the twelve-year-old Jesus defeated the Jewish "doctoris ryth wise and sage" in argument: "The blyssed babe, withoute glose, / Overcam olde clerkys with suych langage / þat þey merveyled" (246–49). The Passion play approaches its subjects with a similar focus on exegetical fulfillment. The N-Town "Last Supper / Conspiracy with Judas" section opens with Jesus announcing the destruction of Jerusalem in terms that also make it the figure of all cities:

> O Jherusalem, woful is þe ordenawnce
> Of the day of þi gret persecucyon!
> Thu xalt be dystroy with woful grevans
> And thi ryalte browth to trew confusyon.
> (486–89)

The lament ends with "Both templys and towryrs, they xal down cleen / O ceté, ful woful is thin ordenawns!" (500–501). Even though the theatrical setting of Bury is here momentarily identified with the Old Jerusalem, doomed to "gret grevauns" (488), the scene of exegetical conversion that follows almost immediately redefines the city as a Christian space, the worldly foreshadowing of the New Jerusalem.

Following the scenes of Judas's conspiracy with the Jewish judges, Jesus presides over the eating of the paschal lamb as a "sacryfyce":

> þis figure xal sesse; anothyr xal folwe þerby
> Weche xal be of my body, þat am youre hed,
> Weche xal be shewyd to ȝow be a mystery
> Of my flesch and blood in forme of bred.
> (846–49)

He then reads his own body "be ghostly interpretacyon" (880) as the fulfillment and supercession of the "carnal" lamb, "comawndyd be my fadyr to Moyses and Aaron" (836):

> And as in þe old lawe it was comawnded and precepte
> To ete þis lomb to the dystruccyon of Pharao unkende
> So to deystroy ȝoure gostly enmye þis xal be kepte
> For ȝoure paschal lombe into the werdys ende.
>
> (869–72)

Finally Jesus "performs" the sacrifice of the Eucharist for his disciples, saying to each except Judas, "This is my body, flesch and blode / That for þe xal dey upon þe rode" (449–50). In the N-Town play's narrative, Scripture and sacrament become transparent in apparent defiance of what Sarah Beckwith has recently described as the Eucharist's "tension between the seen and unseen at its most impossible and contradictory."[36] Not only is Christ here both exegete and text—a true feat of theory-heavy "performance art"—but his body appears in both forms, natural and sacramental, at the very historical moment that the Old Law is "converted" into the New. The most detailed treatment of the Eucharist that survives from a medieval cycle, the first N-Town Passion play perfectly illustrates the typological, apologetic understanding of history and the vision of sacramental wholeness that ideally structured urban Corpus Christi drama. In this annual vision, Old Testament Jews seamlessly become "figures" of New Testament truth, Jesus' Jewish disciples become Christians, and the Jewish judges and torturers who star in the following sequence of Passion plays are already doomed to destruction with Jerusalem.

If, as Sophia Menache has argued, the expulsion of the Jews was the founding moment for a discourse of English self-definition that developed in the course of the fourteenth century, a "unifying element of national consciousness" in which the "Israel of the flesh" was removed to enable England to become "the Israel of the Spirit," much the same dynamic is at work at a local level in the N-Town plays.[37] In the context of Bury St. Edmunds, the abbey's early expulsion of the Jews similarly echoes in the much later Christian urban identity produced by the dramatic narrative. The absence of unconverted Jews allows for an undisturbed mapping of a typological temporality onto the urban theatrical space of the play cycle and hence for the exegetical expression of the wealthy guilds' mercantile ideology. The English city, free of Jews in both reality and interpretation, is, then, poised

between the Old and New Jerusalems, historically reenacting the Old while await-
ing the New.

It is within this context of urban self-definition that the Croxton Play was
most likely originally written for a religious guild at either Croxton (fourteen
miles north of Bury) or another rural parish dependent on the East Anglian market cities for its basic needs.[38] The play is possibly connected to the Cluniac priory
at Thetford (two miles south of Croxton), which later in the fifteenth century
made payments for touring theater in local villages; this provenance would also
explain the playwright's apparent familiarity with at least some of the earlier,
French accounts of host desecration.[39] An apocalyptic dramatic voice from outside
the city, the play advances a position that devastatingly undermines the hermeneutic and ideological claims of contemporary urban theater. As opposed to a Corpus Christi cycle, like the York plays or N-Town plays, that presents the identity
of the Eucharist and Scripture as socially legible by a local Christian community
and aligns the work of exegesis with mercantile wealth, the Croxton Play removes
Scripture from this entire symbolic context of urban power by reassigning it to
Jews. The Jews, in their continual historical refusal of Christian exegesis, become
the Croxton Play's vehicle for an apocalyptic teleology that demands its own critical understanding of a fissure between Scripture and sacrament. To understand
how the Croxton Play uses its diasporic Jews to work against the typological cer-
tainties of the cycle plays in its doctrinal treatment of the Eucharist, Old Testament
allegoresis, and the conversion of non-Christians, I will read the play through an
authoritative and widely circulated set of intertexts—Nicholas of Lyra's two anti-
Judaic tracts and his monumental *Literal Postill on the Bible*. It is in Lyra's works,
above all, that the Jews take center stage not only as readers and misreaders of
Scripture but as critics of the Eucharist.

LYRA'S JEWS

As Jeremy Cohen has shown in *The Friars and the Jews,* Lyra's two polemics
against the Jews served to summarize and popularize the monumental work of
Raymond Martini, the *Pugio Fidei.* [40] For Cohen, Martini's argument represents
a new definition of the historical break between the Old Testament Jews and the
"modern" rabbinic Jews (*Judei Moderni*), who, by means of their "traditiones"—
specifically the Talmud and Midrash—seek to undermine Christian doctrine.[41]
Martini's methodology, the translation and incorporation of rabbinic sources into

an immense handbook for mendicant preachers seeking to convert Jews, is aimed directly at what he calls "modern" Jewish "perfidy"—not only the deliberate scribal corruption and distortion of Old Testament texts but the misinterpretation of the Bible in Jewish glosses and polemics.[42] Allowing that some of the rabbinic "traditions," however, actually prove the truth of Christian doctrine (since as he says, "honey is the spittle of bees"), Martini undertakes a total appropriation *and* refutation of Jewish exegesis; the original text and meaning of the Bible, lost to modernity, can be recovered only by a Christianizing reading of the *targumim* (Aramaic translations of the Hebrew Bible) and the rabbinic commentaries themselves.

Lyra, in the course of his systematic historicizing exegesis of the whole Bible, translates the rabbinic "modernity" of Martini's historical scheme into a foundational concern with problems of lost text and a melancholic engagement with Jewish history and textuality. In the extremely influential *Second Prologue* to his *Postilla Litteralis,* Lyra laments the erosion of the historical sense of Scripture, necessary for Christian exegesis:

> One should, moreover, bear in mind that the literal sense, which should be our starting-point, as I have said, seems to be greatly obscured in these modern times. This is partly through the fault of scribes who, misled by similarities between letters, have in many places written something which differs from the true reading of the text (*veritas textus*). Partly it is the fault of lack of skill on the part of correctors, who in several places have punctuated where they should not, and have begun and ended verses where they should not begin or end, and for this reason the meaning of the text (*sententia literae*) is inconstant.[43]

Moreover, the Latin translation, as Lyra quotes St. Jerome's *Hebrew Questions on Genesis,* "often has something quite different from the meaning of the Hebrew text." To establish the true text, one needs the Hebrew manuscripts; however, he cautions, the Jews have "corrupted" various passages of the Old Testament that speak of the divinity of Christ "to defend their own erroneous doctrine."[44] The meaning of the Bible, Lyra continues, has likewise been obscured by Christian interpreters who have ignored the literal sense in favor of allegorical readings; his remedy for this will be to consult the readings of Jewish teachers, "especially Rabbi Solomon (Rashi) who . . . has put forward the most reasonable arguments." But he adds, "I shall also sometimes include those teachings of the Jews which are very absurd, not in order that they should be adhered to or followed, but that they may show the prevalence of blindness in Israel, as St. Paul says in Romans 11."[45] Writing decades after the expulsion of the Jews from France in 1306, Lyra remarkably transforms the assertions of earlier polemics. While the *Pugio Fidei* had attacked the "modern Jews'" deliberate distortions of Scripture, Lyra extends these claims of textual corruption into an all-encompassing hermeneutics of loss that includes both Jewish and Christian scribes and readers.

It is, of course, in Lyra's own polemics that his nervous *pas de deux* with the Jews is most evident, to the point where he abandons exegetical argument in favor of eucharistic miracle. In the first tract, the *Quaestio de Adventu Christi,* on "Whether One Can Use Scripture Received from the Jews to Prove Our Savior Was Both God and Man," Lyra runs through proof after scriptural proof— including lengthy passages from the *targumim* and *midrashim*—for the Trinity, largely based on the plurality of the noun *Elohim* (God); the incarnation of Christ; and the advent of Christ in the past rather than the future.[46] As Cohen points out, Lyra makes an extreme claim for the Jewish corruption of the *Hebraica Veritas* by positing "lost" authentic texts. Typical of Lyra's tendentious exegesis is his conclusion that the Vulgate version of Jeremiah 23:6, "Et hoc est nomen quod vocabunt eum, dominus justus noster" [And this is the name that they will call him, our righteous lord], is a passage about the divinity of Jesus the Messiah, and that it has been obscured by the "deception of the Jews" (*falsitas Judaeorum*), who claim that in Hebrew it reads "vocabit" (single and active) and refers to God alone, who will call the Messiah.[47] As he asserts, "Yet although I myself have not seen any bible of the Jews which has not been corrupted, I have faithfully heard from those worthy by reason of their lives, consciences, and knowledge, who swear on an oath that they have seen it thus [in agreement with the Vulgate] in ancient bibles."[48] By contrast, he proves his reading from the "Chaldaic translation" [*Targum*] of Jeremiah 23:5, "which is authentic according to [the Jews]": " 'Ecce dies veniunt dixit dominus et suscitabo David Messiam justum [Behold, the days are coming says the Lord when I will raise up for David a righteous Messiah]', where we have, 'germen justum [a righteous branch].' From this, it is clear that this authority is understood to be about Christ literally and in the Chaldaic translation this follows: 'Et hoc est nomen quod ipsi appellabunt eum, dominus justus noster'" [And this is his name, by which they will call him, our righteous lord].[49] The tract ends, however, with Lyra's admission that such textual "proofs" have not in fact succeeded in converting the Jews, not only because of their greed and habitual hatred for Christians and Christian law, which they curse in synagogue every day, but because of their difficulty in understanding the sacrament of the Eucharist itself as anything other than the worst kind of idolatry.[50]

In his second anti-Jewish tract, the *Responsio ad Quemdam Judaeum,* a rejoinder to the Jewish polemicist Jacob ben Reuben's arguments against Christian doctrines, Lyra returns to the problem of the Eucharist in greater depth.[51] Here he counters the Jewish charge of idolatry with an explanation of transubstantiation: since the substance of bread "converts" to the substance of Christ's body, the worship of the consecrated host as "truly man and truly God" is proper *latria,* not *idolatria.*[52] He then takes up the more problematic objection that the Eucharist involves the brutally cruel eating of a human body:

> It is argued, furthermore, that Christians eat the body of Christ, which is horrible: this would be true if it were received in its own species, but to accept it under the species of bread is not horrible, but rather pleasant and venerable. It is not really Christ himself or his body that in this consumption is broken and ground up and mangled by one's teeth, *as the Jews imagine,* but only the appearances of bread are broken and ground up; once these have been consumed, the body of Christ ceases to be present, but the effect of this sacrament remains, which is the nourishment of the soul by the increase of grace. (emphasis added)[53]

Lyra hence reaffirms the orthodox Thomistic or Bonaventuran doctrine of eucharistic conversion from bread to body, but in such a way as to highlight the ongoing anxieties of debates over eucharistic terminology.[54] The consecrated bread and wine fully become the substance of Christ's body and blood but retain their appearances, "lest" as Aquinas had put it, "this sacrament might be derided by unbelievers (*ab infidelibus irrideretur*), if we were to eat our Lord under his own species."[55] Interestingly, Lyra concludes his defense of the eucharistic miracle with a textual proof from Psalm 71 that hinges on a Christian scribal error in Jerome's so-called "Gallican Psalter," translated from the Septuagint, as opposed to his later "Hebrew Psalter":

> *There will be a firmament on the earth on the tops of the mountains.* Where the Hebrew letter has: *There will be abundant grain in the land on top of the mountains.* And Jerome's translation according to the Hebrew has: *There will be a memorable name of grain on top of the mountains.* And the Aramaic translation has: *There will be an offering of grain on the earth.* From these three passages

we see that our literal sense has been corrupted by scribes putting *firma-mentum* for *frumentum* because of the similarity of the words. From what has been said, it is clear what was predicted about the King Messiah in this psalm, namely, that there would be grain on the earth on the tops of the mountains, or an offering of grain on the earth on top of the mountains. This is fulfilled in the sacrament of the eucharist, in which Christ is contained in the form of bread made of grain and is elevated above the head of priests in order that he may be adored by people; priests, therefore, are called mountains on account of the height of their status.[56]

Lyra here draws attention to Jerome's own discussions of textual inaccuracies in his two translations of the Psalter.[57] To prove the essential identity of the eucharistic bread with the Messiah of the Psalms who is Christ, Lyra himself must once again abandon the Vulgate and turn to the final prophetic authority of the *targum*.

As is apparent even from this brief summary, the Jews in Lyra's exegesis are omnipresent and multivalent, figures both necessary to the understanding of textual origins and, together with various Christians, responsible for "modernity" in the sense of the irreparable loss of origins. Following Martini, Lyra presents Jewish commentary as the ultimate threat to the coherence of the Christian historical narrative because of the Jews' refusal, above all, to accept Jesus as the Messiah. However, for Lyra, the Christian allegorists similarly threaten a historical incoherence that requires his recourse to the eleventh-century "literal" commentator Rashi for philological meaning on every page of his gloss. Moreover, since for Lyra a truly complete reception of biblical history is impossible, doomed by so many layers of sabotage, fragmentation, translation, and misinterpretation—the very multiplicity of bibles—the Jews, by denying the Eucharist and refusing conversion, also represent a challenge to the sacrament that itself transcends temporality and textuality in the "Real Presence" of Christ. The unbelieving Jew relentlessly pressures the language available to describe the sacrament, forcing the paradoxical double explanation of the Eucharist as Christ incarnate, yet eaten as what appears to be bread. As a response to this Jewish literalizing "imagination" characterized by doubt and cruelty, it is not surprising that Lyra turns to apocalyptic solutions in his *Postillae,* including the commentary on Isaiah 63, the prooftext most central to the difference of Jewish and Christian understandings of the end of history that is also the crux of the Croxton Play.

CROXTON'S JEWS

Lyra's phantasmic diasporic Jews, at once everywhere and nowhere, reappear
in the Croxton Play as jarring reminders to an audience more accustomed to
the patriarchs, torturers, and Christs of the mystery cycles. The Croxton Play
seeks to recover and represent the lost origins of both Jewish Scripture and—
by extension—English Jewish history in what Joseph Roach in *Cities of the Dead*
describes as the performance of memory as "surrogation," or, in his wonderfully
suggestive phrase, "the doomed search for originals by continuously auditioning
stand-ins."[58] And, by analogy to certain of the urban performances of Roach's
circum-Atlantic paradigm, the Croxton Play constructs a kind of communal identity *outside* the city by contrast to an alien and increasingly remote Other. As Chris
Bongie defines the project of nineteenth-century exoticism in relation to "the scenario of loss" presented by "a pessimistic and nostalgic evaluation of modernity":
"exoticism necessarily presumes that, at some point in the future, what has been
lost will be attained 'elsewhere.'"[59] A similar discursive dynamic is at work in the
Croxton Play's reinscription of "exotic" diasporic Jews into English history. The
Jews, who represent both the promise of authentic scriptural understanding and
historical loss in contemporary exegetical discourse, reappear here as exoticized yet
familiar tormentors, figures re-created from the traces in chronicles, hagiogra-
phies, and—of course—mystery plays.

    The Croxton Play's Jews, like Lyra's, embody a historically continuous resis-
tance to Christian polemic: as Jonathas says as he contemplates buying the host,
responding to the Pauline and patristic rhetorical tradition of the "blindness of
Israel," "Thus by a conceyte, þe worlde makes us blynd" (203).[60] He later refers to
the sold Eucharist in the same terms: "Thys merchant from the Crysten temple /
Hathe gett us thys bred that makes us thus blynd" (387–88). Through these shadowy Jews, the entire historical and doctrinal problem of the expulsion is relived
and renegotiated in the theatrical process that Roach calls "the pleasures and tor-
ments of incomplete forgetting."[61] The history at stake in the Croxton Play is, however, unlike in the urban N-Town plays, pointedly apocalyptic, seeking to fulfill
and transcend both universal and local historical narratives in its representation
of the sacramental miracle.

    The uneasy yet necessary textual exchanges between Jews and Christians that
are central to Lyra's exegesis are reproduced in the commercial transaction that
opens the Croxton Play. From the beginning of the merchant Aristorius's speech,
a catalog of the ports from Antioch to Prussia where he does business, we are in

the space of universal history as well as trade, the geographical basis for the sacred and national narratives that will culminate in the world's end, or, in Higden's terms, the final time of "reconciliation."[62] In Aristorius's expanding yet de-
clining world, however, the church appears to have become the temple of the
Old Jerusalem, from which Jesus expelled the moneychangers—the "buyers
and sellers": "In Rome to St. Peter's temple," Aristorius brags, "I am knowen
certenly for bying and sellyng" (107–8). He further identifies himself with the
desires of Bury's wealthiest merchants to join the landed gentry and to align their
business with public piety:

> No man in this world may weld more rychesse;
> All I thank God of hys grace, for he þat me sent;
> And as a lordys pere thus lyve I in worthynesse
> My curate wayteth upon me to knowe myn entent.
>   (117–20)

In Jonathas's long catalog of the many things he buys and sells, including
jewels and spices of all kinds, we are in the falling Babylon of Revelation 18, except without the "cargo of human souls," which is here replaced with the host,
sold by the Christian merchant in a drawn-out bargain that begins at twenty
pounds and concludes at a hundred. Aristorius then steals the consecrated host
after distracting a priest with a parodically carnal eucharistic meal of "a drawte
of Romney red" and a "lofe of lyght bred" (340–42). Like the Jews who interpret the Eucharist carnally as a "cake" and insist that "in bred for to be blode yt
ys ontrewe" (215), the Christians are likewise removed from true sacramental effi-
cacy. The thinly disguised prosperous urban mercantile world of Bury and Norwich is, from the author of the Croxton Play's perspective, a confusion of Christian
and Jew through the idiom of exchange, a market so decadent as to anticipate the
apocalypse.[63]

As soon as Jonathas and the Jews have the host, they lay it out on a tablecloth
and, standing around, make it the proof of their scriptural interpretations while
"blindly" reenacting the Last Supper.[64] Like good anti-Christian polemicists, they
recite both the story of the Last Supper and the life of Jesus, including an extra
"accidental" consecration of the host, by recounting Jesus' *comedite corpus meum.*
As Beckwith points out of Jews' dramatic invocation of Christ, "[T]he theatrical effect of his presence works to blur the boundaries of identity, as it blurs the
boundaries of direct and indirect speech. The words are uttered by Jonathas the

Jew, and in that moment he becomes both Christ and priest."[65] The Jews' polemics are, as they are in Lyra's texts, self-consuming. The Jews conclude with Malchus's denial of the Christian apocalyptic program, based on a refusal to identify the Messiah, Jesus Christ, with the Eucharist: "Yea yet they say as false, I dare lay my head / How they that be ded shall com agayn to Judgement, / And our dredfull Judge shalbe thys same brede" (433–35). Jonathas, getting ready to stab the wafer, offers one final and all-important scriptural passage as a challenge:

> Now, serys, ye have rehersyd the substance of ther lawe,
> Bot this bred I wold myght be put in a prefe
> Whether þis be he that in Bosra of us had awe.
> Ther stayned were his clothys, þis may be belefe;
> Thys may we know, ther had he grefe,
> For owr old bookys veryfy thus.
> Theron he was jugett to be hangyd as a thefe —
> *Tinctis Bosra Vestibus.*
>
> (441–48)[66]

Interestingly, this passage, Isaiah 63:1–4, is in Lyra's *Postilla* and the texts it answers, a crucial site for Jewish-Christian polemical showdown over eschatology, conversion, and the historical and allegorical interpretations of blood. Here is the full reference:

> Who is this that cometh from Edom, in dyed garments from Bosra, this beautiful one in his robe, walking in the greatness of his strength? "I, that speak justice, and am a defender to save." Why then is thy apparel red, and thy garments like theirs that tread in the wine press? "I have trodden the winepress alone, and of the Gentiles there is not a man with me; I have trampled on them in my indignation and have trodden them down in my wrath, and their blood is sprinkled upon my garments, and I have stained all my apparel. For the day of vengeance is in my heart, the year of my redemption is come." Isaiah 63:1–4 (Douay version)

Lyra begins his commentary on this passage by observing that both Jews and Christians interpret the figure as the Messiah: Rashi, he says, claims that the blood is that of "the inhabitants of the world," or more specifically Rome, whom the vengeful Messiah will kill, subjecting the rest to the Jews.[67] Lyra is accurate here: this is close to what Rashi and later Jewish exegetes, especially after the anti-Jewish persecutions of First Crusade in 1096, actually do say about the spectacularly bloody triumph of Jews over non-Jews and the apocalyptic end of Jewish exile.[68] Indeed, the thirteenth-century poet Meir of Norwich uses the idea of a "vengeful messiah" in Isaiah 63 to stunning effect in his "Put a Curse on My Enemy," a work that describes the worsening conditions for English Jews: "Let their victory [blood] spatter Your garment / for your beloved's heart is distressed."[69]

Most previous Christian exegetes, Lyra continues, have read the passage as concerning Christ immediately after the Passion, stained with his own blood, spilled at the behest of the Jews. For Lyra himself, however, in direct response to Rashi's apocalypticism, the Messiah is the triumphant Christ of the final judgment, and the blood is Antichrist's. Once Antichrist is revealed and defeated, the Jews "will convert to the Christian faith, performing acts of penance"—a different end of exile.[70] In this text, as the possible readings multiply, Lyra envisions what he previously could not articulate by means of either exegetical polemic or eucharistic doctrine: that is, actual Jewish conversion. The Croxton Play's Jews similarly enact the polemical anxiety of Lyra's text, refuting the possibility of Rashi's counternarrative of a universal conversion of non-Jews. While they appear to refer to the standard Christian interpretation of the text and the "modern" Jewish polemics against it from their rabbinic "old books," the Jews are already performing Lyra's apocalyptic script. And as in the text from Isaiah and its glosses, their conversion is ultimately soaked in blood that changes metaphorical meaning with each new apocalyptic conception of history.

The sheer amount of blood generated by the Jewish and Christian exegesis of Isaiah 63 helps to explain the Croxton Play's excessively gory vision, a staging that goes far beyond any other account of host desecration in its mingling of Christ's blood with Jonathas's. And in the next scene of the Croxton Play, the blood really does begin to splatter. The Jews perform a reenactment of the Passion with the wafer, mimicking in the violence of their language, as Spector has pointed out, the roles of the vicious torturers of the N-Town *Crucifixion* play.[71] When they stab the host five times, eucharistic blood spurts forth; Jonathas exclaims, "Yt bledyth as yt were woode iwis; / but if ye helpe, I shall dyspaire" (483–85), thereby conflating his own sudden madness with the host's "crazy" bleeding. The even more interesting miracle that follows confirms this confusion of identities: when Jonathas tries to throw the host into a cauldron of boiling oil, his hand adheres to the host. Echoing the Jews' earlier desire to "exile" the host from Christian hands, Jonathas, "running wood," now howls, "I may not avoyd it out of my

hond!" (500). If, as Katherine Rowe has argued, the image of the hand in medieval and early modern texts is emblematic of the problems at the intersection
of material and metaphoric agency, Jonathas's hand literally becomes a fusion of
the "exiled" sacrament and the Jewish reader.[72] The wafer itself is here a sign that
reflects the polemical struggle exemplified by Lyra's own sleight of hand in his
arguments about the Jews and the Eucharist. When the Jews then "recrucify" both
Jonathas and the host, nailing both to a post, his hand is torn from his arm, or indeed "exiled" from his body, signaling the bloody fragmentation of Jewish hermeneutic agency in the scene. There is an extraordinary resonance between this
scene and the celebrated twelfth-century Anglo-Norman *Jeu d'Adam*. The prophet
Isaiah, in that play's vision of Christian supercession, disputes with an unbelieving Jew and then tells him from looking at his hand like a physician that he is
sick with error.[73]

In answer to the moment of hermeneutic and eschatological crisis represented by the Jews' citation of Isaiah 63, the host's blood here recapitulates the flow
of Lyra's commentary. Moving from the allegorical to the anti-Judaic anagogical
reading, the blood becomes both eucharistic and triumphant, the blood both of
Christ and of the defeated Jews. Jonathas's hand — now freely attached to Christ's
body — becomes part of the sacramental miracle of "conversion," since the Jews
can no longer coherently interpret the host when it appears in its active, sacramental form. When the Jews then throw hand and host together into the oil, the host —
Christ's flesh and blood — is unscathed, but Jonathas's hand — his remaining
interpretive agency — is "soden, the fleshe from þe bones" (706). The Jewish, or
carnal reading is boiled away in a parodic and miraculous baptism of blood.

It is in the midst of these scenes of the Jews attempting to free Jonathas from
the host that the strangest part of the Croxton Play occurs, a brief interlude during which Colle, the assistant of a physician who "can gyff a judgyment aright
as he þat hath noon eyn" (540), "advertises" the services of his drunken master,
"Brundyche of Braban," who then appears, drunk and drinking. Looking both
to the Christian audience of the play and to the Jews from the previous scene,
Brundyche observes, "Here ys a grete congregacyon, / And all be not (w)hole"
(601–2); this "leche"—"a man of all syence" (529), or doctor — is, appropriately
enough, a parodic version of any number of "doctors" or expositors from the
mystery plays, the narrator-figures who, among other things, ensure the correct
reading of the Old Testament as Christian allegory.[74] Brundyche, needless to say,
merely reinforces the Croxton Play's critical assessment of the cycles' hermeneutic style by failing to cure Jews, Christians, or the abrupt break in time, space, and

"historical" narrative. The doctor has Colle enumerate the diseases he can treat in a catalog that parodically echoes Aristorius's and Jonathas's complementary opening speeches, offering, rather than the power and wealth of exotic places and commodities, an extensive anatomy of decay and death:

> Who hat þe canker, þe collyke or þe laxe
> The tercian, þe quartan or þe brynnung axs—
> For wormys, for gnawyng, gryndyng in þe wombe or in þe boldyro—
> All manner red eyn, bleryd eyen, and the myegrym also
>
> (612–15)

Colle finishes his "declaracion" by telling the audience that if they want to talk to Brundyche, "inquyre to the colkote, for there is his loggyng, A lytll besyde Babwell Myll, yf ye wyll have understanding" (620–21). In this interlude, then, we are not only in the immediate geographic area of Bury St. Edmunds rather than the imaginary "Heraclea" but in the historical present, figured here as an instant appeal to the audience's physical experience of pain. It is this historical moment, as well, that in theatrical time divides a distant memory of Jews in England from the future apocalyptic conversion of the Jews.

The moment of the 1460s in Bury was, as Gibson notes, marked by "resentment against the virtual commercial invasion of Flemings"; the drunken and incompetent Brundiche reflects a stereotypical view of the Flemish, Dutch, and Brabantine immigrants who had been moving to East Anglia since the mid–fourteenth century to work as weavers, dyers, fullers, and, occasionally, brewers.[75] In his article, "In Flaundres," David Wallace offers a constellation of new interpretations of the "discourses of Flanders" as both a center of England's international wool trade and a focus of English economic and cultural anxieties. For Wallace, "Flaundres," as the setting of Chaucer's *Pardoner's Tale,* represents riot and bodily excesses of all kinds, from the supposed wild drunkenness of Flemings to the counterfeit English coins produced in Flanders in the late 1380s to Flanders' own "unnatural," entirely mercantile economy and environment.[76] As Wallace writes of the Pardoner, that sterile seller of counterfeit relics, "[T]here is a convergence here between that which the Pardoner embodies or unembodies, and the land of which he speaks."[77] Much the same is true of Brundyche's selling of the image of a diseased and fragmented body; as a "counterfeit" physician who lives near the Bury landmark of St. Savior's hospital at Babwell, his "Brabant" is, like "Heraclea," another aspect of a deeply troubled, haywire Bury.

Speaking theatrically from "Babwell Mill," the northern border that divides Bury's banleuca from the outlying region that extends finally up to Thetford and Croxton, Brundyche embodies the current-day urban center. Like Jonathas's catalog of wares that actually echoes Revelation, Brundyche's catalog identifies Bury as a type of new Babylon, a city of mercantile wealth about to fall, in the immanent future, in a fiery Last Judgment. Like both the dismembered Jonathas and the "congregation" or audience, Brundyche of Brabant is a sign of all that is not "whole" in Bury. Like the Jews, made blind by metaphor, and offering, as Lyra characterizes them, "blind" readings of Scripture, Brundyche, literally blind, also offers blind judgments: the hermeneutic and, especially, the theatrical work of the contemporary city. While there are no Jews in the present moment of the 1460s, Jonathas reenters the action at the very end of the interlude as Brundyche's potential "patient," a reminder that the Jew's "lost hand," embodying the entire problem of Jewish interpretation, is in fact central to the play's local and national eschatological vision.

The final torture and miracle is the explosion of the apocalyptic oven, echoing the fires of the last judgment where Christ does in fact "return" in theatrical form, as an "image." Jesus' first words, loosely borrowed from Lamentations 1:12, are spoken both as Christ and, literally, as the fallen city of Jerusalem:

> *O mirabiles Judei, attendite et videte*
> *Si est dolor sicut dolor meus?*
> O, ye merveylous Jewys,
> Why ar ye to yowr kyng onkind,
> And I so bytterly bowt yow to my blysse?
> (717–21)

While Jesus returns to the Jews as their king, recapitulating his first entry into Jerusalem, he also addresses—*from* the village of "Croxton"—the urban audience implied in the actual passage from Lamentations: "O all you who pass by in the street, look and see if there is any sorrow like my sorrow." Unlike the N-Town Passion play's historical Jerusalem, the Croxton Play's theatrical space can only become the Jerusalem of Lamentations, the city that has already fallen, leaving the diaspora and its attendant sorrowful problems of "modern" hermeneutics. Lyra interestingly provides a scathing commentary on this same passage in his *Postilla Moralis,* explaining it as the lament of the "allegorical Jerusalem," the militant church, "which has much declined from its original perfection" in both the clergy and the secular princes and laypeople. "In these modern times," Lyra continues, "many of the number of the faithful have abandoned the church."[78] Hence, the Christian Aristorius's mercantile sin of putting a price tag on the Eucharist and the Priest's careless disregard of his church and the host are as much problems of the losses of modernity as the Jews' enduring disbelief.[79]

When Christ finally miraculously heals Jonathas's severed hand by having him stick it back into the cauldron of oil, he associates the Jews with a violent agency:

> No, Jonathas, on thyn hand thow art but lame
> And it is thorow thyn own cruelnesse
> For thyn hurt thou mayest þiselfe blame,
> Thow woldyst preve thy powre me to oppresse.
> But now I considre thy necesse
> Thow wasshest thy hert with gret contrycion,
> Go to the cawdron—þi care shal be the lesse—
> And towche thyn hand to thy salvacion.
>
> (770–77)

Jonathas's "cruelnesse" and "power to oppress" are an almost perfect inversion of Lyra's account of Jewish objections to the Eucharist itself as torture, the painful eating of Christ's flesh. It is the Jew, not the Christian, who not only imagines sacramental cruelty but performs it. Likewise, the exiled Jewish "hand" can be restored only by a form of conversion that explicitly renounces Jewish interpretation.

DIASPORIC THEATRICALITY

When the Jews in the Croxton Play finally do convert following Jesus' miracle of bursting forth from the oven's flames with bleeding wounds, they apocalyptically concede all of the Jewish polemical ground on both Scripture and sacrament: the messianic Isaiah passage becomes entirely Christian, and the Eucharist, subjected to Jewish rather than Christian torment, miraculously transforms into Christ, come again to judge the Jews—and the Christians. As Jesus tells the Jews after they kneel before him reciting passages from the Psalms, "*Ite et ostendite vos sacerdotibus meis*" (765); this citation of Luke 17:14, originally spoken to lepers, recalls

Brundyche's catalog of illnesses, St. Savior's hospital at Babwell, and all who are not "whole" in the city.

The Jews' conversion is also the city's, and Jonathas's language when he hails Jesus as the "king of Jerusalem" certainly echoes a text like the N-Town Passion play's "Entry into Jerusalem" episode, in which four "cetesynys" go to meet Christ barefoot and barelegged, singing "Gloria laus":

> Thow sone of David, þu be oure supporte
> At oure last day whan we xal dye!
> Wherefore we alle atonys to þe exorte
> Cryeng mercy! Mercy! Mercye!
>   (454–57)

Above all, Jonathas's final address concedes the central conflict between Jewish and Christian exegesis by celebrating Jesus as the Messiah:

> "Oh thow my Lord God and Savyowr, osanna!
> Thow Kyng of Jews and of Jerusalem!"
> O thow myghty strong Lyon of Juda
> Blyssyd be the tyme that þou were in Bedlem!
>   (778–81)

This apocalyptic dramatic gloss on the "Entry," however, ultimately counters the mystery plays' typological scheme and tone of civic celebration, as the return of Christ, the Fall of Jerusalem, and the diaspora are all once again conflated in the play's ending. The "modern" Jews, the Croxton Play ultimately contends, will remain until the real End. In the play's final apocalyptic pronouncement, "modernity" itself ends with a vision of historical and textual coherence that puts an end to worldly commerce and to the city itself.

For the rest of the play, a bishop presides over the action, which includes the image of Christ returning to the form of the consecrated host and being taken back to church in a formal Corpus Christi procession. This procession, however, "with a gret menye of Jewys," far from performing its usual symbolic function of defining and celebrating urban society, concludes with the absolute destruction of the city.[80] Following a warning derived from Revelation 20 to anticipate the final apocalyptic struggle, "be strong in batayll gostly / For to fyghht agayn the fell serpent" (868–69), the bishop sentences Aristorius "nevermore for to bye nor sell" and to "chastys thy body" (915–16). He then "crystens" the Jews, who, despite their baptism, are pointedly *not* integrated into a Christian city through conversion. The Jews' diasporic movement begins anew as Jonathas announces:

> Now ar we bownd to kepe Chrystys lawe
> And to serve þe Father, þe Son, and þe Holy Gost.
> Now wyll we walk by contré and cost,
> Our wyckyd lyvyng for to restore:
> And trust in God, of myghtys most,
> Never to offend as we have don befor.
> Now we take owr leave at lesse and mare—
> Forward on owr vyage we wyll us dresse.
>
> (962–69)

When the "baptized" Jews leave the city at the end of the Croxton Play, this new expulsion from East Anglia undermines any untroubled reading of the play as an affirmation of "penance and healing acceptance."[81] Yet this reiterated diaspora is not simply a necessary repetition of either the Fall of Jerusalem or of English history. The diasporic resolution, in which the city is emptied of both the Jews and the merchant, in fact duplicates the Croxton Play's own "traveling" theatricality, in which the players leave to play again elsewhere. The unanchored space created by the Croxton Play, a few miles removed from an actual urban center and its resources, is a multivalent and moving city, as ephemeral as the "Jews" themselves. The "crystened" Jews, setting out on their "vyage," become a figure of the play's own theatrical imagination, which puts diaspora in the service of an apocalyptic vision: the Jews will leave and return again until the end of history. The unfixed dramatic and didactic space of the Croxton Play, then, is itself the harshest assessment of the exegetical performance of urban biblical theater. In its creation of a critical eschatological time and space, the diasporic play continually reinscribes and erases Jewish exegesis, the narrative forever haunting—in Lyra's interpretation—the Christian understanding of Scripture and sacrament.

Croxton's diasporic theater, in which the wealthy secular city falls in anticipation of the Final Judgment, is a radical departure from the urban cycle drama that creates and celebrates its own Jerusalem, a city whose historical fall is elided by typology and sacramentality. The Croxton Play's urban setting, at once "modern" Aragon and Bury, "old" Jerusalem and Babylon, is finally like the N-Town play's city, looking toward the New Jerusalem. However, in the play's final vision from outside the walls, the city is desolate, as both the Jews and the Christian merchant leave in a new penitential exile. The Croxton Play's diasporic Jews, then, return to East Anglia's historical and exegetical memory at great cost to Christian society. The N-Town play's sacrament, a celebration of urban devotion to *Corpus Christi,* gives way to a sacrament that, exiled into a city of "modernity" and Jewish interpretation, can be fully restored to Christian hands only at the End of Days.

c h a p t e r   s i x

The Mixed Life in Motion

Wisdom's Devotional Politics

In his 1458 will, the bibliophile Thomas Chaworth, knight of Nottingham-shire, bequeathed to his executor, Richard Byngham, Justice of the King's Bench, "an English booke called *Orilogium Sapienciae*." To another executor, Master Gull, Doctor of Divinity, he willed "a boke writen in Latin called *Poli-c[hr]onicon,* or ellys a rose peece with a coverkill," an ornate gilded bowl. This legal document, in which a literate layman not only inventoried the Domini-can Heinrich Suso's allegorical dialogue along with his down pillows and sil-ver candlesticks but also put the book into the hermeneutic clutches of an em-inent lawyer, suggests the limits of asceticism among this emerging class of readers.[1] In *The Seven Poyntes of Trewe Wisdom,* as Suso's *Horologium Sapientiae* was also called in its much-reduced Middle English version, the allegorical figure of Wisdom — at once *Sapientia,* the soul's bride, and Jesus — exhorts the disciple seeking spiritual perfection to "learn to die":

> þou schalte first with-draw þe from yvel felawschypes and noyous famy-
> liarities and fro alle men þat wolde lette þy good purpos; sekyng alle-wey

opportunite, where and what-tyme þou mayste a place of reste and þere take þe prive silences of contemplacyone and flee the periles of turblaunce of þis noyous world. Alle-tymes it longith to thee principally to studye to have the clannes of herte, þat is to saye, so þat closynge thy fleschly wittes, þou be turned into þyselfe and þat þou have, in als myche as hit is possibil, þe dores of thyne herte bisily closed fro þe formes of oute-warde things and ymagynacyouns of erthely þings — ffor, sooþly, amonge alle goostly exercises clennes of herte hath þe pricipalite, as a fynalle entencyone and rewarde of alle þe travailes þat a chosen knyghte of Criste is wonte forto receyve.

(353–54)[2]

Like many of the great works of Middle English mysticism, including Walter Hilton's *Scale of Perfection* and the *Chastising of God's Children, The Seven Poyntes* is directed to a female religious reader, a "goostly douȝhter" (325). In his sweeping revisions, however, Suso's translator clearly anticipated a wider lay audience.[3] This passage's oppositions between interior and exterior realities, contemplation and business, recur again and again, with various nuances, in most vernacular spiritual guides. Suso's original Latin version of this passage, however, counsels obedience to religious vows in moderating between solitude and society, while in *The Seven Poyntes* the pious layperson must take this responsibility upon herself or himself as an inner judgment.[4] While we can know nothing of his heart, it would appear that the knight Chaworth, on the evidence of his unusually cluttered will, was unable to maintain such distinctions and thus could not become Suso's "chosen knyghte of Christ."

The social logic by which a text that counsels renunciation of all worldly things could itself become a kind of commodity is one of the underlying subjects of the roughly contemporary East Anglian play *Wisdom. Wisdom* (c. 1470), in a strange hybrid of static and riotous theatrical styles, narrates the fall of a soul into sin within a frame of excerpts from English devotional texts, including, from its opening lines, *The Seven Poyntes of Trewe Wisdom*.[5] In what amounts to an overview of available vernacular works, Wisdom confronts the spirituality and the spiritual pretensions of an increasingly literate, book-owning gentry and merchant class. As much as it is about the fall of a representative "Anima," *Wisdom* is about the fall of spiritual writings from their relatively controlled original textual communities into a society of lay readers with a multiplicity of interpretive strategies. In his Latin prologue to the *Horologium,* Suso relates how he, "the Disciple," considered suppressing his collection of private insights altogether for fear

that "envious men" would accuse him of unorthodoxy; in *Wisdom* this same eso-
teric work has become incorporated into the public discourse of a theatrical performance.[6] Likewise, Suso's original work follows the mystical ascent of a "novice"
who first hears the sapiental books of the Old Testament read by a lector in his
convent;[7] *Wisdom*'s borrowings from devotional writing serve to underline the
reader's distance from Scripture itself in these works' larger reception. The subject or "Anima" whose corruption, fragmentation, and redemption *Wisdom* stages
is, above all, an inept reader of such devotional texts, who, exposed to too much
vernacular theology too quickly, falls victim to the devil's exegetical and rhetorical finesse.

Important studies by Malcolm Vale, Jeremy Catto, and Michael Sargent,
among others, have shown the growing popularity of vernacular devotional writings among lay readers in the late fourteenth and fifteenth centuries, including
the "common profit books" that circulated among wealthy London guild members.[8] Roger Lovatt has charted the wide lay dissemination of *The Seven Poyntes
of Trewe Wisdom* through wills and manuscript anthologies, characterizing the
translation of Suso as "remodelled to the pattern of contemporary English piety";
the reviser, that is, emphasized the "prosaic" over the "flamboyant" in a way that
suggests that he himself felt that the original work had subversive or unortho-
dox potential.[9] *Wisdom,* preserved both in the Macro manuscript and in a partial
version in Oxford MS Digby 133, seems to have been composed specifically to
address the new problem of runaway devotion among England's social elites.[10]
The play is, indeed, a kind of polemical response to a text addressed directly in
English to powerful lay readers, Walter Hilton's *Epistle on the Mixed Life,* which
pointedly warns its audience that "charite unruled turneth sumtyme into vice"
(112).[11] I conclude my book, then, by examining a play that itself recapitulates some
of my main themes: the manifold problems presented by secular exegesis of Scripture in late medieval England and the related social dangers involved in transforming extravagant allegories like Suso's into either popular spiritual handbooks
or theatrical representations. This final chapter approaches *Wisdom* through the
English and Latin intertexts that supply its characters with so many of their lines
that this piece, unique among "morality plays," imagines a soul literally constructed by texts.

Hilton's concept of the "mixed life" is central to *Wisdom*'s paradoxical theatrical
vision. As a Middle English play performed for laypeople, *Wisdom* participates
in Hilton's ideal of vernacular instruction in contemplative values; however, its

author makes Lucifer himself the advocate of a "mixed" active and contemplative spiritual practice and identifies it with the cynicism of corrupt lords and lawyers. Hilton's *Epistle on the Mixed Life,* read alongside a number of passages in *The Scale of Perfection,* has itself most often been taken as his attempt to prevent misunderstandings among vernacular readers of Richard Rolle's and his followers' style of fervently interior affective mysticism.[12] Written to a wealthy layman who had apparently decided to renounce his worldly life in favor of contemplation, the *Epistle* argues that "oure Lord hath ordeyned thee and sette the in the staat of sovereynte over othir men . . . and lente the habundaunce of worldli goodis for to rulen and sustene speciali alle thise that arn undir thi governaunce and thi lordschipe, of thi myght and kunnynge" (116). Given his bond of prior responsibility to his tenants, servants, and children, the recipient of the *Epistle* cannot, Hilton warns, "yeve thee hooli to goostli occupaciouns of preiers and meditaciouns, as it were a frere, or a monk" (112). A worldly sovereign cannot truly become a contemplative without inflicting social injustice on his dependents.

Hilton continues his argument with an analogy between his addressee's mundane responsibilities and the traditional pastoral "mixed" or "medlyd life" of spiritual sovereigns like bishops and curates. According to Hilton, the layman must temper his contemplative desires by managing his wealth to support his subjects:

> And therefor departe wiisli thi livyng in two: o tyme to oon, another tyme to that othere. For, wite thou weel, yif thou leve nedefull bisynesse of actif liyf, and be reklees, and take noo keep of thi wordli goodes, hou thei are spendid and keped, ne haste no force of thi suggettis and of thyne evene-Cristene bicause of wille and desire that thou hast onli to yeve thee to goosteli occupacion, wenynge that thou art bi that excused—yif thou do soo, thou doost not wiseli. (116)

Needless to say, Hilton's "medlyd life" is, with its inherent doubleness, an uneasy and even self-contradictory spiritual model, which essentially warns the rich layman to abandon all inner desire or "covetise" for "veyne worschipes and richesse of this world" (128), yet not to forego the power and possessions themselves.[13]

No sooner does Hilton establish the layman's duties to his family and subjects than he turns to the new problem of how a sovereign's psychology may hamper his spiritual goals. Advising the layman to meditate on God's manhood, Hilton warns: "This thought is good and spedeful, nameli whan it cometh freeli of Goddis yifte, with devocioun and fervour of the spirit: elles a man mai not lightli have savour ne devocioun in it I hoolde it not spedeful to a man for to prese thanne to moche therupon, as yif he wolde gete it by maistrie, for he schal mowe breke his heed and his bodi, and he schal nevere be the neer" (125).[14] Accustomed to commanding, the layman would likely try to control his own interior life and imagination with that kind of force or "mastery" that Hilton here opposes to true contemplation. As is furthermore clear from this passage, the *Epistle*'s ideological strain manifests itself in a marked anxiety about the body, which can be destroyed by a spiritual regimen that is exterior, visible, and forced. Hilton opens this text by reminding the layman that "as Seint Poul seith, 'As woman was maad for man and not man for woman,' right so bodili worchynge was maad for goosteli, and not goostli for bodili" (110). He ends it with a call for discretion regarding the kinds of sensual meditative experiences associated with the women mystics as well as the *fervor, dulcor* and *canor* from Rolle's works: "Loke aftir noon other feelynge in thi bodili wittes; ne seke after noon other bodili suettenesse, neither sowynyg, ne savoryng, ne wondirful light, ne angelis sight; ne though oure Lord himself (as unto thi sight) wolde appere bodili to thee, charge it but a litil" (122).[15] For Hilton, the rhetorical and political challenge of the "mixed life" is how to govern spiritually those who must govern others bodily and who furthermore understand devotion in those terms. The *Epistle*'s implicit message is that the contemplative efforts of sovereigns are always in danger of falling into a kind of material misrule in which the body governs the spirit like a woman governing a man.

Wisdom dramatizes the very fissures that threaten Hilton's ideal of a responsible and charitable ruling class. As Lucifer announces before presenting the Soul with his account of the "mixed life": "þe flesche of man þat ys so changeable / That wyll I tempte" (360–61).[16] The "changeable flesh" of humanity is both the principle of theatricality, body shaped into narrative, and the principle of interpretation, flexible according to bodily desire. The "plot" of the play, if one can call it that, is worth recounting in some detail. Wisdom, Suso's *Sapientia,* appears on stage dressed as a monarch in ermine, wearing a "ryche imperyall crown þerwpon sett wyth precyus stonys and perlys"; the Soul, Anima, appears "as a mayde" in a fur-trimmed white "clothe of golte" with a black cloak. The two exchange around a hundred lines of "bridal mysticism" taken from the English version of Suso's *Horologium.* Wisdom reminds the Soul that their erotic language, ultimately derived from the apocryphal *Wisdom of Solomon* and the *Song of Songs,* is strictly allegorical and warns the Soul that reason must always rule sensuality. The five "wyttes" of the soul enter as virgins singing "Nigra sum sed formosa filia Jerusalem," already glossed as referring to her "fowll" and "fayer" inclinations.

Anima then "splits" into the three Augustinian faculties of the Soul—Mind, Understanding, and Will (treated by Hilton in the *Scale of Perfection* as the "myghtes" mynde, resoun, and wille), who identify themselves in turn with the attributes of Father, Son, and Holy Spirit. The middle section of the play begins with the appearance of Lucifer, who explains his plan and declares that "I xall never rest tyll þe Soule I defyle" (380). He accomplishes this by changing into the costume of "a goodly galont" and then presenting the three faculties with a definitive misinterpretation of Hilton's *Epistle on the Mixed Life* one that stresses the virtues of gaining wealth: "Beholde how ryches dystroyt nede" (458). Almost instantly, as we might expect, the allegory of the soul collapses and the faculties transform into social vices. Mind turns into "Maintenance," attended by corrupt retainers; Understanding becomes "Perjury" with double-faced jurors; and Will becomes "Lechery," followed by an orgiastic dance of gallants and matrons. In their new identities, the three interact as a parody of the English legal system instead of as a unified soul. In conclusion, Wisdom re-enters, telling Anima to "Take hede!" (900), and the process of penance begins. Wisdom finally instructs the Soul by reciting around seventy lines of *Novem Virtutes,* a vernacular text on charity once ascribed to Rolle. The play ends with the abject and contrite Soul reconciled to God.

Wisdom is a peculiar production in its equal attention to staging and exegesis; part doctrine and part dumbshow, the play is an allegory in motion and a self-aware polemic on the impossibility of staging the stable referents of allegory.[17] In its attention to specific devotional works, the play is a journey through a library, in which texts become vehicles for both fall and redemption. The division or fragmentation of the female Anima into the male faculties Mind, Understanding, and Will parallels the dissemination of vernacular texts like the *Seven Poyntes* from their intended female religious audience to a wider audience of men of the world who, at their worst, resemble the array of Vices. The misguided reading associated with the "mixed life" is imbricated with what Marlene Clark, Sharon Kraus, and Pamela Sheingorn, in a coauthored article, call "the homosocial order of the fifteenth-century manor, courtroom, and battlefield."[18] Likewise, literary forms are crucial to the drama: Suso's erotic metaphors spin out of control onstage, but in the end the reading subject is recuperated by the *Novem Virtutes'* unadorned rules for the proper Christian life.[19]

The Soul's distinctive "fall" into political chaos has led Gail Gibson both to imagine a monastic audience at Bury St. Edmunds decrying Hilton's "mixed" spiritual ideal and to suggest that the play, with its kingly Wisdom, could have been occasioned by a visit by Edward IV to the abbey in 1469.[20] Milton Gatch has argued that *Wisdom*'s detailed legal satire identifies it with the London Inns of Court and pious common lawyers seeking a "mixed life."[21] However, given that the play is clearly, as Pamela King notes, "visually sumptuous" and also specifically demands the participation of women in the dance of Lechery's entourage, I would agree instead with Alexandra Johnston's more plausible suggestion that *Wisdom* was designed for an aristocratic venue. As Johnston persuasively argues, the play, even if originally composed by a monk of Bury, was a professional production for the court of a great East Anglian magnate, intended for an audience of gentry and clergy alike.[22] This is the audience that potentially included patrons of the great works of lay piety, literate "sovereigns" like Chaworth and the lawyer Byngham, who owned and likely read books like the *Seven Poyntes*. The play is, as I will argue at length later in this chapter, a searching critique of the "mixed life," engaged with the social and political dangers that ensue from these readers' interpretations of mystical texts. If Hilton's *Epistle on the Mixed Life* cautiously guides the wealthy layman toward a correct response to a body of allegorical works by Rolle, Suso, Bridget of Sweden, and Richard of St. Victor among others, *Wisdom* rebukes a gentry who not only misinterpret such texts but willfully read allegory in the most literal sense to advance specific political ends.

The historical specificity of *Wisdom* emerges, appropriately enough, when Mind, Understanding, and Will fall into their debauched political roles and revel in their abuses of various legal institutions, including the vague "quest of Holborn," the civil law courts of the Knight-Marshall and the Admiralty, and the royal common law courts that met at Westminster Hall.[23] As Understanding, having become Perjury, describes his manipulation of documents and bribing of juries:

> At Westmyster, wythowt varyance,
> þe nex terme xall me sore avawnce,
> For retornys, for enbraces, for recordaunce.
> Lyghtlyer to get goode kan no man on lyve.
>
>   (789–92)

By staging the actual corruption of the retainers and lawyers of the 1460s and 1470s as in some sense a consequence of the devotional and textual ideals promoted by the "mixed life"—however distorted these are in Lucifer's account—*Wisdom* presents a deeply pessimistic view of the gentry's spiritual potential. To understand the specifically legal cast of the satire, it is instructive to look beyond the play-wright's direct English borrowings to Hilton's Latin letter to a repentant civil lawyer, *Epistola ad Quemdam Seculo Renunciare Volentem.*[24] Hilton attempts, here as in all his texts, to define the relationship between the interior realm and the po-litical world in terms of clashing discourses. This is likewise the peculiar quality of his devotional style most strongly reflected in *Wisdom,* when the eternal soul falls into temporality. Like the vernacular *Epistle on the Mixed Life,* this text at-tempts to define a "mixed life" as Hilton simultaneously advises his friend against joining a religious order and persuades him to renounce wealth and ambition.

As a class, both canonists and civil lawyers, clerics who served in the civil law-based courts of Chivalry and Admiralty, were notable for their extensive libraries. John Neuton, a contemporary of Hilton's at Cambridge, owned some of his class-mate's works as well as those of Rolle and Bridget of Sweden. John Dygon, an Oxford-trained civil lawyer who, unlike Hilton's correspondents, actually suc-ceeded in becoming a recluse around 1435, likewise owned an array of devo-tional texts, including an English *Imitatio Christi* that he copied himself.[25] In the *Epistola,* Hilton, who refers in passing to his own career as a canonist, treats devo-tional and legal thinking as opposites in an effort to explain divine justice. While both civil law and contemplative practice, as Hilton recognizes, attempt in dif-ferent ways to discern the interior condition of a person — particularly in terms of *intention* — law remains a public rhetorical exercise inseparable from worldly vanity:[26] "You should therefore leave the school of Justinian and the courts of law and enter the school of Christ through penitence and various corporal and spiri-tual exercises, with a true humility of heart. Don't let the fear of poverty slow you down; Christian poverty is indeed always precious."[27] In an argument more com-plex and nuanced than that of the vernacular *Epistle on the Mixed Life,* Hilton con-centrates on the psychological condition of the convert, in particular his adherence to legalistic rules rather than his own heart. In Hilton's writings, as in William Flete's *Remedies against Temptations,* a text he almost certainly knew, intention is far more important than action.[28] On the sacrament of confession, he admon-ishes: "[D]o not desire a confession of crimes by means of your voice, but rather de-sire and hope for a conversion of heart."[29] Hilton further warns the lawyer to avoid the "many words" (*multiloquium*) associated with his profession in his prayers, the language of custom (*consuetudo*) rather than true contrition. "God is not ver-bal but real; therefore, one should not put hope in verbal expression. Nor does He pay attention to many words where a pure unadorned heart is offered to Him. See the example in the gospel: 'And in praying,' Christ says, 'do not talk excessively as the Gentiles do, who think they will be heard for their many words' [Matthew 6:7]."[30] Hilton concludes the letter by trying to direct the lawyer away from his anxiety over vows he made verbally but cannot actually keep and toward his inner "intention": in other words, away from the legalistic sense of his transgression and toward his real spiritual condition. He must turn his "spiritual eye" from "exterior acts" and "carnal sins" to "spiritual vices," above all, his "inordinate love of this world."[31] Hilton concludes his advice with the Pauline image, which also appears throughout the *Scale of Perfection,* of putting off the old animal skins that represent bestial, irrational sin and putting on the new clothing of Christ.[32]

In both books of his extremely popular *Scale of Perfection,* Hilton uses the ideas of clothing and disguise to illustrate the double-edged exterior and interior senses of the term *likenes.*[33] In the opening chapter of *Scale*'s book 1, Hilton uses *likeness* to denote at once the surface of the body, and hence the ground of hypocrisy, and the true spiritual goal of turning to Christ:

> For wite thu weel, a bodili turnynge to God without the herte folwynge is but a figure or a likenes of vertues and no soothfastnesse. Wherfore a wrecchid man or a woman is he or sche that leveth al the inward kepinge of hymself and schapith hym withoute oonli a fourme and likenes of hoolynesse, as in habite and in speche and in bodili werkes, biholdynge othere mennys deedys and demyng here defaughtes, wenynge hymsilf to be aught whanne he is right nought, and so bigileth hymsilf. Do thou not so, but turne thyne herte with thy body principali to God, and schape thee withinne to His likenesse bi mekenesse and charité and othere goostli vertues, and thanne art thou truli turned to Hym. (31)[34]

Hilton goes on to illustrate his central Augustinian theological concept, the "reforming" of the soul to God's image, by the aristocratic metaphor of Jesus' "livery": "Forthi schape thee for to be araied in His likenes, that is in mekenesse and charite, whiche is His livery, and thanne wole He hoomli knowe thee and schewe to thee His privytee."[35] Hilton's distinction between interior and exterior "likeness" was, however, apparently unclear enough in *Scale*'s book 1 that he begins book 2 with a strong clarification grounded in Scripture:

> And in the bigynnynge, yif thou wole witen pleynli what I mene bi this image, I telle thee forsothe that y understonde not ellis but thyn owen soule;

for thi soule and my soule and everi resonable soule is an image, and that a
worthi image, for it is the ymage of God, as the apostel seith: *Vir est imago dei*
[1 Corinthians 11:7]. That is, man is the image of God and maad to the image
and to the liknesse of Him, *not in bodili schap withoutin* [emphasis added],
but in the myghtes of it withinne, as Holi Writ seith: *Formavit deus hominem
ad similitudinem suam* [Genesis 1:27]. That is, oure Lord God schoop in soule
man to the ymage and liknesse of Him. (134)

David Bevington has taken up *Wisdom*'s use of Hilton's concepts of likeness and image in the context of a larger argument that "the fifteenth-century
morality play . . . derives its theatrical form from the visualizing of metaphor,
from the concretizing of homiletic and scriptural proposition."[36] While Bevington
notes Lucifer's theatrical manipulations of appearance and costume in the play,
he nonetheless asserts that "such a perception of falsity in images does not gain-
say the moral dramatist's ability, nonetheless, to speak with unambiguous visual
meaning."[37] I would argue, however, that it is this very concreteness, the attempt
to erase ambiguity from metaphors by giving them "bodily shape," that *Wisdom*
identifies as the main spiritual danger for readers of allegorical texts. To understand the dynamic of figuration that the play distorts for dramatic effect, it is instructive to turn to Suso's own original theorizing. In Suso's Latin *Horologium
Sapientiae,* Wisdom tells her Disciple, who has strayed into the Augustinian "land
of unlikeness" (*in regionem dissimilitudinis*),[38] that "the human intellect cannot
understand simple truths about matters that are most sublime, and therefore it
is necessary to convey them through images and accepted comparisons."[39] For
Wisdom and her lover in the friar's daring and erudite dialogue, this includes
quoting passages of Ovid's *Ars Amatoria* and *Remedia Amoris* to each other. In
his cautionary prologue to this text, however, Suso is at pains to explain how
the figurative language of bridal mysticism works, including Christ's fluidity of
gender:

It should also be noted that I have used the device of questions and answers
between the disciple and Wisdom only to convey matters more vividly. It is
not to be understood that there will ever be just such a disciple as this, or
that Wisdom will be concerned with him to everyone else's exclusion, or that
he, more than all others, will love her so much, or that she will do so many
great things only for him, but take him to represent everyone who is like
him. . . . And so the style changes from time to time, to suit what is then the

subject. Sometimes the son of God is presented as the spouse of the devout soul; then later the same Son is introduced as Eternal Wisdom, wedded to the just man.[40]

In response to the exegetical efforts of writers like Suso and Hilton, the play enacts its drama of misinterpretation at just this level of figurative language. While the *Epistle on the Mixed Life* opposes the layman's sovereignty to a full access to contemplative experience, *Wisdom* uses a variety of theatrical resources to oppose the concept of sovereignty itself to the complexities of allegory and allegorical understanding.

From *Wisdom*'s opening, it confronts the coinciding epistemological and political limits of a theatrical representation of mystical language:

WISDOM: Yff ȝe wyll wet þe propyrtye
          Ande þe resun of my nayme imperyall,
          I am clepyde of hem þat in erthe be
          Everlastynge Wysdom, to my nobley egalle;
          And most to me ys convenyent,
          Allthow eche persone of þe Trinyte be wysdom eternall
          And all thre one everlastynge wysdome togedyr present.
          Nevertheles, forasmoche as wysdom ys propyrly
          Applyede to the Sune by resune,
          And also it fallyt to hym specyally
          Bycause of hys hye generacyon,
          Therfor þe belowyde Sone hath this sygnyficacyon:
          Custummaly Wysdom, now Gode, now man,
          Spows of the chyrche and wery patrone,
          Wyff of eche chose sowle. Thus Wysdom begane.
ANIMA: "Hanc amavi et exquisivi":
          Fro my yougthe thys have I sowte
          to have my spowse most specyally,
          For a lover of yowr schappe am I wrowte.

                                                        (1–20)

Suso's allegorical exchange between Wisdom and Anima, drawn from the eroticized spiritual reading associated with the Cistercians, has become grotesquely literalized in its visual realization: the *Horologium*'s Wisdom, at once female and male, *Sapientia* and Christ, "mayster" and "maystresse," lover and "moder of love," is here always a king in full regalia, who, calling himself the "wyffe of eche chose sowle," is still in patriarchal "imperial" drag, with—as the unusually detailed stage directions specify—"a berde of gold of sypres curled."[41] Similarly, Wisdom's explanation to the soul "as a mayde" of their "play of love" in this context draws attention to the erotic and financial pull of the embodied, bejeweled sovereign, a reanimated Solomon—or perhaps, ironically, an Edward IV—more than Bernard of Clairvaux's spiritualized deity.[42]

While as Bevington argues, the image of the regal Christ derives ultimately from parts of Suso's own text, in *Wisdom* the figure has become static and curiously alienated from the discourse that he is required by the textual sources to deliver. The icon of Christ in majesty, a remote eschatological figure, incongruously *speaks* here as the very different, ambiguously gendered Christ of bridal mysticism: "Beholde now, Sowll, with joyful Mynde / How lovely I am, how amyable, / To be halsyde and kyssyde of mankynde" (42–43). This in turn confuses Wisdom's next pronouncement, clothed as he is in the trappings of worldly desire: "The prerogatyff of my love ys so grett / þat who tastyt therof the lest droppe sure / All lust and lykyngys worldly xall lette" (49–51). Then in come the "Daughters of Jerusalem," or "virgins," or interior "senses," the guardians of reason, themselves already precariously embodying that most contested of allegories, the Song of Songs. One might expect the corresponding "fyve outwarde wytts" or bodily senses, to appear separately as well, yet these are never visually represented but are only verbally mentioned in Wisdom.[43] That the allegorical "senses" perform a double job as inner and outer experience, however, in itself characterizes the play's opening polemical "fall." The binary distinctions that ground Hilton's spiritual understanding in the *Scale*—interior and exterior, reason and sensuality, soul and body—are here compromised by a forced matching of Suso's elusive figurative text to picture. Inner and outer faculties, imagination and sensual experience, are here already confused. Although Suso's translator's words are not significantly altered in this scene, their allegorical assumptions and ambiguities have been reduced to material images that demonstrate the possibilities of radical misreading.

It is precisely through the "wits," the imaginative faculties acting here as the spectatorial "daughters of Jerusalem," that Anima comes to temptation. Within the space of a few admonitory lines from Wisdom, Hilton's central idea of the soul as the "figure" of God becomes an invitation to identify with the actor's royal splendor. Two of the three "myghts" that form the play's Trinitarian soul, Mind and Will, announce themselves as, respectively, "the veray figure of the Deyte" and "Off the Godhede, lyknes and fygure," but Wisdom makes Anima's mis-recognition of herself in God concrete:

> Lo thes thre myghtys in one Soule be
> Mynde, Wyll, and Wndyrstondynge
> By Mynde of Gode þe Fadyr knowyng have ye;
> By Wndyrstondynge of Gode þe Sone ye have knowynge;
> By Wyll, wyche turnyt into love brennynge,
> Gode þe Holy Gost, þat clepyde is lowe:
> Not thre Godys but one Gode in beynge
> Thus eche clene soule ys symylytude of Gode abowe
>
> . . . .
>
> *Thys þe clene soule stondyth as a kynge*
>
> > (277–84, 289, emphasis added)

The Soul's subsequent misinterpretation and adoption of Wisdom's metaphor of sovereignty, by means of a combination of outer and inner senses, forms the middle section of *Wisdom* with its explicit evocations of courtly pageantry. The entire opening of the play could be taken as a gloss on another greatly influential discussion of "wisdom" within an exegesis of "Nigra sum, sed formosa, filiae Jerusalem," Bernard of Clairvaux's Sermon 25 on the *Song of Songs*. In this contemplative reading, Bernard opposes the beauty of wisdom to the empty allure of wealth and power:

> Therefore the soul of Paul was adorned with brightness, and wisdom dwelt there, to enable him to impart wisdom among the mature, a wisdom hidden in mystery, which none of the rulers of this world understood. This wisdom and righteousness of Paul were either produced or merited through the outward impairment of his little body, worn out by constant labors, by frequent fastings and vigils. Hence this ugliness of Paul is more beautiful than jewelled ornaments, than the raiment of kings. No physical loveliness can compare with it, no skin however bright and glowing; not the tinted cheek for which corruption waits, nor the costly dress that time wears out; not the lustre of gold nor sparkle of gems, nor any other creature: all will crumble into corruption. It is with good reason then that the saints find no time for the glamor of jewellry and the elegance of dress that lose their appeal with every passing hour; their whole attention is fixed on improving and adorning the inward self that is made to the image of God, and is renewed day by day.[44]

Wisdom here is a concept defined only negatively, removed by metaphor itself from the realm of possible metaphoric representations and figured in direct opposition to both body and political power.

The play's boldest polemical move is to propose that "sovereign" readers of mystical texts have an interest in appropriating and depicting figurative discourse to serve their political ends. This continual distortion of metaphor in turn fuels the play's own theatrical flourishes and innovations. Hence, Lucifer's theory of temptation is to encourage misapprehension, "undyr colors all thynge perverse":

> Of God man is þe fygure / His symylytude, his pyctowre,
> Gloryosest of ony creature / þat ever was wrought
> Wyche I will dysvygure / Be my fals conjecture
> Yff he tend my reporture / I xall brynge him to nought.
>   (349–56)

The soul's fall in this demonic strategy will be from an understanding of her place in the figurative economy of Hilton's *Scale* to the spiritual "nothingness" of a carnal, literal level of interpretation. Lucifer, apparently armed with Hilton's complete works, characterizes his own displacement by the Soul with the Augustinian's central term, *reforming:*

> In reformynge of my place ys dyght
> Man, whom I have in most dyspyght,
> Ever castynge me wyth hem to fyght
> In þat hewynly place he xulde not dwell.
>   (337–40)

Hence, Lucifer "re-forms" or "dis-figures" the Soul by making her and her faculties face the spiritual consequences of what the play itself has already visually staged, the misrecognition of sovereignty in the reification of metaphors. Lucifer's subsequent argument, based on a specious version of *Imitatio Christi,* follows logically as another type of "disfiguring" substitution.

Lucifer's rhetorical onslaught against Mind, who, like Hilton's correspondents in the *Epistle on the Mixed Life* and the *Epistola ad Quemdam Seculo Renunciare Volentem,* apparently aspires to a purely contemplative life, is to draw on the weaknesses of Hilton's tightrope-walking argument. If, in the *Epistle,* the layman's interior condition defines his relation to his wealth and power, Lucifer plays on "the flesch of man that is so changeable" to manipulate Anima's psychological faculties. He cites Hilton's claim that Christ himself followed the "medlyd life" as an example to others:

Sumtyme wyth synners he had conversacyon
Sumtyme wyth holy also comunycacyon
Sumtyme he laboryde, preyde; sumtyme tribulacyon;
Thys was *vita mixta* þat Gode here began
And þat lyff xulde ye here sewe.

(424–29)

Although Mind briefly holds to the contemplative ideal, Lucifer shrewdly re-works Hilton's arguments against joining religious orders to emphasize the very fears of God's wrath that the canon's conscience-stricken friends harbor. In Lucifer's legalistic version, which plays on the sovereign's fear of "mastering" his spiritual life, act entirely overshadows intention:

Contemplatyff lyff for to sewe
Yt ys grett drede, and se cause why:
They must fast, wake, and prey, ever new,
Wse harde lywynge and goying wyth dyscyplyne dew,
Kepe sylence, wepe, and surphettys eschewe,
And yff þey fayll of thys þey offende Gode hyghly.
Wan þey have waystyde by feyntnes,
Than febyll þer wyttys and fallyn to fondnes,
Sum into dyspeyr and sum into madnes.

(431–39)

Lucifer soon convinces Mind to "be in þe worlde" (442), to adhere to a "common" life that in fact involves neither active nor contemplative spirituality. To Will, the desiring faculty, he adds that this is the only way to avoid the confusion of body and spirit that Hilton at the opening of the *Scale* calls hypocrisy; in the devil's account, however, body must rule:

Lewe your stodyes, þow ben dyvyn;
Your prayers, your penance, of ipocryttys þe syne,

Ande lede a comun lyff.
What synne ys in met, in ale, in wyn?
What synne is in ryches, in clothynge fyne?
All thing Gode ordeynde man to inclyne.

(470–75)

The subsequent "fall" of Mind, Understanding, and Will into explicitly political roles is not that of the clueless "everyman" lured into sensuality by a persuasive evil but rather that of the gentry as a class, having finally found a devotional slogan in the Latin *vita mixta* that licenses them to carry on worldly "bisynesse" as usual. Lucifer, apparently armed here only with Hilton's collected writings and his own psychological acuity, is as much spin-doctor as seducer.

As Pamela King points out, Lucifer, with his "inherently deceitful and unstable nature," represents a kind of principle of theatricality in *Wisdom,* as he presides over both elaborate changes of costume into "livery" and fundamental "distortions of identity."[45] Lucifer in fact effects a kind of catastrophic deallegorization of the play's previous scenes. The mystical metaphors of Suso's *Horologium,* the allegorical "sovereignty" of Wisdom as Christ and His love for the Soul, are recast starkly as literal power and sex. In *Wisdom*'s discursive imagination, the combination of allegorical language with political and legal corruption is the very essence of a profane worldly pageantry — exemplified by the song-and-dance extravaganza at the play's center. The concept of the *vita mixta* itself is literally realized as well, as each of the faculties splits into two distinct identities, its "contemplative" name and its corresponding "active" vice. Above all, Lucifer reveals the theatrical potential of Hilton's *Epistle* in his orchestration of this fall; the text, he implies, shows the aristocratic reader how to claim an inner piety while holding on to his inevitably corrupt wealth and power. An already unstable model, the "mixed life" quickly devolves into a masked ball.

The stage suddenly shifts from the interior *psychomachia* to the exterior world of the contemporary gentry, judges, and lawyers, the social reality that exists just beyond the pages of Hilton's devotional texts. This is, of course, the aristocratic audience's own world of rampant legal corruption, focused in particular on the practices of maintenance and livery.[46] *Wisdom* stages a political spectacle that we can imagine as something like that of the Pastons, embroiled in their well-documented legal battles with Lord Moleyns and his retainers over the manor at Gresham, trying to favorably "interpret" metaphoric terms, or that of the common lawyer Byngham curling up with his newly inherited copy of Suso.[47] Mind, the trinitarian faculty associated with the "lordly" power of the Father (*Scale* 43), runs amok as Maintenance:

> This ys cause of my worshyppe:
> I serve myghty lordeschyppe
> And am in grett tenderschyppe;
> Therfor myche folk me dredys.
> Men sew to my frendeschyppe
> For mayntnance of her schendeschyppe.
>
> (629–34)

Mind's musical pageant turns Hilton's Pauline metaphor of Christ's "livery" back into the actual livery of current-day maintenance; as the stage directions indicate, "Here enter six disguised in the sute of Mynde, wyth red byrdys, and lyons rampaunt on here crestys and eche a warder in hys honde." Here Hilton's theme of the reforming of humanity to divine "likeness" has finally been perversely returned to a concrete image of political affinity.

Understanding, the faculty associated most with reason and language, adds his support as "Perjury," a skilled lawyer who knows how to sell himself and to buy a "trusted" jury panel:

> And I use jorowry,
> Enbrace questys of perjury,
> Choppe and chonge with symonye
> And take large yeftys.
> Be þe cause never so try,
> I preve it fals, I swere, I lye,
> With a quest of myn affye.
>
> (637–43)

Similarly, Understanding's pageant—an interpretive dance by a jury of various forms of deceit—plays on the doubleness or hypocrisy of legal language addressed by Hilton's *Epistola:* "Here entre the six jorours in a sute, gownyde, wyth hodys abowt her nekys, hattys of meyntenance þerupon, vyseryde dyversly." The "wisdom" of the son, a unity of meaning, splits into the interpretive multiplicity of "legal" authority; or, in the sense of Hilton's rebuke to the civil lawyer, the "real" fragments into the "verbal."

Finally, Will, or, in Augustinian terms, "Amor," follows suit into carnal desire, in a pageant that calls for the unusual presence of cross-dressed female dancers onstage, representing various sensual vices: "here entreth six women in sute, thre dysgysyde as galontys and thre as matrones, wyth wondyrfull vysurs conregent." Especially if five of these "fortherers of love" or whores are the erstwhile Daughters of Jerusalem or Inner Wits, the parody of mystical Song of Songs commentary is clear. Providing the most literal possible reading of the Song as a kind of sex manual, Will even echoes the Wits' earlier quasi-liturgical singing of "Nigra sum sed Formosa" and "Tota Pulchra Es":[48]

Cum slepers, Rekeleshede and Idyllnes,
All in all, Surfet and Gredynes,
For þe flesche, Spousebreche and Mastres,
With jentyll Fornycacyon
Yowyr mynstrell a hornepype mete
þat fowll ys in hymselff but to the erys swete.

(753–58)

In this burlesque of the *Song,* Wisdom considers the specifically exegetical dangers of a "mixed life" in which Hilton's active-contemplative laymen have access to English devotional texts like the *Seven Poyntes* but not necessarily to the tradition of Scripture and allegorizing commentary that inform them. Toward the end of *Scale*'s book 2, Hilton explains how his distinction between exterior and interior realities translates into hermeneutic theory:

Thanne for as moche as the soule of a lovere is maad meke thorugh inspiracion of grace bi openynge of the goostli iye, and seeth that it is not in itself, but oonli hangeth on the merci and the goodnesse of God, and lastyngeli is born up bi favour and helpe of Hym oonli and truli desirynge His presence: therfore seeth it Jhesu, for it seeth sothfastnesse of Holi Writte wondirfulli schewed and opened, aboven studie and traveile and resoun of mannes kyndeli wit. . . . Right so the goostli presence of Jhesu openeth the witte of His lovere that brenneth in desire to Him, and bryngeth to his mynde bi mysterie of angelis the wordes and sentence of Holi Writ, unsought and unavised, oon aftir anothir, and expouneth hem redili, be thei never so hard or so privei. (250–51)

In its imagination of a "mixed life" that privileges the "active," *Wisdom* reverses the logic of Hilton's contemplative theory of reading. Rather than illuminating

Holy Writ, the "mixed life's" appropriation of devotional language only obscures the possibilities of allegorical interpretation. According to Hilton, the true apprehension of Scripture is by definition beyond visual representation, even in the clerical realm of study; in the dramatic space of the "mixed life," Holy Writ immediately falls victim to the temporal forces represented by the Vices.

Theater, the realm of the bodily rather than the "spiritual eye," as the *Miller's Tale* raucously demonstrates in its account of Absolon's ill-fated encounter with the Song of Songs, resists the dynamic of Hilton's mystical exegesis to secure "the priveté of Holi Writ." While Clark et al.'s article calls attention to the "gender slipperiness" of this moment in *Wisdom* as a subversive theatricality in which "gendered characteristics seem to be in free play rather than bound to sexed bodies," I read this passage as less a "refusal of the law" than—in Hilton's terms—a legalistic literal gloss.[49] Suso's bigendered figure of Wisdom—the Christ of mystical readings of the *Song*—is here parodied by cross-dressing women, and the burning love of God by the "flesh" of the Song's literal meaning. The idea of the abstract feminine *Sapientia* signifying the son is carnally represented by a woman counterfeiting a "galont"; the divine doubleness of mystical understanding has been reduced to another form of hypocritical disguise, conceptually similar to maintenance and perjury.

The pageant's emphasis on legal satire characterizes the gentry's limits as readers; legal language is, in *Wisdom*'s terms as well as Hilton's *Epistola*'s, the inverse of contemplative "understanding"; in theory it seeks to find Truth, but it uses knowledge only to lie effectively.

> Jorowrs in one hood beer to facys
> Fayer speche and falshede in on space ys.
> Is it not ruthe?
> The quest of Holborn cum into þis placys
> Ageyn þe ryght ever þey rechases.
> Off wom þey holde not, harde hys grace ys.
> Many a tyme have dammyde truthe.
>   (719–24)

The doubleness inherent in all allegory as *alieniloquium*, "speaking other" in order to represent spiritual truth, in this worldly court becomes the doubleness of legalistic hypocrisy.[50] The distance between word and meaning here works not for transcendence but for corruption, a lawyer's rhetorical figure rather than a mystic's exercise. Understanding/Perjury's subsequent mention of the specialized civil law courts of Admiralty and Chivalry ("Marschalsi") underlines the play's larger theme of a political and spiritual chaos supported by legal misinterpretation at the highest levels of government. The lawyers who participated in these courts are, as Hilton's *Epistola* forcefully reminds us, the same readers of theology in danger of confusing their two discourses of legal "custom" and inner truth. Allegory, the vehicle for Suso's universalizing treatment of the mystical subject, can itself be another rhetorical tool at the disposal of corrupt sovereigns and their counselors. As the *Epistle on the Mixed Life* fears, the body—literal and fleshly—rules the spirit in the gentry's ideal life. Hilton's intention, to direct the aristocratic reader's desire for "erthli richesse," toward spiritual "richesse," easily and dangerously reverses itself.

Having located the peril of the "mixed life" in lay readers' desire to misconstrue allegorical language in order to pursue worldly ends, the regal Wisdom reappears onstage with more questions than answers: "What have I do? why lowyst þou not me? Why cherysyste þi enmye? Why hatyst þou þi frende? Myght I have done ony more for þe?" (913–15). These are the lamentations of a misread book. As Wisdom/Christ admits, his direct mystical relationship with the lay, vernacular reader has failed miserably; charity unruled *has* become vice. First, he counters the soul's attempts at lay interpretation with a stern order back to the church and sacramental mediation:

> For Gode you have offended hyghly
> And yowr modyr, Holy Chyrche so mylde,
> þerfor Gode you must aske mercy,
> By Holy Chyrche to be reconsylyde.
> Trusting verely ye xall never be revylyde
> Yff you have yowr charter of pardon by confessyon.
> (981–86)

The "answer, " nevertheless, by which Wisdom brings the "fowll" soul back to spiritual understanding is as much stylistic as social. In the play's ending, Wisdom, rather than condemning vernacular devotion altogether—as a "monastic" drama might well do in Gibson's reading, for example—ultimately recuperates Hilton's concept of the "mixed life" by turning to a text written in a much less ambiguous style than the popular *Seven Poyntes*. Unsurprisingly, it is also a text that forecloses any possibility of theatricality.

The ending's central borrowing, together with the numerous citations from Hilton's *Epistle* and *Scale,* is from the anonymous *Novem Virtutes* (or in its surviving English version, "Nine Points"), a set of directives for a moderate spiritual program well suited to the true "mixed life" of contemplation and action.[51] The emphasis of the "nine points" is on spiritual discipline: each "virtue" juxtaposes an extreme physical act with a spiritual act in order to instruct the reader in the logic of charity. In an example clearly directed at the gentry's self-understanding:

> The fourte, Gode sethe: "Wake one owyr for þe love of me,
> And þat to me ys more plesaunce
> Than yff þou sent twelve kyngys free
> To my sepulkyr wyth grett puysschaunce
> For my dethe to take vengeaunce."
> Lo, wakynge is a holy thynge.
> þer yt ys hade wyth goode usance,
> Many gracys of yt doth sprynge.
>
> (1021–28)

In a passage pointedly aimed at the favorite literary entertainments of these vernacular readers, all of the ideology and lore of the crusade romances are subordinated to simple contemplation.

Called into dialogue with the *Seven Poyntes,* the *Novem Virtutes* erases the metaphoric "knyghte of Criste" altogether and inscribes in his place a subject named by spiritual ideals alone. Awareness or understanding, in this passage, must be sovereign over worldly power; Mind, under strict social control, literally cannot function as "Maintenance." Similarly, the text admonishes, having compassion for a "seke and nedy" (1030) neighbor is better than fasting on bread and water for forty years. The hermeneutic opposite of allegory, the text anticipates and erases any possible double understanding. For *Wisdom*'s wayward "Anima," this text's nonallegorical emphasis on practical charity toward equal "neighbors" and "evyn-Chrystens" allows little room for the politically motivated radical disjunction between language and action afforded by Suso's *Horologium* or Hilton's *Scale.* The play attempts to confront such abuses with a tight control over text and interpretation. The *Novem Virtutes,* clearly, is a devotional work that means exactly what the words on the page say; textual interpretation, even by the most "hypocritical" reader is essentially limited to action, and the "vita activa" is securely restored to the "medled" ideal.

Wisdom's polemic, then, is not directed so much against the "mixed life" as against those who would define it in the interest of legitimating the contemporary gentry's oppressive politics. Taking Hilton's own anxious warnings from the *Epistle* and the *Scale* a step further, the onstage figure of Wisdom contends that the body should not be just restrained from the potential excesses of Rolle's "fire of love" but actually forced into its place in a hierarchy of spiritual practices: "Lo Gode is plesyde more with þe dedys of charyte / Than all þe penys man may suffer iwys" (1062–63). Going further than Hilton, *Wisdom* dramatizes the certainty that the "pious" gentry will read the mystical texts in vogue in the late fifteenth century the wrong way; and the play concludes by turning instead to the question of what they might safely read besides the *Polichronicon.*

The Soul's penitence, finally, acknowledges the role of imagination and interpretation—the "inner wits"—as equal to sensuality in her fall:

> In tweyn myghtys of my soule I thee offendyde
> The one by my inwarde wyttys, thow ben gostly
> þe other by my outwarde wyttys comprehendyde
> Tho be þe fyve wyttys bodyle.
>
> (1073–76)

After the recitation of the *Novem Virtutes,* inner and outer faculties are again distinguished from each other and realigned, with Anima's imagination and sensuality yoked to charity. With this distinction secured, the kingly Wisdom pronounces a final strain of bridal mysticism, restoring the Song of Songs to its status as Latin and English Holy Writ, simultaneously translated and glossed:

> Vulnerasti cor meum soror mea, sponsa,
> In uno ictu oculorum tuorum.
> You have wonded my hert, syster, spowse dere,
> In þe tweyn syghys of your ey.
>
> (1083–86)

In a renunciation of the profane pageantry, not only the Soul but the audience must also finally direct its "eye" to Wisdom. The play, however, ends much the same way it begins, with the soul's "likeness" and metaphoric "sovereignty" reinscribed; Mind admonishes the Soul, citing Romans 12:2:

> Conforme yow not to þis pompyus glory
> But reforme in gostly felynge.
> Ye þat were dammyde by synn endelesly,
> Mercy hathe reformyde yow ande crownyde as a kynge.
>
> (1121–24)

Once again this "king," like Scripture itself, seems poised for literalistic appropriation in a repeat performance. Hence, even after prescribing its conservative textual program, the play gestures to the instability of all scriptural interpretation. In *Wisdom*'s exegetical economy, the social justice for which Hilton's *Epistle* strives can be produced only by subjecting the desires of sovereigns—their bodily, spiritual, and literary wills—to a single hermeneutics. But in a world of theater, *Wisdom* demands of us, can there ever be such a discipline?

BIHR	*Bulletin of the Institute for Historical Research*
CCCM	Corpus Christianorum, Continuatio Medievalis
CCSL	Corpus Christianorum, Series Latina
CSEL	Corpus Scriptorum Ecclesiasticorum Latinorum
EETS	Early English Text Society
ELH	*English Literary History*
EWS	*English Wycliffite Sermons,* 5 vols., ed. Anne Hudson and Pamela Gradon. Oxford: Oxford University Press, 1983–96.
JEGP	*Journal of English and Germanic Philology*
JMEMS	*Journal of Medieval and Early Modern Studies*
MED	*Middle English Dictionary,* ed. Hans Kurath, Sherman M. Kuhn, and Robert E. Lewis. Ann Arbor: University of Michigan Press, 1952–.
MLQ	*Modern Language Quarterly*
PL	Patrologia Latina, ed. J.-P. Migne
PMLA	*Publications of the Modern Language Association*
REED	Records of Early English Drama
RS	Rolls Series
SCH	Studies in Church History

INTRODUCTION

1. From *The York Plays,* ed. Richard Beadle (London: Edward Arnold, 1982).

2. Anselm of Canterbury, *Why God Became Man,* trans. Janet Fairweather, in the *Major Works,* ed. Brian Davies and G. R. Evans (Oxford: Oxford University Press, 1998), 278. "Sed quoniam ipse cum patre sanctoque spiritu disposuerat se non aliter quam per mortem celsitudinem omnipotentiae suae mundo ostensurum." Anselm of Canterbury, *Cur Deus Homo,* in *Opera Omnia,* ed. F. S. Schmitt (Stuttgart: Frommann, 1968), 1:62.

3. There has been some much-needed stocktaking recently of the field of study itself, most notably in *A New History of Early English Drama,* ed. John D. Cox and David Scott Kastan (New York: Columbia University Press, 1997), and in the excellent *Cambridge Companion to Medieval English Theatre,* ed. Richard Beadle (Cambridge: Cambridge University Press, 1994), which both summarizes and clarifies the manuscript evidence of the major dramatic texts and thoroughly reviews the last century of scholarship.

4. With the partial exception of *Wisdom,* which, in addition to the Macro Manuscript (Folger Library, MS V.a.354), exists in a second incomplete manuscript (Bodleian Library, Digby MS 133). See Mark Eccles, introduction to *The Macro Plays,* EETS (Oxford: Oxford University Press, 1969), xxvii–xxx.

5. The classic account of the eventual suppression of the cycle plays during the Reformation is Harold Gardiner's *Mysteries' End: An Investigation of the Last Days of the Medieval Religious Stage* (New Haven, Conn.: Yale University Press, 1946). For a helpful reassessment of Gardiner's thesis and an account of how Protestant revisions of the originally Catholic drama fared in the sixteenth century, see Paul Whitfield White, "Reforming Mysteries' End: A New Look at Protestant Intervention in English Provincial Drama," *JMEMS* 29:1 (1999): 89–120. For an illuminating account of the centrality of theater to the cultural

transformations of the Reformation, see Sarah Beckwith, "Theaters of Signs and Disguises: The Reform of the York Corpus Christi Plays," in *Signifying God: Social Relation and Symbolic Act in the York Corpus Christi Plays* (Chicago: University of Chicago Press, 2001), 121–57.

6. All students of medieval theater are indebted to the tremendous efforts of the scholars who have edited regional volumes of the Records of Early English Drama (REED) series. The archival labors of the REED project have revealed an immense amount of dramatic material but have also sparked historiographic controversies over the problems of how to define the legitimacy of a given "record." For an important critique of the positivist methodology of the REED project, specifically of the principles behind the editors' selections of what constitute "dramatic" documents, see Theresa Coletti, "Reading REED: History and the Records of Early English Drama," in *Literary Practice and Social Change in Britain, 1380–1530,* ed. Lee Patterson (Berkeley: University of California Press, 1990), 248–84. For a more positive assessment of the uses of the REED project, particularly in terms of spatial ideas, see Patricia Badir, "Playing Space: History, the Body, and Records of Early English Drama," *Exemplaria* 9:2 (1997): 255–79.

7. Richard Beadle, "The York Cycle," in Beadle, *Cambridge Companion,* 90.

8. See Richard Beadle, introduction to *The York Plays,* 10–45.

9. Alan Fletcher, "The N-Town Plays," in Beadle, *Cambridge Companion,* 171. See also Stephen Spector, introduction to *The N-Town Play,* 2 vols., EETS (Oxford: Oxford University Press, 1991), xiii–xlv. On the medieval theory of *compilatio,* see A. J. Minnis, "Late-Medieval Discussions of Compilatio and the Role of the Compilator," *Beiträge zur Geschichte der deutschen Sprache und Literatur* 101 (1979): 385–421.

10. Michel Foucault, "What Is an Author?" trans. Josué Harari, in *The Foucault Reader,* ed. Paul Rabinow (New York: Random House, 1984), 101–20.

11. Peter Meredith, "The Towneley Cycle," in Beadle, *Cambridge Companion,* 134–62.

12. Eamon Duffy, *The Stripping of the Altars: Traditional Religion in England, 1400–1580,* (New Haven, Conn.: Yale University Press, 1992), 11–52.

13. Quoted in O. B. Hardison Jr., *Christian Rite and Christian Drama in the Middle Ages* (Baltimore: Johns Hopkins University Press, 1965), 36. See also Miri Rubin, *Corpus Christi: The Eucharist in Late Medieval Culture* (Cambridge: Cambridge University Press, 1991), 12–49.

14. V. A. Kolve, *The Play Called Corpus Christi* (Stanford, Calif.: Stanford University Press, 1966), 99. On the hermeneutics of the Glossa Ordinaria, which Kolve draws on heavily, see Beryl Smalley, *The Study of the Bible in the Middle Ages* (Oxford: Blackwell, 1952; reprint, University of Notre Dame Press, 1964), 46–66. Citations are to the 1964 edition.

15. M. R. James, "Ritual, Drama, and the Social Body in the Late Medieval English Town," *Past and Present* 98 (1983): 3–29.

16. Gail McMurray Gibson, *The Theater of Devotion: East Anglian Drama and Society in the Late Middle Ages* (Chicago: University of Chicago Press, 1989), 1–18.

17. Sarah Beckwith, *Signifying God,* esp. 23–41.

18. See David Lawton, "Dullness and the Fifteenth-Century," *ELH* 54 (1987): 761–99.

19. Nicholas Watson, "Censorship and Cultural Change in Late-Medieval England: Vernacular Theology, the Oxford Translation Debate, and Arundel's Constitutions of 1409," *Speculum* 70 (1995): 822–64.

20. Fiona Somerset, "Professionalizing Translation at the Turn of the Fifteenth Century: Ullerston's Determinatio, Arundel's Constitutions," in *The Vulgar Tongue: Medieval and Post-medieval Vernacularity,* ed. Fiona Somerset and Nicholas Watson (University Park: Pennsylvania State University Press, 2003), 145–57.

21. On the related issue of the impact of the suppression of Lollardy on the richness of fifteenth-century English musical production, see Bruce Holsinger, "The Vision of Music in a Lollard Florilegium: *Cantus* in the Middle English *Rosarium theologiae* (Cambridge, Gonville and Caius College MS 354/581)," *Plainsong and Medieval Music* 8 (1999): 95–106.

22. Joseph Roach, *Cities of the Dead: Circum-Atlantic Performance* (New York: Columbia University Press, 1996), 3–4.

CHAPTER I.   DRAMA AFTER CHAUCER: THE *MILLER'S TALE* AND
         THE FAILURES OF REPRESENTATION

1. Throughout this chapter, all quotations from the *Canterbury Tales* are taken from *The Riverside Chaucer,* 3d ed., ed. Larry Benson (Oxford: Oxford University Press, 1988).

2. For a critique of how "Pilates voys" has been interpreted traditionally, see Ralph Hanna III, "Pilate's Voice/Shirley's Case," in *Pursuing History: Middle English Manuscripts and Their Texts* (Stanford, Calif.: Stanford University Press, 1996), 267–79.

3. Pilate has an interesting connection to millers via the *Legenda Aurea,* where he is said to be the illegitimate son of Pila, daughter of the miller Atus (hence the name Pilatus), by King Tyrus. See Jacobus de Voragine, *The Golden Legend,* trans. William Granger Ryan (Princeton, N.J.: Princeton University Press, 1993), 1:211.

4. All quotations from the York plays are from Richard Beadle, ed., *The York Plays* (London: Edward Arnold, 1982).

5. All quotations from the Towneley plays are from Martin Stevens and A. C. Cawley, eds., *The Towneley Plays,* 2 vols., EETS (Oxford: Oxford University Press, 1994).

6. On the different valences of Pilate in the mystery plays, see Seth Lerer, "The Chaucerian Critique of Medieval Theatricality," in *The Performance of Middle English Culture: Essays on Chaucer and the Drama in Honor of Martin Stevens,* ed. James J. Paxson, Lawrence M. Clopper, and Sylvia Tomasch (Cambridge: D. S. Brewer, 1998), 59–76.

7. Throughout this chapter, all quotations from the *Tretise* are taken from Clifford Davidson, ed., *A Tretise of Miraclis Pleyinge* (Kalamazoo, Mich.: Medieval Institute Publications, 1993). For an excellent introduction to the *Tretise,* see Nicholas Davis, "The *Tretise of Myraclis Pleyinge:* On Milieu and Authorship," *Middle English Theatre* 12:2 (1990): 124–51. See also Ruth Nisse, "Reversing Discipline: The *Tretise of Miraclis Pleyinge,* Lollard Exegesis, and the Failure of Representation," *Yearbook of Langland Studies* 11 (1997): 163–94.

8. "Nam in principio cavendum est ne figuratam locutionem ad litteram accipias. Et ad hoc enim pertinet quod ait apostolus, *littera occidit, spiritus autem vivificat.* Cum enim figurate dictum sic accipitur tamquam proprie dictum sit, carnaliter sapitur. Neque ulla mors animae congruentius appellatur quam cum id etiam quod in ea bestiis antecellit, hoc est intelligentia, carni subicitur sequendo litteram. Qui enim sequitur litteram, translata verba sicut

propria tenet, neque illud quod proprio verbo significatur refert ad aliam significationem. . . . Ea demum est miserabilis animae servitus, signa pro rebus accipere et supra creaturam corpoream oculum mentis ad hauriendum aeternum lumen levare non posse." Augustine, *De Doctrina Christiana,* ed. and trans. R. P. H. Green (Oxford: Oxford University Press, 1995), 140–41.

9. V. A. Kolve, *The Play Called Corpus Christi* (Stanford, Calif.: Stanford University Press, 1966).

10. Erich Auerbach, "Figura," in *Scenes from the Drama of European Literature* (Minneapolis: University of Minnesota Press, 1984), 54, 58.

11. Gail McMurray Gibson, *The Theater of Devotion: East Anglian Drama and Society in the Late Middle Ages* (Chicago: University of Chicago Press, 1989), 1–18.

12. [Johannis de Caulibus], *Meditations on the Life of Christ: An Illustrated Manuscript of the Fourteenth Century,* ed. and trans. Isa Ragusa and Rosalie B. Green (Princeton, N.J.: Princeton University Press, 1961), 318. "Sed in quali bello et conflictu, audi et vide. Alius enim apprehendit; alius ligat; alius insurgit, et alius exclamat; alius inpellit, alius blasphemat; alius expuit in eum, alius vexat; alius circumvoliuit, alius interrogat." Johannis de Caulibus, *Meditationes Vitae Christi,* ed. M. Stallings-Taney, CCCM 113 (Turnhout: Brepols, 1997), 253.

13. Hugh of St. Victor, *Didascalicon,* ed. Charles H. Buttimer (Washington, D.C.: Catholic University Press, 1939), 113, and *Didascalicon,* trans. Jerome Taylor (New York: Columbia University Press, 1961), 135.

14. Miri Rubin, *Corpus Christi: The Eucharist in Late Medieval Culture* (Cambridge: Cambridge University Press, 1991), 270.

15. See John Ganim, *Chaucerian Theatricality* (Princeton, N.J.: Princeton University Press, 1990), 41–42. Interestingly, the two main critical treatments of theater from the late fourteenth century—the *Miller's Tale* and the *Tretise*—are also complex reactions to the Peasants' Revolt.

16. For this term and the tenuous boundaries between "ernest" and "game" in medieval French theater, see Jody Enders, "Medieval Snuff Drama," *Exemplaria* 10:1 (1997): 171–206.

17. "Quem apprehensum et quam plurimus injuriis lacessitum perduxerunt ad novem mercatum, ubi per noctem sequentem obprobriis et conviciis illudebant, quandoque enim coram ipso genuflectebant dicentes 'ave raby,' quandoque ei ciphum sine poculo propinabant, quandoque alapis eum cedentes dixerunt 'prophetiza quis est qui percussit te.' Sic que per totum noctis spacium fremebant et stridebant dentibus super eum, sicut in nocte cene judea gens perfida fecerat super Christum." Extracts from John Gosford's chronicle (British Library, BL Cotton Claudius A XII), quoted in Edgar Powell, *The Rising in East Anglia in 1381* (Cambridge: Cambridge University Press, 1891), 140.

18. "[D]ictus scilicet Johannes Wraw, cum praefata turba, ad villam de Bury properant, at, nemine resistente, subintrant, caputque Prioris praenominati in conspectu villarum, tanquam processionaliter cicumeundo, in edito super lanceam perferentes, donec ad collistrigium pervenirent: quo cum accesssissent, in signum antehabitae amicitiae inter Priorem et Johannem Cavendich, et derisionem utriusque personae, capita, modo velut ad auriculan-

dum, jam auasi ad osculandum, invicem super summitates lancearum cum maxima inep-
tia conjunxerunt. Postremo, cum talibus saturati fuissent ludibriis, utriusque caput iterum
super collistrigium posuerunt." Thomas Walsingham, *Historia Anglicana,* ed. Henry T. Riley
(London: Longman, Green, 1864), 2:2–3. Translation in R. B. Dobson, ed., *The Peasants' Revolt of 1381,* 2d ed. (New York: Macmillan, 1983), 245. Gosford's chronicle tells the tale in
much the same fashion, as a churls' game: "Capitibus igitur illudentes caput Prioris applicu-
erunt ad caput Justiciarii nunc ad auriculum quasi consilium postulando, nunc ad os eius
quasi amicicias ostendendo" (141). [Having thus seized the prior's head, the revelers tilted it
toward the judge's head, now to his ear as if asking for advice, now to his mouth as if dis-
playing friendship.]

19. For a brief mention of this event within a larger consideration of the theatrical potential of Corpus Christi, see Steven Justice, *Writing and Rebellion: England in 1381* (Berkeley: University of California Press, 1994), 157–58. Paul Strohm considers the rebels' and the
chronicles' uses of images of revelry and carnival in "'A Revelle': Chronicle Evidence and the
Rebel Voice," in *Hochon's Arrow: The Social Imagination of Fourteenth-Century Texts* (Princeton,
N.J.: Princeton University Press, 1992), 33–56.

20. The rebels' demands were primarily for freedom from the tolls and rents that the
abbey collected from tenants: for the rebels' claims to the "liberties of King Cnut," see Dobson, *Peasants' Revolt,* Strohm, "'A Revelle,'" and Justice, *Writing and Rebellion.*

21. "Priorem insuper Sancti Edmundi de Bury, Dominum Johannem de Cantebriggia,
virum industrium et solertem, Orpheum Thracem, Neronem Romanum, Belgabred Britan-
num, vocis dulcedine, pariter et cantus scientia superantem." Walsingham, *Historia Anglicana,* 2:2. Translation in Dobson, *Peasants' Revolt,* 244–45.

22. Suetonius, *Works,* rev. ed., ed. and trans. J. C. Rolfe (Cambridge, Mass.: Harvard University Press, 1997), 2:112–15. See Guillaume de Lorris and Jean de Meun, *Le roman de la rose,*
ed. Daniel Poirion (Paris: Garnier-Flammarion, 1974), lines 6141–88. Although the *Roman
de la rose* is his primary source, Chaucer cites "Swetonius" in the *Monk's Tale* (2465).

23. Paul A. Olson, *Chaucer and the Good Society* (Princeton, N.J.: Princeton University
Press, 1986), 75, and see also 49–84 on the revolt. On the 1381 rebels' letters, see Justice, *Writing and Rebellion,* 13–66.

24. Lee Patterson, "The Miller's Tale and the Politics of Laughter," in *Chaucer and the
Subject of History* (Madison: University of Wisconsin Press, 1991), 244–79.

25. Lerer, "Chaucerian Critique," 74.

26. Langland's "goliardeis, a gloton of wordes" appears in William Langland, *Piers
Plowman: The B Version,* rev. ed., ed. George Kane and E. Talbot Donaldson (Berkeley: Uni-
versity of California Press, 1988), Prologue, 139; see Jill Mann, *Chaucer and Medieval Estates
Satire* (Cambridge: Cambridge University Press, 1973), 160–62. On the two terms, see Wil-
liam A. Quinn, "Chaucer's Janglerye," *Viator* 18 (1987): 309–20, and P. G. Walsh, "'Golias' and
Goliardic Poetry," *Medium Aevum* 52 (1983): 1–9.

27. See esp. Marshall Leicester, "Newer Currents in Psychoanalytic Criticism, and the
Difference 'It' Makes: Gender and Desire in the *Miller's Tale*," *ELH* 61 (1994): 473–99; Mark
Miller, "Naturalism and Its Discontents in the *Miller's Tale*," *ELH* 67 (2000): 1–44; and

David Lorenzo Boyd, "Seeking 'Goddes Pryvetee': Sodomy, Quitting, and Desire in *The Miller's Tale*," in *Words and Works; Studies in Medieval English Language and Literature in Honor of Fred C. Robinson,* ed. Peter Baker and Nicholas Howe (Toronto: University of Toronto Press, 1998), 243–60.

28. Leicester, "Newer Currents," 491.

29. *A Pistle of Discrecioun of Stirings,* in Phyllis Hodgson, ed., *Deonise Hid Diuinite and Other Treatises on Contemplative Prayer Related to The Cloud of Unknowing,* EETS (London: Oxford University Press, 1955), 69.

30. See Sandra Prior, "Parodying Typology and the Mystery Plays in the *Miller's Tale*," *Journal of Medieval and Renaissance Studies* 16 (1986): 57–73.

31. On the suppression of the "carnal" literal sense of the Song of Songs in favor of allegorical readings, see Ann Astell, *The Song of Songs in the Middle Ages* (Ithaca, N.Y.: Cornell University Press, 1990), esp. 25–41; and Denys Turner, *Eros and Allegory: Medieval Exegesis of the Song of Songs* (Kalamazoo, Mich.: Cistercian Publications, 1995), esp. 108–23. In the formulation of Gregory the Great to explain the language of the Song of Songs: "For in this book are described kisses, breasts, cheeks, limbs; and this holy language is not to be held in ridicule because of these words. Rather we are provoked to reflect on the mercy of God; for by his naming of the parts of the body by which he calls us to love we must be made aware of how wonderfully and mercifully he works in us; for he goes so far as to use the language of our shameful loves in order to set our heart on fire with a holy love." Turner, *Eros and Allegory,* 217–18. The literalist and historicist Nicholas of Lyra takes a similar position, denying that the Song of Songs is about Solomon and the daughter of Pharoah, since "such a love has a certain dishonorable and improper quality about it." Nicholas of Lyra, *The Postilla of Nicholas of Lyra on the Song of Songs,* ed. and trans. James George Kiecker (Milwaukee, Wis.: Marquette University Press, 1998), 28.

32. For an extremely learned reading of the Songs of Songs as an intertext in the *Miller's Tale,* which, however, preserves the "heterosexuality" of all concerned, see R. E. Kaske, "The *Canticum Canticorum* in the *Miller's Tale*," *Studies in Philology* 59 (1962): 479–500. On the sleazy clerical politics of the literal sense of the Song of Songs, see Patterson, *Chaucer,* 260–62.

33. See Miller, "Naturalism," on the centrality of the kiss and its relations to the problems of "naturalistic" understandings in the *Tale.*

34. Patrick J. Gallacher, ed., *The Cloud of Unknowing* (Kalamazoo, Mich.: Medieval Institute Publications, 1997), 89–90.

35. Ibid., 92.

36. Bernard of Clairvaux, Sermon 53, in *On the Song of Songs,* vol. 3, *Sermons 47–66,* trans. Kilian Walsh and Irene M. Edmonds (Kalamazoo, Mich.: Cistercian Publications, 1979), 61. "Pingemus nobis, sive in Psalmis ista legentes, sive in praesenti Cantico, virum gigantem procerae staturae, absentis cuiuspiam muliericulae amore captum, et dum properat ad cupitos amplexus, transilientem montes collesque hos, quos videmus mole corporea super plana terrae tanta altitudine eminentes, ut et supra nubes aliqui illorum verticem extulisse cernantur? Verum non decet istiusmodi corporeas phantasias imaginari, praesertim trac-

tantes hoc Canticum spirituale; sed nec licet omnino nobis, qui meminimus legisse in Evangelio, quia *Spiritus est Deus, et eos qui adorant eum opoprtet in spiritu adorare.*" Bernard of Clairvaux, *Opera,* ed. J. Leclerq, C. H. Talbot, and H. M. Rochais (Rome: Editiones Cisterciences, 1958), 2:97–98; for a discussion of this passage and its conflicting hermeneutic ideas, see Jeffrey Hamburger, "The Visual and the Visionary: The Image in Late Medieval Monastic Devotions," in *The Visual and the Visionary: Art and Female Spirituality in Late Medieval Germany* (New York: Zone Books, 1998), 111–48.

37. On the exegetical possibilities associated with Absolon through his notorious namesake and his rebellion, see Paul Beichner, "Absolon's Hair," *Mediaeval Studies* 12 (1950): 222–33. Beichner focuses on Absolon's "feminine beauty" and overall "excesses."

38. Bernard of Clairvaux, Sermon 56, in *On the Song of Songs,* 3:87–88. "Caro paries est, et appropiatio Sponsi, Verbi incarnatio. Porro cancellos et fenestras, per quas respicere perhibetur, sensus, ut opinor, carnis et humanos dicit affectus, per quos experimentum cepit omnium humanarum necessitatum. . . . Humanis ergo affectionibus sensibusque corporeis pro foraminibus usus est et fenestris, ut miserias hominum homo factus experimento sciret, ut misericors fieret." Bernard of Clairvaux, *Opera,* 2:114–15.

39. See R. Howard Bloch, *The Scandal of the Fabliaux* (Chicago: University of Chicago Press, 1986), esp. 59–100.

40. Jean-Claude Schmitt and Jerome Baschet, "La 'Sexualité du Christ,'" *Annales* (1991): 337–46.

41. Nicholas of Lyra, *The Postilla,* 35. "Quia meliora sunt ubera tua vino, in Hebraeo habetur: Quia meliores sunt amores tui, nomen enim Hebraicum hic positum equivocum est ad amores et ubera. Hebraei sequuntur unam significationem, translatio nostra aliam, sed in hoc videntur Hebraei melius dicere, quia secundum proprietatem Hebraici sermonis sponsa hic alloquitur sponsum, in commendatione vero sponsi non videtur decenter fieri mentio de uberibus. Potest tamen dici quod per ubera sponsi hic intelligitur plenitudo misericordiae Dei. Est igitur sensus secundum Hebraeos, cum dicitur: Quia meliores sunt amores tui vino, id est sapidiores menti devote quam quodcumquam sapidum corporale gustui corporali. Et secundum translationem nostram: Meliora sunt ubera tua vino, id est, tuae misericordiae plenitudo dulcior est humanae menti quam vinum gustui quod inter corporalia est magis sapidum." Nicholas of Lyra, *The Postilla,* 34. The Hebrew words for *loves* (*dod'im*) and *breasts* (*dad'im*) can appear to be the same without pointing.

42. For a description of the mystical experience of a violent, penetrating, and fragmenting love based on a reading of this passage of the Song of Songs, see Richard of St. Victor, *De IV Gradibus Violentae Caritatibus,* ed. Gervais Dumiege (Paris: Vrin, 1955).

43. The characterization of Absolon as an "effeminate small-town dandy" is Beichner's ("Absolon's Hair," 222).

44. On the symbolism of Noah's Ark, see V. A. Kolve, *Chaucer and the Imagery of Narrative* (Stanford, Calif.: Stanford University Press, 1984), 158–216. On Hugh's *De Arca Noe Moraliter,* with its suggestive distinction—in the context of the *Miller's Tale*—between "the eye of the flesh" and the "eye of reason," see Bernard McGinn, *The Growth of Mysticism* (New York: Crossroad, 1994), 376–85.

CHAPTER 2.   STAGED INTERPRETATIONS: CIVIC RHETORIC AND
LOLLARD POLITICS IN THE YORK PLAYS

1. *EWS,* 1:425–26, and, for commentary, 4:299–300. See also *MED* on *pagent.* Wyclif's own Palm Sunday sermon, which argues for the rule of secular lords over the clergy, is almost certainly a source for the English sermon; see John Wyclif, *Sermones,* ed. Johann Loserth (London: Wyclif Society, 1887–90), 1:154–60.

2. Anne Hudson, *The Premature Reformation* (Oxford: Oxford University Press, 1988), 429.

3. For a new look at sacramental culture in the York plays, see Sarah Beckwith, *Signifying God: Social Relation and Symbolic Act in the York Corpus Christi Plays* (Chicago: University of Chicago Press, 2001), 59–71, and "*Sacrum Signum:* Sacramentality and Dissent in York's Theatre of Corpus Christi," in *Criticism and Dissent in the Middle Ages,* ed. Rita Copeland (Cambridge: Cambridge University Press, 1996), 264–88.

4. Ruth Nisse, "Reversing Discipline: The *Tretise of Miraclis Pleyinge,* Lollard Exegesis and the Failure of Representation," *Yearbook of Langland Studies* 11 (1997): 163–94.

5. Ritchie Kendall, *The Drama of Dissent: The Radical Poetics of Nonconformity* (Chapel Hill: University of North Carolina Press, 1986), 50–51. Kendall goes on to argue that, in rivalry over the same lay audience, the Lollards "displaced" cycle drama, transferring the outrages of the so-called "tyrant plays" onto agonistic accounts of heresy trials like Thorpe's *Testimony* and satiric dialogues like *Jack Upland.* In other accounts, the Marxist critic Robert Weimann, in *Shakespeare and the Popular Tradition in the Theater: Studies in the Social Dimension of Dramatic Form and Function* (Baltimore: Johns Hopkins University Press, 1978), 92–94, caps off a tradition of viewing the author of the "Wakefield Plays" in the Towneley cycle as a Lollard-tinged social revolutionary. Lauren Lepow, conversely, in *Enacting the Sacrament: Counter-Lollardy in the Towneley Cycle* (Rutherford, N.J.: Fairleigh Dickinson University Press, 1990), reads these same plays as a step-by-step refutation of Wycliffite theology. By far the most subtle and interesting analysis of the intersections between Lollardy and drama is William F. Bennett's "Interrupting the Word: Mankind and the Politics of the Vernacular" (Ph.D. diss., Harvard University, 1992), esp. his reading of the N-Town *Conception* play's sympathetic treatment of Lollard criticisms of the institutional church and defense of prayer "in campo."

6. Hudson, *Premature Reformation,* 390–445.

7. The third of Arundel's Constitutions, "Quod praedicator conformet se auditorio, aliter puniatur," is printed in D. Wilkins, *Concilia Magnae Britanniae et Hiberniae* (London, 1737), 3:316: "Insuper, sicut bonus paterfamilias tritcum spargit in terram as hoc dispositam, ut fructum plus afferat; volumus et mandamus, ut praedicator verbi Dei veniens juxta formam superius annotatam, in praedicando clero sive populo, secundum materiam subjectam se honeste habeat, spargendo semen secundum convenientiam subjecti auditorii; clero praesertim praedicans de vitiis pullulantibus inter eos et laicis de peccatis inter eos communiter usitatis, et non e contra; alioquin sic praedicans secundum qualitate delicti, per loci ordinarium canonice et acriter puniatur." John Foxe's translation reads: "Moreover, like a good

householder casteth wheat into the ground, well ordered for that purpose, thereby to get the more increase, even so we will command, that the preacher of God's word, coming in form aforesaid, preaching either unto the clergy or the laity, according to his matter proponed, shall be of good behaviour, sowing such seed as shall be convenient for his auditory: and chiefly preaching to the clergy, he shall touch the vices commonly used amongst them; and to the laity, he shall declare the vices commonly used amongst them; and not otherwise. But if he preach contrary to this order, then he shall be sharply punished by the ordinary of that place according to the quality of that offense." John Foxe, *Acts and Monuments,* ed. G. Townsend (London, 1843–49), 3:244. For an incisive consideration of the effects of the 1409 *Constitutions* on vernacular preaching, see H. Leith Spencer, *English Preaching in the Late Middle Ages* (Oxford: Oxford University Press, 1993), 163–88.

8. Nicholas Watson has recently extended Hudson's argument by considering the open controversies over translation and vernacular theology in the decades preceding the Constitutions. See "Censorship and Cultural Change in Late-Medieval England: Vernacular Theology, the Oxford Translation Debate, and Arundel's Constitutions of 1409," *Speculum* 70 (1995): 822–64.

9. On the *Dives and Pauper* author, see also Spencer, *English Preaching,* 161.

10. G. R. Owst, *Literature and Pulpit in Medieval England* (Cambridge: Cambridge University Press, 1933), 471–547; quote is from p. 547. On the tradition of Latin anticlerical reformist preaching, see also Owst's *Preaching in Medieval England* (Cambridge: Cambridge University Press, 1926). For a recent assessment of areas ripe for future work on the influence of preaching on drama, see Marianne Briscoe, "Preaching and Medieval English Drama," in *Contexts for Early English Drama,* ed. Marianne Briscoe and J. Coldewey (Bloomington: Indiana University Press, 1989), 150–72.

11. Owst, *Literature and Pulpit,* 285.

12. Spencer, *English Preaching,* 5.

13. Ibid., 38.

14. Ibid., 278–311.

15. Jonathan Hughes, *Pastors and Visionaries: Religion and Secular Life in Late Medieval Yorkshire* (Woodbridge: Boydell and Brewer, 1988). While this book provides a good overview of religious and cultural movements in fourteenth- and fifteenth-century Yorkshire, it is often inaccurate in specific details.

16. Ibid., 125–26.

17. The Yorkshire manuscript of the expurgated Lollard sermon cycle that Hudson discusses, Bodley MS Don.c.13, includes Rolle's *Expositio Super Oracionem Dominicam;* Trinity College Cambridge MS B.14.38 includes both the Sunday epistle sermons, Rolle's *Form of Living,* and, perhaps of most interest for pointing to the kind of hybrid devotional milieu that I believe influenced the York plays, a version of the Pseudo-Bonaventure *Meditations on the Passion.* Sidney Sussex College MS 74, one of the sets of derivative sermons, includes Rolle's *Pater Noster* (*EWS,* 1:70–74, 87).

18. J. A. F. Thomson, *The Later Lollards: 1414–1520* (Oxford: Oxford University Press, 1965), 195–97.

19. Anne Hudson, "The Expurgation of a Lollard Sermon-Cycle," in *Lollards and Their Books* (London: Hambledon Press, 1985), 201–15. Hudson and Gradon collate the Northern dialect of this expurgated version with the texts of the sermons in their editions; for the contents of the manuscript, Bodleian MS Don. c. 13, see *EWS,* 1:87–88.

20. See Hudson, "Expurgation," 205–9, for specific examples.

21. Rita Copeland, "Rhetoric and the Politics of the Literal Sense in Medieval Literary Theory: Aquinas, Wyclif and the Lollards," in *Interpretation Medieval and Modern,* ed. Anna Torti (Cambridge: D. S. Brewer, 1993), 20. For an excellent analysis of the problems inherent in Lollardy's "democratic vision" see Ralph Hanna III, "'Vae Octuplex,' Lollard Socio-Textual Ideology, and Ricardian-Lancastrian Prose Translation," in *Criticism and Dissent in the Middle Ages,* ed. Rita Copeland (Cambridge: Cambridge University Press, 1996), 244–63.

22. For Wyclif's position on the secular "defense" of the Bible, see, e.g., John Wyclif, "Speculum Secularium Dominorum," in *Opera Minora,* ed. J. Loserth (London: Wyclif Society, 1913), 74–91, and Sermon XXIII, in *Sermones,* vol. 1. See also Hudson's commentary on this sermon in *EWS,* 4:258–63.

23. See also Hudson's commentary in *EWS,* 4:213–14. This antifraternal passage does not appear in the expurgated Northern MS of the sermons.

24. T. H. Simmons and H. E. Nolloth, eds., *The Lay Folks' Catechism,* EETS (London: K. Paul, Trench, Trübner, 1901), 15.

25. *EWS,* 2:64. See also Gradon's commentary in *EWS,* 5:150–51. This passage does not appear in the expurgated Northern MS.

26. For a discussion of scholastic controversies over human will (*voluntas*) in fourteenth-century England, see John M. Bowers, *The Crisis of Will in Piers Plowman* (Washington, D.C.: Catholic University of America Press, 1986), esp. 41–60, and, on ideas of political will, 97–128.

27. Lawrence Clopper, "Lay and Clerical Impact on Civic Religious Drama and Ceremony," in *Contexts of Early English Drama,* ed. Marianne Briscoe and J. Coldewey (Bloomington: Indiana University Press, 1989), 128. See also Lawrence Clopper, *Drama, Play and Game: English Festive Culture in the Medieval and Early Modern Period* (Chicago: University of Chicago Press, 2001), 138–68.

28. Dating the actual composition of the York plays is, of course, a notoriously thorny problem. The manuscript of the whole cycle (BL MS Additional 35290) has been dated by Richard Beadle and Peter Meredith to 1463–77 in "Further Evidence for Dating the York Register," *Leeds Studies in English* 11 (1980): 51–55. Working from comparisons of the descriptions of the plays in the *Ordo Paginarum,* the list of the plays from 1415 recorded in the York *Memorandum Book,* with descriptions from later civic records, Martin Stevens, in *Four Middle English Mystery Cycles: Textual, Contextual, and Critical Interpreations* (Princeton, N.J.: Princeton University Press, 1987), 39–50, guesses at a large-scale revision of the cycle in the early 1440s. Richard Beadle, in his most recent study of the cycle, posits a period of revision in the 1420s–30s. See Richard Beadle, ed., *The Cambridge Companion to Medieval English Theatre* (Cambridge: Cambridge University Press, 1994), 100–104.

29. On the York *Liber Albus,* and the contents of these collections in Norwich and London, see Maud Sellers's introduction to the *York Memorandum Book Lettered A/Y in the Guildhall Munimaent Room,* Surtees Society Publications (Durham: Andrews, 1912–15), 2:viii.

Some of York's records, like the ordinances of the pewterers' guild and the processes of the sheriffs' court, were copied directly from London counterparts. On trade between London and York, see Heather Swanson, *Medieval Artisans: An Urban Class in Late Medieval England* (Oxford: Blackwell, 1989).

30. Susan Reynolds, *An Introduction to the History of Mediaeval English Towns* (Oxford: Oxford University Press, 1977), 160–87, and *Kingdoms and Communities in Western Europe, 900–1300* (Oxford: Oxford University Press, 1984), 155–218.

31. Henry T. Riley, ed., *Liber Customarum,* in *Munimenta Gildhallae Londoniensis,* RS (London: Longman, Brown, Green, Longmans, and Roberts, 1860), 2:16–25. For the fishmonger Horn's career and the political and legal context of this document, see Jeremy Catto, "Andrew Horn: Law and History in Fourteenth-Century England," in *The Writing of History in the Middle Ages: Essays Presented to R. W. Southern,* ed. R. H. C. Davies and J. M. Wallace-Hadrill (Oxford: Oxford University Press, 1981). See also Reynolds's discussion of the Latini passages as evidence for a common vocabulary of rule throughout European town communities in *Kingdoms and Communities,* 197–98.

32. Riley, *Liber Customarum,* 2:19: " Car a ceo guerre et hayne est si multipliee cy ey aillours en cytez et en viles, ceo est par la devisioun des communes, et la diversite de volente des burgeis qi sount en deus parties."

33. Ibid., 2:18: "Car il affiert a gouvenour qil parole mieuz qe nul autre; pur ceo qe touz li moundes tient a sage qi sagement parole."

34. Ibid., 2:22–23: "Autersi, te dois garder de trop rire; car il est escrit, qe ris est en la bouche du fol. Et nepurquaunt, tu pues bien rire et juer aucune foi; mais noun pas a maniere denfaunt ne de femme; ne que semble faus ris ne orgeuillous. Et qi est bon des autres choses, il serra les plus cremuz sil moustre lee la visage, meemement quaunt il est assis a oir plet. Autersi, ne deis tu loer tey mesmes, tout seies tu loe de bons; et ne te chaut si tu nes loe de mauvois. Et garde tei de gaungleours, qi te loent devaunt tey." The custumal here translates Latini's third person into the second person. Translation on 2:525. I have corrected this stilted version with the help of Paul Barrette's and Spurgeon Baldwin's translation of Latini, *The Book of the Treasure* (New York: Garland, 1993), 376. Latini's term *gengelour* is, I think, untranslatable, suggesting the politically menacing sarcasm and riot of a "janglere" like Chaucer's Robin the Miller.

35. Riley, *Liber Customarum,* 2:24–25.

36. On the transmission of Latini's works in England, see Julia Bolton Holloway, "Brunetto Latini and England," *Manuscripta* 31 (1987): 11–21.

37. See in particular Stevens, *Four Middle English Mystery Cycles,* 17–87; Swanson, *Medieval Artisans,* 119–20, and "The Illusion of Economic Structure," *Past and Present* 121 (1988): 29–48; and Beckwith, *Signifying God.*

38. Swanson, *Medieval Artisans,* 121–22; Beckwith, *Signifying God,* 49–51.

39. E. Miller, "Medieval York," in *The Victoria County History of Yorkshire: City of York,* ed. P. M. Tillot (London: Institute of Historical Research, 1961), 77–84.

40. Alexandra F. Johnston and Margaret Rogerson, eds. and trans., *REED: York* (Toronto: University of Toronto Press, 1979), 1:11: "les ditz pagentz sount mayntenez & sustenez par les Comunes & Artificiers demesme la Citee en honour & reverence nostreseignor Iesu

Crist & honour & profitt de mesme la Citee. . . . Et ces matiers suisditz suppliount quelles soient perfourneez ou autrement la dite Jue ne serra my Jueez par les Comunes suisditz." Translation on 2:697–98.

41. Beckwith, *Signifying God,* 53.

42. Johnston and Rogerson, *REED: York,* 1:17.

43. Stevens, *Four Middle English Mystery Cycles,* 50–51.

44. Ibid., 52.

45. Gordon Kipling, *Enter the King: Theatre, Liturgy, and Ritual in Medieval Civic Triumph* (Oxford: Oxford University Press, 1998), 24–26.

46. Ibid., 16–17.

47. Ibid., 315–18.

48. Sellers, *York Memorandum Book,* 2:251–65. Sellers dates this document to before 1396 since it mentions the bailiffs, who were superseded that year by sheriffs when York became a county by royal charter. See also Miller, "Medieval York," 76.

49. Sellers, *York Memorandum Book,* 2:251–52.

50. Ibid., 2:255–56.

51. Ibid., 1:60–61.

52. Reynolds, *Kingdoms and Communities,* 168–96. See also Antony Black, *Political Thought in Europe, 1250–1450* (Cambridge: Cambridge University Press, 1992), 118–20.

53. Swanson, *Medieval Artisans,* 110.

54. Johnston and Rogerson, *REED: York,* 1:20; Swanson, *Medieval Artisans,* 110. On the "truly oppressed elements in society," below the guild structure, see Sarah Rees-Jones, "York's Civic Administration, 1354–1464," in *The Government of Medieval York: Essays in Commemoration of the 1396 Royal Charter,* ed. Sarah Rees-Jones (York: Borthwick Institute of Historical Research, 1997), 108–40.

55. Stevens, *Four Middle English Mystery Cycles,* 59.

56. Richard Beadle, ed., *The York Plays* (London: Edward Arnold, 1982). All quotations follow the line numbering of Beadle's edition.

57. The York custumal gives this description of the "Gardeyns des clieffs dez Portes:" "Item, ait este use et accoustume de eslire ung ou deux prudhommes, lesquelx jures et lours noms enrolles, pour la garde des clieffs de chescune porte de la citee, lesquelx doyvent tous jours estre prestez de faire ce que lour serra commande par la maieur et la communalte." Sellers, *York Memorandum Book* 2:261. [Item, it has been a custom to choose one or two wise men of the city, who, having been sworn in and had their names enrolled to keep the keys for each of the city gates, must be ready every day to do whatever the mayor and the commons command them.] See also Rees-Jones, "York's Civic Administration," 140.

58. Brunetto Latini, *Li livres dou tresor,* bk. 3, pt. 1, ed. Francis J. Carmody (Berkeley: University of California Press, 1948). On Latini and the medieval concepts of rhetoric and politics, see Quentin Skinner, *The Foundations of Modern Political Thought* (Cambridge: Cambridge University Press, 1978), 1:23–48; and Maurizio Viroli, *From Politics to Reason of State: The Acquisition and Transformation of the Language of Politics, 1250–1600* (Cambridge: Cambridge University Press, 1992), 23–30.

59. R. B. Dobson, "The Risings in York, Beverley and Scarborough, 1380–1," in *The English Rising of 1381,* ed. R. H. Hilton and T. H. Aston (Cambridge: Cambridge University Press, 1984), 112–42.

60. Stevens, *Four Middle English Mystery Cycles,* 75.

61. Randolph Starn and Loren Partridge, *The Arts of Power: Three Halls of State in Italy, 1300–1600* (Berkeley: University of California Press, 1992), 19–28.

62. On the political consequences of the Scrope Rebellion, see Miller, "Medieval York," 58. See also Stevens, *Four Middle English Mystery Cycles,* 81–82.

63. The Middle English version of the Gospel of Nicodemus in BL Harley MS 4196 renders the relevant passage as "Crist said: "Ilk man a mowth has fre / To weld at his own will; / thare wordes ful wyde sall wyten be / whether thai be gud or ill." *The Middle English Harrowing of Hell and Gospel of Nicodemus,* ed. W. H. Hulme, EETS (London: Oxford University Press, 1907), 36.

64. For a discussion of the Pilate of the York Passion plays as a "master politician," see Robert Brawer, "The Characterization of Pilate in the York Cycle Play," *Studies in Philology* 68 (1972): 289–303.

65. Johnston and Rogerson, *REED: York,* 1:12 (translation, 2:698).

66. Ibid., 1:49 (translation, 2:734).

67. One of the most trenchant Wycliffite attacks on images as the products of "mannis craft" is in a text preserved in a Northern dialect, the *Apology for Lollard Doctrines,* ed. J. Todd (London, 1842).

68. Riley, *Liber Customarum,* 2:18.

CHAPTER 3.   NAKED VISIONS

1. Richard Beadle, ed., *The York Plays* (London: Edward Arnold, 1982). All quotations follow the line numbering of Beadle's edition.

2. All quotations from the *Liber Celestis* are taken from Bridget of Sweden, *The Liber Celestis of St. Bridget of Sweden,* vol. 1, ed. Roger Ellis, EETS (Oxford: Oxford University Press, 1987). Ellis's edition is based on the earlier of the two complete Middle English versions in BL MS Claudius Bi.

3. As Dyan Elliott notes, when Christ calls Bridget "sponsa mea & canale meum" (my bride and my channel) in her visions, he is punning on the double meaning of *canalis* as both channel and uterine cervix. See Bridget of Sweden, *Den Heiliga Birgittas Revelationes Extravagantes,* ed. Lennart Hollmann (Uppsala: Almqvist & Wiksells, 1956), 162–63; and Dyan Elliott, "The Physiology of Rapture and Female Spirituality," in *Medieval Theology and the Natural Body,* ed. Peter Biller and A. J. Minnis (Rochester, N.Y.: York Medieval Press, 1997), 141–73.

4. On the influence of St. Bridget's Nativity vision in the York play, see J. W. Robinson, "A Commentary on the York Play of the Birth of Jesus," *JEGP* 70 (1971): 241–54, and Rosemary Woolf, *The English Mystery Plays* (Berkeley: University of California Press, 1972), 180–81.

5. See, e.g., V. A. Kolve, *The Play Called Corpus Christi* (Stanford, Calif.: Stanford University Press, 1966), and David L. Jeffrey, "Franciscan Spirituality and the Rise of Early English Drama," *Mosaic* 8 (1975): 17–46.

6. [Johannis de Caulibus], *Meditations on the Life of Christ,* trans. Isa Ragusa and Rosalie B. Green (Princeton, N.J.: Princeton University Press, 1961), 5. "Nam circa divinam Scripturam meditari, exponere et intelligere multifarie, prout expedire credimus possumus." Johannis de Caulibus, *Meditationes Vitae Christi,* ed. M. Stallings-Taney, CCCM 113 (Turnhout: Brepols, 1997). The extremely popular and influential *Meditations* are now attributed to one Johannis de Caulibus; the work was circulated in various versions in Latin and in English translation, including Nicholas Love's *Mirror of the Blessed Life of Jesus Christ.* See Michael Sargent's excellent introduction to his edition of Love's *Mirror of the Blessed Life of Jesus Christ* (New York: Garland, 1992), ix–xx.

7. [Johannis de Caulibus], *Meditations,* 5. On the practice of imaginative exegesis in the *Meditations,* see Robert Worth Frank, "Meditationes Vitae Christi: The Logistics of Access to Divinity," in *Hermeneutics and Medieval Culture,* ed. Patrick J. Gallacher and Helen Damico (Albany: SUNY Press, 1989), 39–50. On the problem of desire and imagination in contemporary hermeneutic debates, see Kantik Ghosh, "Manuscripts of Nicholas Love's The Mirror of the Blessed Life of Jesus Christ and Wycliffite Notions of Authority," in *Prestige, Authority, and Power in Late Medieval Manuscripts and Texts,* ed. Felicity Riddy (Cambridge: D. S. Brewer, 2000).

8. For the *Gesta Pilati,* see K. Tischendorf, *Evangelia Apocrypha* (Leipzig, 1876), 333–88. The *Dream* most closely follows the Middle English version of the *Gesta Pilati;* see William Hulme, ed., *The Middle English Harrowing of Hell and Gospel of Nicodemus,* EETS (London: Oxford University Press, 1907), 23–54.

9. Alexandra Johnston and Margaret Rogerson, eds., *REED: York* (Toronto: University of Toronto Press, 1979), 1:21, 2:707. The tapiters' guild ordinances mention the play though not its content; see Maud Sellers, ed., *York Memorandum Book Lettered A/Y in the Guildhall Munimaent Room,* Surtees Society Publications (Durham: Andrews, 1912–15), 2:191. On the guild itself, see Heather Swanson, *Medieval Artisans: An Urban Class in Late Medieval England* (Oxford: Blackwell, 1989), 38–39.

10. I have room here only to nod to the insights of psychoanalysis into dreams: particularly interesting for my reading of Procula's dream and the York reviser's split stage is Jacques Lacan's treatment of dreams as mediating between the Symbolic and Imaginary orders in *Four Fundamental Concepts of Psychoanalysis,* trans. Alan Sheridan (New York: Norton, 1978), and Slavoj Zizek's consideration of dreams that reveal the absurdity of the "Law" in *The Sublime Object of Ideology* (London: Verso, 1989). My reading has also been influenced by Cathy Caruth's "Traumatic Awakenings," in *Performativity and Performance,* ed. Andrew Parker and Eve Sedgewick (New York: Routledge, 1995), 89–108. The York couch-bed, which my students insist must be represented by a Lazy-Boy, is, of course, an irony of history.

11. The etymology of Pilate's name appears in "The Passion of the Lord" in Jacobus de Voragine, *The Golden Legend,* trans. William Granger Ryan (Princeton, N.J.: Princeton University Press, 1993): "There was a king, Tyrus by name, who seduced a girl named Pyla, daugh-

ter of a miller named Atus, and had of her a son. When her son was born, Pyla gave him a named composed of her own and her father's, and called him Pylatus" (1:211).

12. The York reviser's bedroom-focused staging is likely indebted to Nicholas of Lyra's literal commentary on Matthew 27; he argues that since the gospel calls the dream a *visum,* Pilate's wife must have been asleep, and that she must have still been in bed during the interrogation of Christ the following morning. See Nicholas of Lyra, *Biblia Sacra cvm Glossis, Interlineari, et Ordinaria . . .* (Venice, 1588), 5:84D.

13. Jesse Gellrich, *The Idea of the Book in the Middle Ages: Language, Theory, Mythology, and Fiction* (Ithaca, N.Y.: Cornell University Press, 1985), 214.

14. For a reading of hermeneutic tensions between authorial "entente" and political pressures, see James Simpson, "Ethics and Interpretation: Reading Wills in Chaucer's *Legend of Good Women,*" *Studies in the Age of Chaucer* 20 (1998): 73–100; see also Gellrich, *Idea of the Book,* 202–23.

15. "The apparition (*phantasma* or *visum*) comes upon one in the first moment between wakefulness and slumber, in the so-called 'first cloud of sleep.' In this drowsy condition he thinks he is still fully awake and imagines or sees specters rushing at him or wandering vaguely about, differing from natural creatures in size and shape, and hosts of diverse things, either delightful or disturbing. To this class belongs the incubus, which, according to popular belief, rushes upon people in sleep and presses them with a weight which they can feel." Macrobius, *Commentary on the Dream of Scipio,* trans. William Stahl (New York: Columbia University Press, 1952), 89.

16. Simone Collin-Roset, ed., "Le *Liber Thesauri Occulti* de Pascalis Romanus: Un traité d'interprétation des Songes du XIIe siecle," *Archives d'Histoire Doctrinale et Litteraire du Moyen Age* 30 (1963): 111–98. On the classification of dreams as literary forms, see Steven Kruger, *Dreaming in the Middle Ages* (Cambridge: Cambridge University Press, 1992), 130–40.

17. For an influential interpretation of Pilate's wife's dream as the classic "demonic" vision, see Robert Holkot, *Super Libros Sapientiae,* Lectio 201 (Hagenau, 1494); Kruger, *Dreaming,* 95–96.

18. This image (2 Corinthians 11:14) appears in virtually all writings on dreams and visionary experience. As the Cloud-author's *Tretis of Discresyon of Spirites* puts it, "And it is ful needful & speedful to knowe his queintyse and not for to unknowe his doelful deseites. For somtyme he wol, that wickid cursid wight, chaunge his licnes into an aungel of light, that he may, under colour of vertewe, do more dere. But yit thanne, and we loke rediliche, it is bot seed of bittirnes and of discorde that he schewith, seem it never so holi ne never so feire at the first schewing." In Phyllis Hodgson, ed., *Deonise Hid Diuinite and Other Treatises on Contemplative Prayer Related to The Cloud of Unknowing,* EETS (London: Oxford University Press, 1955), 85–86.

19. For an excellent summary of the contradictions involved in the Cloud-author's project of writing a vernacular work for an apparently strictly limited group of contemplatives, see Nicholas Watson, "The Middle English Mystics," in *The Cambridge History of Medieval English Literature,* ed. David Wallace (Cambridge: Cambridge University Press, 1999), 552–55. As Watson puts it, "[T]he Cloud-author never resolves the tensions inherent in his role as me-

diator between learned and lay, or reconciles his elitism with his desire to universalize the system. Outside the circle for which his works were written, the community of vernacular readers he envisages remains crucially ambiguous and vulnerable to challenge" (554).

20. All citations to the *Cloud* are from Patrick Gallacher, ed., *The Cloud of Unknowing* (Kalamazoo, Mich.: Medieval Institute Publications, 1997).

21. Both Vincent Gillespie and Michael Sargent have written a number of illuminating articles tracing how texts originally written for enclosed communities like the Carthusians and Bridgettines—works such as Hilton's *Scale of Perfection*—were adapted and translated for a wider clerical and lay audience. See esp. Vincent Gillespie, "Vernacular Books of Religion," in *Book Production and Publishing in Britain, 1375–1475,* ed. Jeremy Griffiths and Derek Pearsall (Cambridge: Cambridge University Press, 1989), 317–44, and Sargent's introduction to his edition of Nicholas Love's *Mirror of the Blessed Life of Jesus Christ* (New York: Garland Press, 1992). While there is no evidence for a wide circulation of the *Cloud*-author's works, there are some intriguing transmissions. Peter Jolliffe has edited two contemplative tracts that borrow from the *Cloud of Unknowing* and other *Cloud* treatises; these texts are both in mid-fifteenth-century Carthusian manuscripts, one of which, BL MS Additional 37790, also contains works by Rolle, the unique short version of Julian of Norwich's *Revelations,* the Middle English *Mirror of Simple Souls,* and a note of St. Bridget's *Revelations.* P.S. Jolliffe, "Two Middle English Tracts on the Contemplative Life," *Mediaeval Studies* 37 (1975): 85–121. Of more direct relevance to the civic context of the York plays is Sargent's discussion of the four surviving "Common Profit" manuscripts made in the early to mid–fifteenth century by London merchants: one of these, Cambridge UL MS Ff. vi. 31, contains the Cloud-author's treatises on *Discretion of Spirits* and *Discretion of Stirrings* and *Epistle of Prayer.* Michael Sargent, "Walter Hilton's Scale of Perfection: The London Manuscript Group Reconsidered," *Medium Aevum* 52:2 (1983): 189–216. On the textual culture of York and the role of the Mount Grace charterhouse in providing vernacular pastoral works and spiritual anthologies for the secular clergy of the York Minster, see Vincent Gillespie, "The *Cibus Anime* Book 3: A Guide for Contemplatives?" *Analecta Cartusiana* 35 (1983): 90–117. For more on the relationship between the clergy of the York diocese and the circulation of contemplative writings, see Jonathan Hughes, *Pastors and Visionaries: Religion and Secular Life in Late Medieval Yorkshire* (Woodbridge: Boydell and Brewer, 1988), 191–208.

22. Richard of St. Victor, *Richard of St. Victor,* ed. and trans. Grover Zinn (New York: Paulist Press, 1979), 67, and *Opera Omnia,* ed. J.-P. Migne, PL 196 (Paris: Garnier, 1880), cols. 10–11: "Res enim invisibiles, per rerum visibilium formas describunt, et earum memoriam per quarumdam concupiscibilium spiecierum pulchritudinem mentibus nostris imprimunt."

23. On the valences of *naked* in the Cloud-author, see John P. H. Clark, *The Cloud of Unknowing: An Introduction,* Analecta Cartusiana 119:5 (Salzburg, Austria: Institut für Anglistik und Amerikanistik, Universität Salzburg, 1996), 2:25–29.

24. On the problem of imagination in the *Cloud of Unknowing,* see J. A. Burrow, "Fantasy and Language in the *Cloud of Unknowing,*" in *Essays on Medieval Literature* (Oxford: Oxford University Press, 1984), 132–47; and A. J. Minnis, "Affection and Imagination in *The Cloud of Unknowing* and Hilton's *Scale of Perfection,*" *Traditio* 39 (1983): 323–66.

25. This is similar to David of Augsburg's description of deceptive erotic perceptions of Christ and the Virgin Mary in book 3, ch. 66 of *De Exterioris et Interioris Hominis Compositione,* on visions and revelations. David of Augsburg, *De Exterioris et Interioris Hominis Compositione* (Rome: Quaracchi, 1899), 359–60. For a translation of this text into English, see David of Augsburg, *Spiritual Life and Progress,* trans. Dominic Devas (London: Burns, Oates & Washbourne, 1936), 2:188–206. See also Caroline Walker Bynum, "The Female Body and Religious Practice in the Late Middle Ages," in *Fragmentation and Redemption* (New York: Zone Books, 1991), 181–238.

26. Hodgson, *Deonise Hid Diuinite,* 67–69.

27. Richard of St. Victor, *Richard of St. Victor,* 124–30, and *Opera Omnia* (chs. 67–72).

28. On the foundation of Syon, see Richard Rolle, *The Incendium Amoris of Richard Rolle,* ed. Margaret Deanesley (Manchester: Manchester University Press, 1915), 91–144, and David Knowles, *The Religious Orders in England* (Cambridge: Cambridge University Press, 1948–59), 2:175–82. On Bridget's vision in support of the English claim (*Revelations,* book 4, chs. 103–5) and its origins in the reign of Edward III, see Eric Colledge, "Epistola Solitarii ad Reges: Alphonse of Pecha as Organizer of Bridgettine and Urbanist Propaganda," *Mediaeval Studies* 18 (1956): 19–49. Bridget's *Revelations* were also used by later anti-Lancastrian writers to denounce Henry IV's usurpation of the English crown; see Roger Ellis, "Flores ad Fabricandum . . . Coranam: An Investigation into the Uses of the Revelations of St. Bridget of Sweden in Fifteenth-Century England," *Medium Aevum* 51 (1982): 163–86.

29. Jeremy Catto, "Religious Change under Henry V," in *Henry V: The Practice of Kingship,* ed. G. L. Harriss (Oxford: Alan Sutton, 1985), 110–11.

30. On the surviving manuscripts of Bridget's *Revelations,* see Ellis's introduction to Bridget of Sweden, *Liber Celestis,* ix–xv. See also Hughes, *Pastors and Visionaries,* 92–93, on Bridget in Yorkshire; Ellis, "Flores," on the wide circulation of Bridgettine materials; and F. R. Johnston, "The English Cult of St. Bridget of Sweden," *Analecta Bollandiana* 103 (1985): 75–93. For an overview of the dissemination of Rolle, Hilton, and other devotional texts, see Gillespie, "Vernacular Books."

31. The best compendium of attacks on Bridget's sanctity is contained in Adam Easton's *Defense* of Bridget's rule, written before her canonization in the 1380s. See James Schmidke, "Adam Easton's *Defense of St. Birgitta* from Bodleian Ms. Hamilton 7 Oxford University" (Ph.D. diss., Duke University, 1971). Easton presents a defense of women's authority by prophetic exemplars, including Mary Magdalene, St. Agnes, and St. Agatha. He likewise compares Bridget to St. Paul, although into their lives were "perhaps not equal in every merit," as persons who had a gospel or rule dictated to them by Christ (47).

32. Alfonso of Jaén, *Alfonso of Jaén: His Life and Works with Critical Editions of the Epistola Solitarii, the Informaciones and the Epistola Servi Christi,* ed. Arne Jonsson (Lund: Lund University Press, 1989), 117–22. See also Colledge, "Epistola," 40–41.

33. Rosalynn Voaden edits the text of the Middle English *Epistola* from BL MS Cotton Julius Fii as an appendix in *God's Words, Women's Voices: The Discernment of Spirits in the Writing of Late-Medieval Women Visionaries* (York: York Medieval Press, 1999), 159–81; see 163. Augustine sets out his hierarchy of visions, of which the highest is *intellectual,* in book 12 of *The*

Literal Meaning of Genesis, on Paul's vision of Paradise; see Augustine, *The Literal Meaning of Genesis,* trans. Paul Hammond Taylor, S.J. (New York: Newman Press, 1982), 2:178–231.

34. Voaden, *God's Words,* 79–93.

35. On the translator's censorship, see ibid., 162.

36. The manuscripts of the *Chastising* illustrate perfectly the complexities of the transmission of devotional works: the antiheretical *Chastising* exists in two manuscripts, with the Middle English translation of Marguerite Porete's heterodox *Mirror of Simple Souls.* See Joyce Bazire and Eric Colledge, introduction to *The Chastising of God's Children and the Treatise of the Perfection of the Sons of God* (Oxford: Blackwell, 1957), 1–90. All citations to the *Chastising* are to this edition. As suggested by Nicholas Watson in "Censorship and Cultural Change in Late-Medieval England: Vernacular Theology, the Oxford Translation Debate, and Arundel's Constitutions of 1409," *Speculum* 70 (1995): 822–64, contemplative devotion in the late fourteenth and early fifteenth centuries was a tightrope walk between heresy and orthodoxy.

37. Jean Gerson, *De Probatione Spirituum,* in *Oeuvres completes,* ed. P. Glorieux (Tournai: Desclee, 1965), 9:177–85.

38. On the position of the English delegation at Constance, led by Robert Hallam, the Bishop of Salisbury, see F. R. Johnston, "English Defenders of St. Bridget," in *Studies in St. Birgitta and the Brigittine Order,* Analecta Cartusiana 35:19 (Lewiston, N.Y.: Edwin Mellen Press, 1993), 1:263–75.

39. Gerson, *De Probatione Spirituum,* 184. For the verse translation of *Aeneid* IV, 5–6, see Virgil, *The Aeneid of Virgil,* trans. Allen Mandelbaum (New York: Bantam, 1972), 81.

40. For the accusation against Bridget that she "publicized" her visions too much by going to her spiritual father, see also Schmidtke, "Adam Easton's *Defense,*" 76.

41. Marilynn Desmond, *Reading Dido: Gender, Textuality and the Medieval Aeneid* (Minneapolis: University of Minnesota Press, 1994), 74–98.

42. Ibid., 85.

43. Thomas Hoccleve, *The Regiment of Princes,* ed. Charles R. Blyth (Kalamazoo, Mich.: Medieval Institute Publications, 1999); cited by line number.

44. Ann Warren, *Anchorites and Their Patrons in Medieval England* (Berkeley: University of California Press, 1985), 203–6. For the famous late-fifteenth-century illustration of this event in British Library MS Cotton Julius E IV, see Viscount Dillon and W. H. St. John Hope, eds., *The Pageant of the Birth, Life and Death of Richard Beauchamp, Earl of Warwick, 1389–1439* (London: Longmans, 1914), 93–94.

45. Margery Kempe, *The Book of Margery Kempe,* ed. Sanford Brown Meech and Hope Emily Allen, EETS (Oxford: Oxford University Press, 1940), 47.

46. See Ruth Shklar [Nisse], "*The Book of Margery Kempe* and the Power of Heterodox Thinking," *MLQ* 56:3 (1995): 277–304.

47. For the various legal and hermeneutic senses of *entente,* see the entry in the *MED.*

48. Richard Firth Green, *A Crisis of Truth: Literature and Law in Ricardian England* (Philadelphia: University of Pennsylvania Press, 1999), see esp. 1–40.

49. Perhaps the most influential fifteenth-century formulation of treason as crime of language is set out in the accusations before the King's Bench in the first year of Henry V's

reign against those "liars and gossipmongers" who claimed, in "unceasing murmuring," that Richard II was still alive and the legitimate king. See G. O. Sayles, ed., *Select Cases in the Court of the King's Bench under Richard II, Henry IV, and Henry V,* Selden Society Publications, vol. 88 (London: B. Quaritch, 1971), 7:212–15. On these treasonous "rumors" of Richard's afterlife, see Paul Strohm, "The Trouble with Richard: The Reburial of Richard II and Lancastrian Symbolic Strategy," *Speculum* 71 (1996): 87–111. See also Green, *Crisis of Truth,* 206–47, on the shifting meanings of the Ricardian "keywords" *truth* and *treason.* R. H. Helmholtz, *Select Cases of Defamation to 1600,* Selden Society Publications (London: B. Quaritch, 1985).

50. Woolf, *English Mystery Plays,* 245.

51. The Cloud-author's translation, *A Tretyse of the stodye of Wysdome that Men Clepen Beniamyn,* reads: "And thus it is wel provid that Bala is a foule jangeler. & also sensualite is evermore so thristy that al that affeccioun her lady may fele may not yit slecken hir thirst, The drinke that sche desireth is the luste of fleschly, kyndly, & worldly delices, of the which, the more that sche drinketh, the sorer sche thristeth. . . . And thus it is wel provid that Zelfa is evermore dronken & thristy." Hodgson, *Deonise Hid Diuinite,* 13–14.

52. Quoting from William of St.-Thierry's *Epistola ad Fratres de Monte Dei,* the *Meditations* explains the relationship between manual work and spiritual studies: "Man is not made for woman but woman for man (I Cor. Xi, 9). Spiritual exercises are not made for the corporal, but the corporal for the spiritual." [Johannis de Caulibus], *Meditations,* 280.

53. On the idea, from Macrobius, of the incubus who in a *visum* sexually assaults a sleeper, see above, n. 15; see also Kruger, *Dreaming,* 70.

54. Robert Hanning, "You Have Begun a Parlous Pleye: The Nature and Limits of Dramatic Mimesis as a Theme in Four Middle English Fall of Lucifer Cycle Plays," in *Drama of the Middle Ages: Comparative and Critical Essays,* ed. Clifford Davidson, C. J. Gianakaris, and John Stroupe (New York: AMS Press, 1982).

55. Barbara Newman's fascinating article on female demoniacs, "Possessed by the Spirit: Devout Women, Demoniacs, and Apostolic Life in the Thirteenth Century," *Speculum* 73 (1998): 733–70, demonstrates their spiritual authority and their similarity to prophetic saints.

56. Green, *Crisis of Truth,* 206–47.

57. I am indebted here to Page DuBois's influential discussion of the epistemological claims of torture in *Torture and Truth* (New York: Routledge, 1991).

58. Jody Enders, *The Medieval Theater of Cruelty: Rhetoric, Memory, Violence* (Ithaca, N.Y.: Cornell University Press, 1999), 58.

59. Elliott, "Physiology of Rapture," 152–53.

60. Ibid., 142.

61. See Isak Collijn, ed., *Acta et Processus Canonizacionis Beate Birgitte* (Uppsala: Almquist & Wiksells, 1924–31), esp. 105–64.

62. In the manuscript, the play is immediately preceded by a genealogical chart for Mary, similar to the ones in the Middle English lives of St. Anne. See Stephen Spector, ed., *The N-Town Play,* EETS (Oxford: Oxford University Press, 1991), 1:70; and Peter Meredith, ed., *The Mary Play,* 2d ed. (Exeter: University of Exeter Press, 1997), 9–12. See also Roscoe Parker, ed., *The Middle English Stanzaic Versions of the Life of St. Anne,* EETS (London: Oxford

University Press, 1928). For the larger cultural role of St. Anne, see Kathleen Ashley, "Image and Ideology: Saint Anne in Late Medieval Drama and Narrative," in *Interpreting Cultural Symbols: Saint Anne in Late Medieval Society,* ed. Kathleen Ashley and Pamela Sheingorn (Athens: University of Georgia Press, 1990), 111–30.

63. There is little evidence in the extant records for determining the gender of performers. On sixteenth-century evidence for men playing female roles in mystery cycles, see Meg Twycross, "Transvestism in the Mystery Plays," *Middle English Theatre* 5:2 (1983): 123–80. P. J. P. Goldberg argues for women's participation in the York plays in "Craft Guilds, the Corpus Christi Play and Civic Government," in *The Government of Medieval York,* ed. Sarah Rees-Jones (York: Borthwick Institute of Historical Research, 1997), 141–63.

64. These plays are numbered 8–13 in the sequence of the N-Town cycle in BL MS Cotton Vespasian D VIII, omitting the later interpolated play 12, "Joseph's Doubts." On the style and authorship of the plays, see Meredith, *The Mary Play,* 1–23. For more on the development of the unique manuscript, see also Spector, *The N-Town Play,* 2:537–43, and Alan Fletcher, "The N-Town Plays," in *The Cambridge Companion to Medieval English Theatre,* ed. Richard Beadle (Cambridge: Cambridge University Press, 1994), 163–88.

65. See Meredith, *The Mary Play,* 4–5; Spector, *The N-Town Play,* 2:537–49.

66. On the distinct authorship and style of *Passion Play II,* see Spector, *The N-Town Play,* 2:506.

67. The universal identification of "Contemplacio" as a male figure seems primarily indebted to M. Patricia Forrest's influential article "The Role of the Expositor Contemplacio in the St. Anne's Day Plays of the Hegge Cycle," *Mediaeval Studies* 28 (1966): 60–76. Forrest writes, "[T]his enigmatic prologuist . . . enacts the parts of commentator, priest, and prophet, often with far-reaching implications" (61). For Forrest, these roles all demand a male gender, even in an allegorical person. Woolf, in *English Mystery Plays,* similarly refers to Contemplacio as male, an analogue to the expositors in continental drama; yet in the very next paragraph she mentions a female analogue, "Oraison," in the *Passion de Valenciennes* (164).

68. Moreover, the *Mary Play* is replete with female allegorical figures, particularly in its staging of the debate of the four daughters of God, Veritas, Justicia, Miseriacordia, and Pax; one of the main sources for this play, *The Charter of the Abbey of the Holy Ghost,* includes Contemplacion as one of the twenty-nine "ghostly ladyes" who live in the cloister. C. Horstmann, ed., *Yorkshire Writers: Richard Rolle and His Followers* (London, 1895), 1:337–62. For more on Contemplacio, see Christiana Whitehead, "Making a Cloister of the Soul in Medieval Religious Treatises," *Medium Aevum* 67 (1998): 1–29.

69. All quotations from the *Mary Play* are taken from Meredith, *The Mary Play,* and cited by line number.

70. Richard of St. Victor, *Richard of St. Victor,* 161. "In imaginatione contemplatio nostra tunc procul dubio versatur, quando rerum istarum visibilium forma, et imago in considerationem adducitur, cum obstupescentes attendimus, et attendentes obstupescimus, corporalia ista quae sensu corporeo haurimus quam sint multa, quam magna, quam diversa, quam pulchra vel jucunda, et in his omnibus creatricis illius superessentiae potentiam, sapientiam munificientiam mirando veneramur, et venerando miramur. Tunc autem contemplatio nostra in imagina-

tione versatur, et secundam solam imaginationem formatur, quando nihil argumentando quae-rimus vel ratiocinando investigamus, sed libera mens nostra huc illucque discurrit, quo eam in hoc spectaculorum genere admiratio rapit." Richard of St. Victor, *Opera Omnia,* col. 70.

71. The *Myroure of Oure Ladye,* an exposition of the Syon liturgy, is in part a translation of and commentary upon Bridget's *Sermo Angelicus* by an anonymous author; it survives in two fifteenth-century manuscripts and a printed edition (1530). The latter is the basis for John Henry Blunt's EETS edition (London: Oxford University Press, 1873). Since this text has been dated from the early fifteenth century to c. 1450, it is difficult to argue for its direct influence on the *Mary Play;* more likely is the well-read playwright's familiarity with the same Bridgettine concepts of Marian devotion from the *Revelations* and the *Sermo* that the *Myroure* collects and extends. On the dating of the *Myroure,* see Roger Ellis, *Syon Abbey: Spiri-tuality of the English Bridgettines,* Analecta Cartusianana (Salzburg, Austria: Institut für An-glistik und Amerikanistik, Universität Salzburg, 1984), 115–23. My reading of the Bridgettine texts is indebted to the brilliant analysis of the relationship between the *Sermo* and the *My-roure* in Laura S. King's 1989 manuscript "Through a Glass Clerkly: Manipulation of Brid-gettine Models in the *Myroure of Oure Lady.*" I thank her for sharing this essay with me.

72. Nicholas Watson, "Conceptions of the Word: The Mother Tongue and the Incar-nation of God," *New Medieval Literatures* 1 (1998): 85–124, 101.

73. As in the texts that Watson considers in "Conceptions of the Word"—including *Piers Plowman* and Julian of Norwich's *Revelation of Love*—the idea of the superiority of the vernacular in the *Myroure* and the *Mary Play* is distinctly non-Lollard but also stands in op-position to Nicholas Love's condescension to the vernacular in the *Mirror of the Blessed Life of Jesus Christ.*

74. "Et sic stans dictam lecturam, idest infrascriptas lecciones legendas in matutinis in dicto monasterio, que tractant de excellentissima excellencia ab eterno beate Marie Virginis, pise dictabat distincte et ordinate in lingua materna beate Birgitte." Bridget of Sweden, *Sermo Angelicus,* vol. 2 of *Sancta Birgitta Opera Minora,* ed. Sten Eklund (Uppsala: Almquist & Wik-sells, 1972), 75–76.

75. "I am not wyser then was seint Hierome that in the drawying of holy scripture from other language to latyn, sayth how he was compellyd at eche boke to answer to bak-bytinge of them that depraved his laboure. But for that I know myne owne feoblenes, as well in connyng as in verteu; therefore I will neyther seke defaulte in other, ne maynteyne myne owne; but lowely I submyt me and all oure wrytynges, and other werkes to the correccyon of oure mother holy chyrche, & of the prelates annd fathers therof, and of all that are wyser and can fele better." Blunt, *Myroure,* 8. King elaborates further on this passage in her essay "Through a Glass Clerkly."

76. Bridget of Sweden, *Sermo Angelicus,* 96–99.

77. On the anticlericalism of this play, see William F. Bennett, "Interrupting the Word: 'Mankind' and the Politics of the Vernacular" (Ph.D. diss., Harvard University, 1992), 165–98.

78. Walter Cahn, "Architecture and Exegesis: Richard of St.-Victor's Ezekiel Commen-tary and Its Illustrations," *Art Bulletin* 76 (1994): 53–68; Patrice Sicard, *Diagrammes medievaux et exegese visuelle* (Turnhout: Brepols, 1993).

79. Nicholas of Lyra, *Prologue to the Commentary on the Psalter,* in *Medieval Literary Theory and Criticism, c. 1100–c. 1375: The Commentary Tradition,* ed. A. J. Minnis and A. B. Scott (Oxford: Oxford University Press, 1988), 271. "[Q]uia David, qui fecit psalmos saltem pro maiori parte, non solum dicitur propheta, sed etiam eximus prophetarum." Nicholas of Lyra, *Biblia Sacra cvm Glossis,* 3:83E.

80. Nicholas of Lyra, *Prologue,* 272. "Alii prophetae per quasdam rerum imagines, atque verborum tegumenta prophetaverunt. David autem solius spiritu santi instinctu sine omni exteriori adminiculo suam edidit prophetiam." Nicholas of Lyra, *Biblia Sacra cvm Glossis,* 3:83F.

81. Nicholas of Lyra, *Prologue,* 271. "Principalis est ipse Deus revelans mysteria in hoc libro descripta. Instrumentalis autem est ipse David." Nicholas of Lyra, *Biblia Sacra cvm Glossis,* 3:83E.

82. A. J. Minnis, *Medieval Theory of Authorship: Scholastic Literary Attitudes in the Later Middle Ages,* 2d ed. (Philadelphia: University of Pennsylvania Press, 1988), 91. On ideas of David's prophetic authorship in the Middle Ages, including a discussion of Rolle's English Psalter commentary, see Michael Kuczynski: *Prophetic Song: The Psalms as Moral Discourse in Late Medieval England* (Philadelphia: University of Pennsylvania Press, 1995), 3–19.

83. For a provocative interpretation of Mary's composition of the *Magnificat* as the focus for anxieties about the woman writer, see Susan Schibanoff, "Botticelli's Madonna del Magnificat: Constructing the Woman Writer in Early Humanist Italy," *PMLA* 109 (1994): 190–206.

84. Note that Mary's descent by blood from Jesse/David is only mentioned briefly in the play (unlike the source, the *Legenda Aurea*).

85. Meredith, *The Mary Play,* 105.

86. Richard Rolle, *The Psalter or Psalms of David and Certain Canticles, with a Translation and Exposition in English by Richard Rolle of Hampole,* ed. H. R. Bramley (Oxford: Clarendon Press, 1884), 4. Rolle wrote the English Psalter for his friend Margaret Kirkeby, a Cistercian nun and anchoress; see Nicholas Watson, *Richard Rolle and the Invention of Authority* (Cambridge: Cambridge University Press, 1991), esp. 242–48.

87. The *Charter of the Abbey of the Holy Ghost* appears in the mid-fifteenth-century Bridgettine manuscript Lambeth MS 432, together with various Marian texts including the "Wordys of the Bleesed Virgin Our Lady Seint Mary to Saint Burgitt of the Incarnation and Passion of Oure Lord Jesu Crist." Domenico Pezzini, "The Meditation of Oure Lordis Passyon and other Bridgettine Texts in MS. Lambeth 432," in *Studies in St. Birgitta and the Brigittine Order,* Analecta Cartusiana 35:19 (Lewiston, N.Y.: Edwin Mellen Press, 1993), 1:276–95.

88. Nicholas of Lyra, *Prologue,* 272, and *Biblia Sacra cvm Glossis,* 3:83F. See also Cassiodorus, *Expositio Psalmorum I–LXX,* ed. M. Adriaen, CCSL 97 (Turnhout: Brepols, 1958), 3–25, and *Explanation of the Psalms,* ed. and trans. P. G. Walsh (New York: Paulist Press, 1990), 1:34–35. David Mills points out that as Mary studies the psalter, Contemplacio appears on stage to begin the next play. In this transition, "he is the externalization of Mary's own contemplation as she reads and meditates upon the psalm, and it is her plea for mercy which

prompts the ensuing action." David Mills, "Religious Drama and Civic Ceremonial," in *The Revels History of Drama in English,* vol. 1, *Medieval Drama,* ed. A.C. Cawley et al. (London: Methuen, 1983), 198.

89. Mills, "Religious Drama," 198.

90. The play's source in the *Charter of the Abbey of the Holy Ghost* reads: "& þan wente Isaye the prophete & souȝte the abbesse & here covent many days & fele & he fond hem nouȝt; & þanne he seyde þus: "*Utinam dirumperes celos et descenderes,* wolde god, he seyd, þou woldest bresten hevene & come adoon, & helpen us for to maken aȝen þe abbeye of þe holy gost & fynden up þe covent þat is þus goon aweye." Horstmann, *Yorkshire Writers,* 1:347.

91. Bynum, "The Female Body," esp. the fascinating illustration on 208.

92. Ibid., 204. This accords with Meredith's eucharistic reading, with reference to Ludolph of Saxony's *Vita Christi* (Meredith, *The Mary Play,* 107).

93. See Bynum on Thomas Aquinas in "The Female Body," 226–31.

CHAPTER 4.   LABOR'S END: THE WAKEFIELD MASTER'S POOR THEATER

1. All citations to the Towneley plays are from Martin Stevens and A.C. Cawley, eds., *The Towneley Plays,* 2 vols., EETS (Oxford: Oxford University Press, 1994), and follow the line numbering of that edition.

2. The classic discussion of Christ's forgiveness of the unknowing, "game-playing" torturers is V.A. Kolve's *Play Called Corpus Christi* (Stanford, Calif.: Stanford University Press, 1966), 175–205.

3. Richard Beadle, ed., *The York Plays* (London: Edward Arnold, 1982), cited by line numbers.

4. See Sarah Beckwith, *Signifying God: Social Relation and Symbolic Act in the York Corpus Christi Plays* (Chicago: University of Chicago Press, 2001), 53–54.

5. My translation of Nicholas of Lyra, *Postilla Litteralis,* on Luke 23:34: "*Pater dimitte illis: qui nesciunt quod faciunt.* Erant enim ibi aliqui simplices & illiterati a sacerdotibus judaeorum decepti, qui persequebatur christum zelo legis: & pro istis oravit Christus. Alii autem erant literati qui ipsum esse Christum probabiliter noverant: seu agnoscere debuerant: sed ex odio & invidia fuerunt excaecati & ipsum persecuti sunt usque ad mortem & pro illis non oravit." In Nicholas of Lyra, *Biblia Sacra cvm Glossis, Interlineari et Ordinaria . . . ,* 6 vols. (Venice, 1588), 5:180H.

6. Martin Stevens, *Four Middle English Mystery Cycles: Textual, Contextual, and Critical Interpretations* (Princeton, N.J.: Princeton University Press, 1987), 161.

7. Robert Weimann, *Shakespeare and the Popular Tradition in the Theater: Studies in the Social Dimension of Dramatic Form and Function* (Baltimore: Johns Hopkins University Press, 1978), 96–97.

8. For a summary, see Peter Meredith, "The Towneley Cycle," in *The Cambridge Companion to Medieval English Theatre,* ed. Richard Beadle (Cambridge: Cambridge University Press, 1994), 134–62.

9. Barbara Palmer, "'Towneley Plays' or 'Wakefield Cycle' Revisited," *Comparative Drama* (1988): 318–48.

10. While this interpretation of the "cycle's" development is contrary to P. J. P. Goldberg's new idea of the Wakefield plays as "the creation of a specific moment in history" when the "borough elite" sought a mark of urban identity, I do agree that the later absorption of the work into a "luxury volume" at the end of the fifteenth century represents a "statement of urban pride." See P. J. P. Goldberg, "Performing the Word of God: Corpus Christi Drama in the Northern Province," in *Life and Thought in the Northern Church, c. 1100–c. 1700,* ed. Diana Wood, SCH, Subsidia 11 (Rochester, N.Y.: Boydell Press, 1999).

11. For a discussion of these issues, see Lawrence Clopper, "English Drama: From Ungodly Ludi to Sacred Play," in the *Cambridge History of Medieval English Literature,* ed. David Wallace (Cambridge: Cambridge University Press, 1999), 739–66.

12. The image of Christ's poverty at birth took on, of course, a new polemical significance in the course of thirteenth-century Franciscan debates over the meaning of the order's vow of poverty. For a discussion of Peter John Olivi's *Treatise on Usus Pauper,* for instance, see David Burr, *Olivi and Franciscan Poverty: The Origins of the Usus Pauper Controversy* (Philadelphia: University of Pennsylvania Press, 1989), 57–87.

13. Goldberg, "Performing the Word," 170.

14. As Palmer points out, even the Wakefield place-names that the playwright includes, like the "ayll of Hely" and "Horbery shrogys," are actually references to surrounding villages; only Cain's defiant demand that he be buried in "Gudeboure at the quarrell head" recalls the town itself, here as a "refuge" for the plowman turned murderer who "sets not a fart" by anyone (Palmer, "'Towneley Plays,'" 336).

15. Beckwith, *Signifying God,* 42–55.

16. Ibid., 53.

17. On this "redemptive" theory of human labor, see George Ovitt Jr., *The Restoration of Perfection: Labor and Technology in Medieval Culture* (New Brunswick, N.J.: Rutgers University Press, 1987), 107–63; On Hugh of St. Victor's newly positive theory of the mechanical arts, see Elspeth Whitney, *Paradise Restored: The Mechanical Arts from Antiquity through the Thirteenth Century* (Philadelphia: American Philosophical Society, 1990), 75–145.

18. For a discussion of Piers Plowman as a new valuation of the peasant, see Elizabeth Kirk, "Langland's Plowman and the Recreation of Fourteenth-Century Religious Metaphor," *Yearbook of Langland Studies* 2 (1988): 1–21. On the many medieval stereotypes of peasants as animalistic or ruled by appetite alone, see Paul Freedman, *Images of the Medieval Peasant* (Stanford, Calif.: Stanford University Press, 1999), 133–56.

19. Weimann, *Shakespeare,* 85–97.

20. See I. M. W. Harvey, *Jack Cade's Rebellion of 1450* (Oxford: Oxford University Press, 1991), particularly ch. 6, "Popular Revolt in the 1450s" and the "Bills of Complaint" in the Appendix A, which protest against a range of abuses by the gentry and royal officials.

21. Rosemary Woolf, *The English Mystery Plays* (Berkeley: University of California Press, 1972), 183.

22. Annabel Patterson, *Pastoral and Ideology: Virgil to Valéry* (Berkeley: University of California Press, 1987), 8. For Patterson's longer discussion of Virgil's politics of authorship in the First Eclogue and his criticism of Octavian's land confiscations in 40–38 BCE through the personae of Meliboeus and Tityrus, see 19–42. See also Michael Winterbottom, "Virgil and the Confiscations," *Greece and Rome,* 2d ser., 23 (1976): 55–59.

23. Medieval interpretation of the *Eclogues* (or *Bucolica*) for the most part closely follows Servius's fourth-century reading of the poems as biographical and political allegory, as set forth in the preface to his commentary. See Domenico Comparetti, *Virgil in the Middle Ages* (1895; reprint, Princeton, N.J.: Princeton University Press, 1997), 50–74. On English reception of the *Eclogues,* see Christopher Baswell, *Virgil in Medieval England: Figuring the Aeneid from the Twelfth Century to Chaucer* (Cambridge: Cambridge University Press, 1995), 36–40, and for his description of a fourteenth-century annotated *Eclogues* manuscript, BL Harley 4967, ff. 126v–138v, see 300–301.

24. "Ille meas errare boves, ut cernis, et ipsum / ludere quae vellem calamo permisit agresti" (Eclogue 1, 9–10), in Maurus Servius, *Servii Grammatici Qui Feruntur in Vergilii Carmina Commentarii,* ed. Georg Thilo and Hermann Hagen (Leipzig, 1881–87), vol. 3, pt. 1, "Ludere Scribere," 6.

25. No less a reader of Langland than Elizabeth Salter compares the Wakefield "shepherd-exegetes'" laments to the complaint of Pees against Wronge in *Piers Plowman* B, Passus IV. Salter also argues that the shepherds participate in the literary tradition of Virgil's *Eclogues* and *Georgics* and notes that there were two copies of these works at the Augustinian Friary at York. Elizabeth Salter, "The Anunciation to the Shepherds in Later Medieval Art and Drama," in *English and International Studies in the Literature, Art and Patronage of Medieval England,* ed. Derek Pearsall and Nicolette Zeeman (Cambridge: Cambridge University Press, 1988), 272–92.

26. Claire Sponsler, *Drama and Resistance: Bodies, Goods, and Theatricality in Late Medieval England* (Minneapolis: University of Minnesota Press, 1997), 136–60.

27. I am indebted here to Laura S. King's reading of Mak and Gill as paradigmatic theatrical actors and directors and their sheep rustling as "a species of purveyance" in "'A Good Bowrde': *The Second Shepherds' Play* and the Defense of Drama in Late Medieval England," unpublished manuscript, 1998.

28. See Christopher Dyer, *Standards of Living in the Middle Ages* (Cambridge: Cambridge University Press, 1989), 144–45. On enclosure and the economic depression of the mid–fifteenth century, see E. B. Fryde, *Peasants and Landlords in Later Medieval England* (New York: St. Martin's Press, 1996), 145–68; See also R. H. Hilton, *The English Peasantry in the Later Middle Ages* (Oxford: Oxford University Press, 1975), 161–73.

29. See Salter, "The Annunciation," 278–80.

30. Nicholas Watson, "Censorship and Cultural Change in Late-Medieval England: Vernacular Theology, the Oxford Translation Debate, and Arundel's Constitutions of 1409," *Speculum* 70 (1995): 849.

31. A. I. Doyle, "Remarks on Surviving Manuscripts of Piers Plowman," in *Medieval English Religious and Ethical Literature: Essays in Honor of G. H. Russell,* ed. G. Kratzmann

and James Simpson (Cambridge: Cambridge University Press, 1986), 35–48. Doyle suggests that one B-Text manuscript, Cambridge University Library Dd.i.17, might be from York. For the wills of Walter de Brugge, canon of York Minster, and John Wyndhill, Rector of Arncliffe, see Ralph Hanna III, *William Langland* (Aldershot: Ashgate, 1993), 35.

32. Anne Middleton, "The Audience and Public of 'Piers Plowman,'" in *Middle English Alliterative Poetry and Its Literary Background,* ed. David Lawton (Cambridge: D. S. Brewer, 1982), 104.

33. On the development of "Piers's" afterlife as a character, see Anne Middleton, "William Langland's 'Kynde Name': Authorial Signature and Social Identity in Late Fourteenth-Century England," in *Literary Practice and Social Change in Britain, 1380–1530,* ed. Lee Patterson (Berkeley: University of California Press, 1989), 15–82; Steven Justice, *Writing and Rebellion: England in 1381* (Berkeley: University of California Press, 1994), 102–39; and Anne Hudson, "Piers Plowman and the Peasants' Revolt: A Problem Revisited, " *Yearbook of Langland Studies* 8 (1995): 85–106. For a provocative reading of a radical, dissenting fifteenth-century reception of Piers Plowman in the visual program of the Anglo-Irish Douce manuscript (Oxford, Bodleian Library, MS Douce 104), see Kathryn Kerby-Fulton and Denise Despres, *Iconography and the Professional Reader: The Politics of Book Production in the Douce Piers Plowman* (Minneapolis: University of Minnesota Press, 1999).

34. In recent readings of *Piers Plowman,* David Aers and Anne Middleton have emphasized Langland's responses to legislative efforts, in the series of Statutes of Laborers from 1349 to 1388, not only to control the wages and movements of the labor force but to define subjects bureaucratically according to their place in the market economy. Aers argues that *Piers Plowman* ultimately embraces a "doomed . . . neo-Franciscan ethos" of poverty and an evasive "withdrawal from the field of material production." David Aers, *Community, Gender and Individual Identity: English Writing, 1360–1430* (London: Routledge, 1988), 66–67. Middleton's article, to which I am indebted for my reading of the "Langlandian" aspects of the Wakefield shepherds' plays, brilliantly demonstrates how Langland explores the ethical basis of his own identity as a literary "maker" of fictions through a phantasmic encounter with the vagrancy statute's production of new, fluid, and "false" socioeconomic identities. Anne Middleton, "Acts of Vagrancy: The C-Version 'Autobiography' and the Statute of 1388," in *Written Work: Langland, Labor, and Authorship,* ed. Steven Justice and Kathryn Kerby-Fulton (Philadelphia: University of Pennsylvania Press, 1997), 208–317.

35. This is perhaps a late ironic echo of the thirteenth-century seigneurial equation of the peasant with his belly or appetite: see Justice's discussion of the "anthropology of the peasant" implied in "the maxim that villeins possessed *nihil extra ventrem*" (Justice, *Writing and Rebellion,* 142–43).

36. The following passage is from ch. 8 of Francis's Earlier Rule (*Regula Non Bullata*): "Unde nullus fratrum, ubicumque sit et quocumque vadit, aliquo modo tollat nec recipiat nec recipi faciat pecuiam aut denarios neque occasione vestimentorum nec librorum nec pro pretio alicuius laboris, immo nulla occasione, nisi propter manifestam necessitatem infirmorem fratrum; quia non debemus maiorem utilitatem habere et reputare in pecunia et denariis quam in lapidibus. . . . Et si forte, quod absit, aliquem fratrem contigerit pecuniam vel de-

narios colligere vel habere, excepta solummondo praedicta infirmorum necessitate, omnes fraters teneamus eum pro falso fratre et apostata et fure et latrone et *loculos habente,* nisi vere poenituerit." Francis of Assisi, *Opuscula,* ed. Kajetan Esser, in *Fontes Franciscani,* ed. Enrico Menesto and Stefano Brufani (Assisi: Edizioni Porziuncola, 1995), 193. "Therefore, none of the brothers, wherever he may be or wherever he goes, should in any way carry, receive, or have received [by another] either money or coins, whether for clothing, or books, or payment for any work — indeed for no reason — unless it is for the evident need of the sick brothers; for we must not suppose that money or coins have any greater value than stones. . . . And if by chance — which God forbid — it should happen that some brother has collected or is hoarding money or coins, with the sole exception of the needs of the sick as mentioned above, all the brothers are to consider him as a false brother and an apostate, and a thief and a robber, and as the one who held the purse (cf. John 12.6), unless he has truly repented." Francis of Assisi, *Francis and Clare: The Complete Works,* ed. and trans. Regis J. Armstrong and Ignatius C. Brady (New York: Paulist Press, 1982), 116. On the importance of the bag (*loculi*) carried by Judas in Franciscan interpretations of poverty, see M. D. Lambert, *Franciscan Poverty: The Doctrine of the Absolute Poverty of Christ and the Apostles in the Franciscan Order, 1210–1323* (London: SPCK, 1961; rev. ed., St. Bonaventure, N.Y.: Franciscan Institute, 1998), 67–70. All citations are to the 1998 edition.

37. On Bonaventure's formulations, see Lambert, *Franciscan Poverty,* 132–48.

38. Ibid., 144.

39. Apropos of the learned man who does not "in some way"renounce his learning: "For in no way does a man perfectly renounce the world who keeps the bag of his own interpretation in the secret places of his heart" (*Legenda Maior,* vii, quoted in Lambert, *Franciscan Poverty,* 65). "Nequaquam enim saeculo perfecte renuntiat qui proprii sensus loculos intra cordis arcane reservat" (Bonaventura de Balneoregio, *Legenda Maior,* in Menesto and Brufani, *Fontes Franciscani,* 833).

40. For an excellent introduction to the Spiritual Franciscans, see Burr, *Olivi and Franciscan Poverty.*

41. William Langland, *Piers Plowman: The C-Version,* ed. George Russell and George Kane (Berkeley: University of California Press, 1997). All citations are by line number.

42. For a thorough discussion of Langland's Franciscan influences and intertexts, see Lawrence Clopper, *Songes of Rechelesnesse: Langland and the Franciscans* (Ann Arbor: University of Michigan Press, 1997), esp. ch. 5, "Idiotae, Viri Apostolici, 'Lunatyk Lollares' and Piers the Plowman," 181–217. On the Spiritual Franciscans' connections between revelation and poverty, and the implications of visionary experience among absolutely poor *viri spirituales,* see the important article by David Burr, "Olivi, Apocalyptic Expectation and Visionary Experience," *Traditio* 41 (1985): 273–85.

43. *Pierce the Ploughman's Crede,* in Helen Barr, ed., *The Piers Plowman Tradition* (London: Dent, 1993). See also Helen Barr, *Signes and Sothe: Language in the Piers Plowman Tradition* (Cambridge: D. S. Brewer, 1994), 86–94, and Christina Von Nolcken, "Piers Plowman, the Wycliffites, and Pierce the Plowman's Creed," *Yearbook of Langland Studies* 2 (1988): 71–102.

44. Middleton, "Acts of Vagrancy."

45. Margery Morgan treats the theme of invisibility as central to both Towneley Shepherds' Plays; the visible world (including theatrical representation) that leads the mind to God is itself the "high fraud" that ultimately emphasizes the "reality" of Christ. Margery Morgan, "'High Fraud': Paradox and Double-Plot in the English Shepherds' Plays," *Speculum* 39 (1964): 676–89.

46. Sarah Beckwith, "*Sacrum Signum:* Sacramentality and Dissent in York's Theatre of Corpus Christi," in *Criticism and Dissent in the Middle Ages,* ed. Rita Copeland (Cambridge: Cambridge University Press, 1996), 264.

47. Ibid., 274.

48. See, e.g., A. C. Cawley, "The Grotesque Feast in the *Prima Pastorum,*" *Speculum* 30 (1955): 213–17.

49. For these Aristotelian definitions of the imaginative faculty, see Thomas Aquinas's *Summa Theologica* 1, Q. 78, Article 4; Jean de la Rochelle, *Tractatus de Divisione Multiplici Potentiarum Animae,* ed. Pierre Michaud-Quantin (Paris: Vrin, 1964), 75–77. See also Alastair J. Minnis, "Langland's Ymaginatif and Late-Medieval Theories of Imagination," *Comparative Criticism* 3 (1981): 71–103.

50. See Woolf, *English Mystery Plays,* 185–93.

51. On the place of poaching game as part of the "Peasant Ideology" of ancient liberties that informed the 1381 uprising, see Rosamond Faith, "The 'Great Rumor' of 1377 and Peasant Ideology," in *The English Rising of 1381,* ed. R. H. Hilton and T. H. Aston (Cambridge: Cambridge University Press, 1984). For Faith, poaching is an act that articulates belief in just the kind of utopian plenitude that the shepherds, however ironically, imagine: "The idea that the peasantry were entitled to what the land naturally provided conflicted with the seigneurial notion that lordship implied dominium over all the assets of the manor" (67). Steven Justice, following Michel De Certeau, puts the term *poaching* to the further ideological work of describing local communities' appropriating the symbolic functions of Corpus Christi. Justice, *Writing and Rebellion,* 157.

52. On the eucharistic implications of the shepherds' feast, see Lauren Lepow, *Enacting the Sacrament* (Rutherford, N.J.: Fairleigh Dickinson University Press, 1990), 80–96, who reads the play within an anti-Lollard frame, and Lois Roney, "The Wakefield First and Second Shepherds Plays as Complements in Psychology and Parody," *Speculum* 58 (1983): 696–723.

53. The most celebrated of these eucharistic events is Thomas Walsingham's account of how the rebels at St. Albans broke and distributed among themselves confiscated millstones that the abbot had used as paving stones. Thomas Walsingham, *Gesta Abbatum Monasterii Sancti Albani,* 3 vols., ed. Henry T. Riley (London, 1867–69). For the larger context, see Margaret Aston, "Corpus Christi and Corpus Regni: Heresy and the Peasants' Revolt," *Past and Present* 143 (1994): 3–47, and Justice, *Writing and Rebellion,* 140–92.

54. Aston, "Corpus Christi," 12.

55. Bonaventure, *Itinerarium Mentis in Deum,* ed. and trans. Philotheus Boehner (St. Bonaventure, N.Y.: Franciscan Institute, 1956).

56. Ibid., 60–61, 40–41.

57. *Sacrum Commercium Sancti Francisci Cum Domina Paupertate,* ed. Stefano Brufani, in Menesto and Brufani, *Fontes Franciscani,* 1705–32. See also John Fleming, *An Introduction*

to the Franciscan Literature of the Middle Ages (Chicago: Franciscan Herald Press, 1977), 78–82. This passage also recalls the "feast" at the beginning of Will's fourth vision in *Piers Plowman* (B.13), which serves to distinguish the gluttonous blancmange-eating "doctor," a hypocritical friar who preaches poverty and "devynes," from Piers Plowman, here a messianic figure vindicating true poverty. On this passage, see Anne Middleton, "The Passion of Seint Averoys [B.13.91]: 'Devynyng' and Divinity in the Banquet Scene," *Yearbook of Langland Studies* 1 (1987): 31–40.

58. The translation of Eclogue IV, lines 6–7 (in reverse order), is from *Virgil: Eclogues, Georgics, Aeneid I–IV,* trans. H. Rushton Fairclough, rev. G. P. Goold (Cambridge, Mass.: Harvard University Press, 1999), 48–49.

59. The Pseudo-Augustine *Sermo contra Judaeos,* one of the most popular texts of the Middle Ages, ultimately derives from Quodvultdeus's *Contra Judaeos, Paganos et Arrianos.* See Quodvultdeus, *Opera,* ed. E. Braun, CCSL 60 (Turnhout: Brepols, 1976), 227–58.

60. For letter 53 to Paulinus of Nola, see Jerome, *Epistulae,* 2d ed., pars I, ed. Isidorus Hilberg, CSEL 54 (Vienna: Verlag der Osterreichischen Akademie der Wissenschaften, 1996), 442–65, and *The Principal Works of St. Jerome,* trans. W. H. Freemantle (1892; reprint, Grand Rapids, Mich.: Eerdmans, 1989), 96–102.

On Jerome's warning against equating the Fourth Eclogue with Scripture in his letter, and his difference from Augustine's position on pagan literature, see Pierre Courcelle, "Les exegeses chretiennes de la Quatrieme Eclogue," *Revue des Etudes Anciennes* 59 (1957): 294–319. See also Sabine MacCormack's brilliant discussion of the patristic reception of the Fourth Eclogue in *The Shadows of Poetry: Vergil in the Mind of Augustine* (Berkeley: University of California Press, 1998), 20–31.

61. Lilian Swinburne, ed., *The Lanterne of Light,* EETS (London: K. Paul, Trench, Trübner, 1917), 55; for more examples of this particular line of antifraternal polemic, see Anne Hudson, *The Premature Reformation* (Oxford: Oxford University Press, 1988), 269–71.

62. Nicholas Trevet's commentary on the Fourth Eclogue, e.g., interprets Saturn as follows: "Similiter etiam *redeunt regan saturnia,* i.e., placata et quieta tempora; secundum enim astronomos opera fixa et stabilia Saturno atribuuntur. Et talis est *etas* fixa christiani nominis et Christi." [Similarly, then, the reign of Saturn returns, that is, calm and peaceful times; indeed, according to the astronomers, fixed and stable deeds are attributed to Saturn. And such is the fixed Christian era, named for Christ.] Nicholas Trevet, *Commentario a las Bucolicas de Virgilio,* ed. Aires Augusto Nascimento and José Manuel Díaz de Bustamante (Santiago: Universidad de Santiago de Compostela, 1984), 121. On the rich medieval mythography of Saturn, in both his good and bad aspects, see Alastair Minnis, *Chaucer and Pagan Antiquity* (Cambridge: D. S. Brewer, 1982), 139–41. Minnis cites Trevisa's translation of Bartholomaeus Anglicus, who characterizes Saturn according to "melancolik humour" (140).

63. For unconvincing iconographic accounts of the meaning of the shepherds' gifts, see Eugene Cantelupe and Richard Griffith, "The Gifts of the Shepherds in the Wakefield *Secunda Pastorum:* An Iconographical Interpretation," *Mediaeval Studies* 28 (1966): 328–35, and Roney, "Wakefield," 721.

64. For Francis's ideal of the friars as "joculatores Domini," see the early fourteenth-century *vita,* the *Speculum Perfectionis,* in Menesto and Brufani, *Fontes Franciscani,* 2013.

65. Anne Hudson, "'Laicus Litteratus': The Paradox of Lollardy," in *Heresy and Literacy, 1000–1530,* ed. Peter Biller and Anne Hudson (Cambridge: Cambridge University Press, 1994), 222–36.

66. Translation in "The Story and Process against Walter Brute, a Briton," in John Foxe, *Acts and Monuments,* ed. G. Townsend (London: Seeley, Burnside and Seeley, 1843–49), 3:139. "Si vero in scriptis meis aliquid boni inveneritis hoc ascribite soli Deo qui ex multitudine misericordie sue aliquando ydiotis et peccatoribus manifestat ea que sanctis et sapientibus occultantur." William W. Capes, ed., *Registrum Johannis Trefnant, Episcopi Herefordensis, 1389–1404* (London, 1916), 290.

67. Foxe, *Acts and Monuments,* 141. "In Ysaya eciam sic scribitur . . . claudet oculos vestros, prophetas et principes vestros qui vident visiones operiet, et erit visio vobis omnium sicut verba libri signati quem cum dederint scienti litteras dicent, lege istum, et respondebit, non possum, signatus est enim. Et dabitur nescienti litteras diceturque ei, lege. Et respondebit, nescio litteras." Capes, *Registrum Johannis Trefnant,* 290.

68. In the manuscript, the play is called the *Coliphizacio* [sic] and interestingly not the *Trial before Annas and Cayphas.*

69. See Seth Lerer, "Representyd Now in Yower Syght: The Culture of Spectatorship in Fifteenth-Century England," in *Bodies and Disciplines: Intersections of Literature and History in Fifteenth-Century England,* ed. Barbara Hanawalt and David Wallace (Minneapolis: University of Minnesota Press, 1996), 37–38, for an extension of Kolve's argument about play and game. Lerer reads Cayphas as an "actor and author" who "theatricalizes" Christ's torture.

70. Jody Enders, *The Medieval Theater of Cruelty: Rhetoric, Memory, Violence* (Ithaca, N.Y.: Cornell University Press, 1999), 174.

71. These terms are from Page DuBois, *Torture and Truth* (New York: Routledge, 1991); see also Enders, *Medieval Theater of Cruelty,* 25–62.

72. Luke 22:63–65: "Et viri qui tenebant illum inludebant ei caedentes et velaverunt eum et percutiebant faciem eius et interrogabant eium dicentes prophetiza quis est qui te percussit et alia multa blasphemantes dicebant in eum." Matthew 26:67–68: "Tunc expuerunt in faciem eius et colaphis eum ceciderunt alii autem palmas in faciem ei dederunt dicentes prophetiza nobis Christe quis est qui te percussit." Robert Weber, ed., *Biblia Sacra Iuxta Vulgatam Versionem,* 3d ed. (Stuttgart: Deutsche Bibelgesellschaft, 1983).

73. This sense of *vayll* is used in the Wycliffite Bible; see, e.g., 2 Corinthians 3:13–15 and *MED.*

74. Clifford Davidson, ed., *A Tretise of Miraclis Pleyinge* (Kalamazoo, Mich.: Medieval Institute Publications, 1993), 102.

75. On the popularity of the image of Christ's sacred heart in fifteenth-century Northern manuscripts of devotional literature, see John Block Friedman, *Northern Medieval Book Owners* (Syracuse, N.Y.: Syracuse University Press, 1995); more generally, see Jeffrey Hamburger, "The Visual and the Visionary: The Image in Late Medieval Monastic Devotions," in *The Visual and the Visionary: Art and Female Spirituality in Late Medieval Germany* (New York: Zone Books, 1998), 111–18.

76. Lerer, "Representyd Now," 38.

CHAPTER 5.   INTO EXILED HANDS: JEWISH EXEGESIS AND URBAN
            IDENTITY IN THE CROXTON *PLAY OF THE SACRAMENT*

1. All citations to the Croxton *Play of the Sacrament* are from the edition by Norman Davis in *Non-Cycle Plays and Fragments,* EETS (Oxford: Oxford University Press, 1970), 58–89.

2. David Nirenberg, *Communities of Violence: Persecution of Minorities in the Middle Ages* (Princeton, N.J.: Princeton University Press, 1996), 217. On Holy Week "ludic violence" and theatrical performances, see ch. 7, "The Two Faces of Sacred Violence," 200–230.

3. The play survives in a single manuscript, Trinity College, Dublin F.4.20, dating from the mid–sixteenth century. In the "Banns" of the Croxton Play, the second Vexillator declares that "Thys maracle at Rome was presented, forsothe, / Yn the yere of our Lord, a thowsand four hundder sixty and on" (57–58), a detail that suggests it was performed in England not long after 1461. On the play as a Tudor document, see Seth Lerer, "Representyd Now in Yower Syght: The Culture of Spectatorship in Late Fifteenth-Century England," in *Bodies and Disciplines: Intersections of Literature and History in Fifteenth-Century England,* ed. Barbara Hanawalt and David Wallace (Minneapolis: University of Minnesota Press, 1996), 29–62.

4. On the plethora of reasons offered for the expulsion of the Jews during the reign of Edward I, including usury, blasphemy, and refusal to convert, see Robin R. Mundill, *England's Jewish Solution: Experiment and Expulsion, 1262–1290* (Cambridge: Cambridge University Press, 1998), 249–85; for a new edition and translation of the "Statute of Jewry," see ibid., 291–93. See also Sophia Menache, "Faith, Myth, and Politics: The Stereotype of the Jews and Their Expulsion from England and France," *Jewish Quarterly Review* 75:4 (1985): 351–74.

5. Miri Rubin, "Desecration of the Host: The Birth of an Accusation," in *Christianity and Judaism,* ed. Diana Wood, SCH 29 (Oxford: Blackwell, 1992), 169–85. On the 1377 host desecration trial in Huesca (Aragon), in which two Jews and a Christian who supposedly sold them the host were executed, see Joaquim Miret y Sans, "El procés de les Hosties contra los Jueus d'Osca en 1377," *Anuari de l'Institut d'Estudis Catalans* 4 (1911–12): 59–80.

6. On the Parisian miracle of 1290, see William C. Jordan, *The French Monarchy and the Jews* (Philadelphia: University of Pennsylvania Press, 1989), 192–94; Menache, "Faith, Myth," 363–64; the version of the story that includes the detail of the Jew's book is preserved in a later source, "De Miraculo Hostiae a Judaeo Parisiis Anno Domini MCCXC," in *Recueil des histoires des Gaules et de la France,* ed. Natalis de Wailly and Leopold Delisle (Paris: Palmé, 1865), 22:32–33.

7. On the church's condemnation of the Talmud in the 1230s–40s, see Jeremy Cohen, *The Friars and the Jews: The Evolution of Medieval Anti-Judaism* (Ithaca, N.Y.: Cornell University Press, 1982), 60–76, and Joel Rembaum, "The Talmud and the Popes: Reflections on the Talmud Trials of the 1240s," *Viator* 13 (1982): 203–23.

8. On the *Mistere,* see Jody Enders, "Dramatic Memories and Tortured Spaces in the Mistere de la Sainte Hostie," in *The Medieval Practices of Space,* ed. Barbara Hanawalt and Michael Kobialka (Minneapolis: University of Minnesota Press, 2000), and Marilyn Aronberg Lavin, "The Altar of Corpus Domini in Urbino: Paoalo Ucello, Joos Van Ghent, Piero Della Francesca," *Art Bulletin* 49 (1967): 1–24.

9. The Jews-as-Lollards argument was first set out by Celia Cutts, "The Croxton Play: An Anti-Lollard Piece," *MLQ* 5 (1944): 45–60. For a recent account, see, e.g., Gail McMurray Gibson, *The Theater of Devotion: East Anglian Drama and Society in the Late Middle Ages* (Chicago: University of Chicago Press, 1989), 32–40. See also Sarah Beckwith, "Ritual, Church and Theater," in *Culture and History, 1350–1600: Essays on English Communities, Identity and Writing,* ed. David Aers (Detroit: Wayne State University Press, 1992), 65–89.

10. Stephen Spector, "Time, Space and Identity in the *Play of the Sacrament,"* in *The Stage as Mirror: Civic Theatre in Late Medieval Europe,* ed. Alan Knight (Cambridge: D. S. Brewer, 1997), 189–200; Robert Clark and Claire Sponsler, "Othered Bodies: Racial Cross-Dressing in the Mistere de la Sainte Hostie and the Croxton Play of the Sacrament," *JMEMS* 29:1 (1999): 61–87.

11. See, e.g., Isidore of Seville, *Allegoriae Quaedam Sanctae Scripturae,* ed. J.-P. Migne, PL 83 (Paris: Garnier, 1850), col. 113: "Roboam, filius Salamonis, et Jeroboam servus, quibus Israel in duas partes divisus est, significant divisionem illam in Domini adventu factam, in qua pars credentium ex Judaeis regnat cum Christo, qui est ex David genere ortus; pars vero secuta Antichristum, cuius ad cultum nefandae servitutis errore constricti sunt." [Rehoboam, the son of Solomon, and Jeroboam his servant, who divided Israel into two parts, signify the division made by the advent of God: of which part are the believers among the Jews who reign with Christ and part are the followers of Antichrist, who are bound in servitude by error to a heinous cult.] Augustine, in *The City of God,* book 17, ch. 22, discusses Jeroboam as the leader of the ten tribes of Israel, whom he led astray with "detestable apostasy" [instituit idolatriam in rego suo et populum Dei secum simulacrorum cultu obstrictum nefanda impietate decepit]. Augustine, *City of God,* trans. Henry Bettenson (Harmondsworth: Penguin Books, 1984), 758, and *De Civitate Dei Libri XXII,* ed. Bernard Domabart and Alphonse Kalb (Stuttgart: Teubner, 1981), 2:252.

12. On the English Jews' refusal to convert as a reason for the expulsion, see Robert C. Stacey, "The Conversion of Jews to Christianity in Thirteenth-Century England," *Speculum* 67 (1992): 263–83.

13. Claudia Rattazzi Papka, "Fictions of Judgment: The Apocalyptic 'I' in the Fourteenth Century" (Ph.D. diss., Columbia University, 1996), 1–2.

14. Bede, "De Temporibus Antichristi," in *De Temporum Ratione,* ed. C. W. Jones, CCSL (Turnhout: Brepols, 1977), 538–39; D. Verhelst, ed., *Adso Dervensis: De Ortu et Tempore Antichristi,* CCCM 54 (Turnhout: Brepols, 1976). On millennial expectations of Jewish conversion, see Richard Landes, "The Massacres of 1010: On the Origins of Popular Anti-Jewish Violence in Western Europe," in *From Witness to Witchcraft: Jews and Judaism in Medieval Christian Thought,* ed. Jeremy Cohen (Wiesbaden: Harrassowitz, 1996), 79–112.

15. Suzanne Lewis, "*Tractatus Adversus Judaeos* in the Gulbenkian Apocalypse," *Art Bulletin* 68 (1986): 543–66.

16. Ibid., 543–44.

17. Richard Morris, ed., *The Pricke of Conscience: A Northumbrian Poem* (Berlin: A. Asher, 1863; reprint, New York: AMS Press, 1973), 123. Citations are from 1973 edition.

18. Any account of the original productions of the Croxton Play is, of course, entirely speculative. For Gibson's idea that the play may have first been performed in Bury itself, see

Gibson, *Theater of Devotion,* 34–35; on the staging of Croxton as "traveling play," see J. Coldewey, "The Non-Cycle Plays and the East Anglian Tradition," in *The Cambridge Companion to Medieval English Theatre,* ed. Richard Beadle (Cambridge: Cambridge University Press, 1994), 189–210; Lerer, "Representyd Now," 47.

19. Gibson, *Theater of Devotion,* 37–38; see also C. Harper-Bill, ed., *Charters of the Medieval Hospitals of Bury St. Edmunds* (Woodbridge: Boydell, 1996), 9–18.

20. Gibson, *Theater of Devotion,* esp. 19–33, 107–35.

21. Robert Gottfried, *Bury St. Edmunds and the Urban Crisis, 1290–1539* (Princeton, N.J.: Princeton University Press, 1982).

22. Ibid., 180–92.

23. Gail McMurray Gibson, "Bury St. Edmunds, Lydgate, and the N-Town Cycle," *Speculum* 56:1 (1981): 56–90.

24. Jocelin of Brakelond, *The Chronicle of Jocelin of Brakelond,* ed. and trans. H. E. Butler (London: Nelson, 1949), 45–46.

25. Antonia Gransden, ed. and trans., *The Chronicle of Bury St. Edmunds, 1212–1301* (London: Nelson, 1964), 58.

26. Ibid., 59.

27. Solomon Grayzel, *The Church and the Jews in the XIIIth Century,* vol. 2, *1254–1314,* ed. Kenneth Stow (Detroit: Wayne State University Press, 1989), 157–58. In contrast to the earlier archbishops of Canterbury, the Franciscan Pecham was actively concerned with prosecuting Jewish apostates. See F. D. Logan, "Thirteen London Jews and Conversion to Christianity: Problems of Apostasy in the 1280s," *BIHR* 45 (1972): 214–29.

28. V. D. Lipman, *The Jews of Medieval Norwich* (London: Jewish Historical Society, 1967), 168–76. On Edward I's prosecutions of Jews for blasphemy, see Mundill, *England's Jewish Solution,* 275.

29. Lipman, *Jews of Medieval Norwich,* 50–57; the classic account of the events surrounding the inception of the cult of William of Norwich is Gavin Langmuir's "Thomas of Monmouth: Detector of Ritual Murder," in *Toward a Definition of Antisemitism* (Berkeley: University of California Press, 1990), 209–36.

30. Joshua Toulmin Smith and Lucy Toulmin Smith, eds., *English Gilds,* EETS (London: K. Paul, Trench, Trübner, 1870), 29–30.

31. This identification was persuasively established by Gibson in "Bury St. Edmunds."

32. Alan J. Fletcher, "The N-Town Plays," in *The Cambridge Companion to Medieval English Theatre,* ed. Richard Beadle (Cambridge: Cambridge University Press, 1994), 163–88.

33. Gibson, "Bury St. Edmunds," 76–78.

34. On the few surviving records of the Norwich Corpus Christi pageants, see Janna Dutka, "Mystery Plays at Norwich: Their Formation and Development," *Leeds Studies in English* 10 (1975): 107–20.

35. All citations of the N-Town plays are from Stephen Spector, ed., *The N-Town Play: Cotton MS Vespasian D.8,* vol. 1, EETS (Oxford: Oxford University Press, 1991).

36. Sarah Beckwith, "*Sacrum Signum:* Sacramentality and Dissent in York's Theatre of Corpus Christi," in *Criticism and Dissent in the Middle Ages,* ed. Rita Copeland (Cambridge: Cambridge University Press, 1996), 264.

37. Menache, "Faith, Myth," 360–61.

38. On the economics of the "greater urban region" of Bury, see Gottfried, *Bury St. Edmunds,* 14–23.

39. Fletcher, "N-Town Plays," 166. On the accounts of Thetford Priory and its payments for theatrical performances, see David Galloway and John Wasson, *Records of Plays and Players in Norfolk and Suffolk, 1330–1642* (Oxford: Malone Society, 1980), 103–4. On the later payments to a "gylde at Crokeston," see 106, 111. On Cluniac monasteries in England in the late Middle Ages, see David Knowles, *The Religious Orders in England* (Cambridge: Cambridge University Press, 1948–59), 2:157–66.

40. Cohen, *Friars and the Jews,* 170–71.

41. Ibid., 136–53.

42. Raymond Martini. *Pugio Fidei Adversus Mauros at Judaeos* (1687; reprint, Farnborough: Gregg, 1967). See esp. Martini's "Proemium," 1–6, and translation of relevant passages in Cohen, *Friars and the Jews,* 137–38. On the history of Christian charges that Jews have changed the text of the Bible, see Irven M. Resnick, "The Falsification of Scripture and Medieval Christian and Jewish Polemics," *Medieval Encounters* 2:3 (1996): 344–80. See also Gilbert Dahan, *Les intellectuels chrétiens et les juifs au moyen age* (Paris: Cerf, 1990), 272–85.

43. "Ulterius considerandum, quod sensus literalis, a quo est incipiendum, ut dictum est, veritur multum offuscatus diebus modernis, partim scriptorum vitio, qui propter similitudinem literarum in multis locis aliter scripserunt, quam habeat veritas textus, partim imperitia aliquorum correctorum, qui in pluribus locis fecerunt puncta, ubi non debent fieri, & versus inceperunt, vel terminaverunt, ubi non debent incipi et terminari. Et per hoc sententia literae variatur." Nicholas of Lyra, *Biblia Sacra cvm Glossis, Interlineari, et Ordinaria . . .* (Venice, 1588), 1:3G. For translation, see Nicholas of Lyra, "Second Prologue to the *Literal Postill on the Bible,*" in *Medieval Literary Theory and Criticism c. 1100–c. 1375,* ed. and trans. A. J. Minnis & A. B. Scott (Oxford: Oxford University Press, 1988), 269–70.

44. Nicholas of Lyra, *Biblia Sacra cvm Glossis,* 1:3G, and "Second Prologue," 269.

45. Nicholas of Lyra, *Biblia Sacra cvm Glossis,* 1:3H, and "Second Prologue," 270. For Lyra's uses of Rashi's biblical commentaries in his *Postillae,* the standard critical work is Herman Hailperin, *Rashi and the Christian Scholars* (Pittsburgh, Pa.: University of Pittsburgh Press, 1963), 137–64. For specific passages of the *Postilla Litteralis* where Lyra accuses Rashi of polemically "corrupting" the text of the Bible — changing the pointing of Hebrew letters, for instance — to erase christological interpretations (Isaiah 9:5; Jeremiah 23:6; Hosea 9:12), see 169–73.

46. Nicholas of Lyra, "Utrum ex Scripturis Receptis a Judaeis Possit Efficaciter Probari Salvatoris Nostrum fuisse Deum et Hominem," in *Biblia Sacra cvm Glossis,* 6:275E–280D. For a consideration of this text within Lyra's larger historical context, see Deeana Klepper, "Nicholas of Lyra's 'Questio de Adventu Christi' and the Franciscan Encounter with Jewish Tradition" (Ph.D. diss., Northwestern University, 1995).

47. Nicholas of Lyra, *Biblia Sacra cvm Glossis,* 6:277BC; Cohen, *Friars and the Jews,* 183–84; see also Hailperin, *Rashi,* 171–72.

48. Nicholas of Lyra, *Biblia Sacra cvm Glossis,* 6:277B; translated in Cohen, *Friars and the Jews,* 184.

49. Nicholas of Lyra, *Biblia Sacra cvm Glossis,* 6:277C. This is a summary of the much longer and more complex argument in Lyra's *Quaestio de Adventu Christi;* for a thorough discussion of the full version, see Klepper, "Nicholas of Lyra's 'Questio,'" 156–61.

50. Nicholas of Lyra, *Biblia Sacra cvm Glossis,* 6:280CD. For this type of Jewish polemic against the Eucharist, see the late thirteenth-century anthology of anti-Christian writings, the *Nizzahon Vetus,* ed. and trans. David Berger as *The Jewish-Christian Debate in the High Middle Ages: A Critical Edition of the Nizzahon Vetus* (Philadelphia: Jewish Publication Society, 1979), 184–85, 225.

51. On Jacob ben Reuben's *Wars of the Lord* (*Milḥamot ha-Shem*), see Cohen, *Friars and the Jews,* 185–86, and David Berger, "Gilbert Crispin, Alan of Lille and Jacob ben Reuben: A Study in the Transmission of Medieval Polemic," *Speculum* 49 (1974): 34–47.

52. Nicholas of Lyra, *Biblia Sacra cvm Glossis,* 6:281A.

53. Ibid., 6:281B: "Quod autem arguitur ultra quod Christiani comedunt corpus Christi, quod est horribile. Dicendum quod verum esset si acciperetur in propria specie, sed ipsum accipere sub speciebus panis non est horribile, sed suave et venerabile. Non enim ipse Christus vel eius corpus in ista comestione frangitur vel atteritur dentibus vel laceretur, sicut imaginantur Judaei, sed sole species panis franguntur vel atteruntur, quibus consumptis, desinit ibi esse corpus Christi, sed remanet huius sacramenti effectus, qui est anime refectio per augmentum gratie." On the Eucharist in Christian and Jewish polemics, see Dahan, *Les intellectuels chretiens,* 502–3.

54. David Burr, *Eucharistic Presence and Conversion in Late Thirteenth-Century Franciscan Thought* (Philadelphia: American Philosophical Society, 1984), 1–15. See also Miri Rubin, *Corpus Christi: The Eucharist in Late Medieval Culture* (Cambridge: Cambridge University Press, 1991), 14–35.

55. Thomas Aquinas, *Summa Theologica* III, Q.75, Article 5.

56. Nicholas of Lyra, *Biblia Sacra cvm Glossis,* 6:281BC: "*Erit firmamentum in terra in summis montium.* Ubi litera Hebraica habet *Erit placenta tritici in terra in capite montium.* Et translatio Hieronymi iuxta Hebraicum. *Erit memorabile nomen triticum in terra in capite montium.* Et translatio Chaldaica habet. *Erit oblatio frumenti in terra.* Ex istis tribus videt quod litera nostra fuerit corrupta per scriptores ponentes firmamentum pro frumentum ex similitudine dictionum. Patet igitur ex dictis quod de rege Messiah praedictum fuerit in hoc psalmo, quod futurum erat frumentum in terra in summis montium, vel oblatio frumenti in terrra in capite montium, quod impletum est in sacramento eucharistiae, in quo Christus sub speciebus panis tritici continetur & super capita sacerdotum elevatur, ut a populo adoretur, qui sacerdotes propter altitudinem status montes nominantur."

57. For Jerome's prefaces to Psalms, see Robert Weber, ed., *Biblia Sacra Iuxta Vulgatam Versionem,* 3d ed. (Stuttgart: Deutsche Bibelgesellschaft, 1983), 767–79.

58. Joseph Roach, *Cities of the Dead: Circum-Atlantic Performance* (New York: Columbia University Press, 1996), 3.

59. Chris Bongie, *Exotic Memories: Literature, Colonialism, and the Fin de Siècle* (Stanford, Calif.: Stanford University Press, 1991), 5.

60. The *locus classicus* for later readings of "the blindness of Israel" and the importance of the Jewish diaspora for proving Christian exegesis is Augustine, *City of God,* 18:46: "When

the Jews do not believe our scriptures, their own scriptures are fulfilled in them, while they read them with blind eyes" (828). [Proinde cum scriptures nostris non credunt, complentur in eis suae quas caeci legunt (329).]

61. Roach, *Cities of the Dead,* 7.

62. Ralph Higden, *Polychronicon Ranulphi Higden,* ed. Churchill Babington and Joseph R. Lumby (London, 1865–86), 1:30.

63. On the blurring of Christian and Jewish identities in the Croxton Play, see Spector, "Time, Space, and Identity."

64. The Croxton Play's Banns, which claim "in an howshold wer convertyd iwys elevyn" (55), suggests that at some point in its production history the table scene involved eleven Jews mirroring the roles of the disciples.

65. Beckwith, "Ritual, Church and Theatre," 74–75.

66. On the possible significance of the citation of Isaiah 63 as part of Holy Week liturgy and on the liturgical settings of other scriptural citations in the *Croxton Play,* see Sister Nicholas Maltman, "Meaning and Art in the Croxton Play of the Sacrament," *ELH* 41 (1974): 149–64.

67. "*Quis est iste.* Both Hebrew and Latin expositiors interpret this chapter to be about Christ, one in one way and the other in another way. Rabbi Salomon, for instance, says: That when this is said: *quis est iste qui venit de Edom,* by Edom the Roman Empire is understood, insofar as it was in its compass when the empire dominated the whole world. He says that the Messiah in his advent will kill many of the world's inhabitants, and will subject all the rest to the Jews; and on account of this his clothing is described as reddened with blood. &. to this he adapts the letter as far as he can." Nicholas of Lyra, *Biblia Sacra cvm Glossis,* 4:101D.

68. On the "Vengeful Messiah" and the Jewish response to the Crusades, see the groundbreaking work of Israel Jacob Yuval, *Shene goyim be-vit neḥ: Yehudim ve-Notsrim — dimuyim hadadiyim* [Two nations in your womb: Perceptions of Jews and Christians] (Tel Aviv: Am Oved, 2000), esp. 108–50. In his critical discussion of Yuval's controversial thesis about the valorization of Jewish martyrdom in the eleventh and twelfth centuries within an English context, Willis Johnson describes the new "vengeful" apocalypticism of Jewish readings of Isaiah 63 after the 1096 Crusade: "The old vision of the messianic age as a return from exile and universal conversion to Judaism was replaced by a vision of revenge and the absolute destruction of Edom." Willis Johnson, "Between Christians and Jews: The Formation of Anti-Jewish Stereotypes in Medieval England" (Ph.D. diss., University of California, Berkeley, 1996). Following Rashi, David Kimchi (c. 1160–c. 1235), e.g., provides the following interpretation of Isaiah 63: "[T]his prophecy is about the future destruction of Rome, because the kingdom of Rome is called by the name Edom . . . and the blessed Almighty is compared to a warrior who wreaks vengeance on his enemies and his clothes are reddened with the blood of slaughter; the destruction [*ḥurban*] of Rome will be the salvation of Israel." Menachem Cohen, ed., *Miḳra'ot Gedolot ḥa-Keter: Isaiah* (Tel Aviv: Bar-Ilan University Press, 1996), 382–83. On Rashi's anti-Christian messianic polemics on the fall of "Edom," see Hailperin, *Rashi,* 161–62. On Jewish apocalyptic thought and its relation to the Christian tradition , see Amos Funkenstein, *Perceptions of Jewish History* (Berkeley: University of California Press, 1993), 70–87.

69. Susan L. Einbinder, "Meir ben Elijah of Norwich: Persecution and Poetry among Medieval English Jews," *Journal of Medieval History* 26 (2000): 145–62. Einbinder includes both a Hebrew edition and her translation of "Put a Curse on My Enemy." In the line that I quote, taken in part from Isaiah 63:3, the Hebrew *niẓḥam*—"their victory"—would also mean, following Rashi's exegesis, "their blood."

70. "And therefore, this first concerns the extermination of Antichrist, and second the execution of the final judgment, in the following chapters. About the first it is known, what Methodius Martyr says & the other doctors alike say about how Enoch and Elias will be sent to reveal the perfidy of the Antichrist. Once he is revealed, the Jews will convert to the Christian faith, performing acts of penance. And therefore the first part is to be understood as referring to the destruction of Antichrist & then the second, to the conversion of the Jews, here: [*I will remember*] *the compassion of the Lord*. About this first, Isaiah foreseeing the future power of the Antichrist, & his sudden destruction by Christ, says in admiration of Christ: *Who is this? It is one who is victorious*." My translation of Nicholas of Lyra, *Biblia Sacra*, 4:101GH.

71. Spector, "Time, Space and Identity," 194.

72. Katherine Rowe, " 'God's Handy Worke': Divine Complicity and the Anatomist's Touch," in *The Body in Parts: Fantasies of Corporeality in Early Modern Europe*, ed. David Hillman and Carla Mazzio (New York: Routledge, 1997), 285–309. Thanks to Laura King for this reference.

73. Paul Aebischer, ed., *Le mystère d'Adam (Ordo Representacionis Ade)* (Geneva: Droz, 1964), 90–91. It is extremely unlikely that the Croxton playwright would have been familiar with this text; the scene nevertheless suggests the continuity of the Isaiah-as-physician motif and the understanding of the Jew's "hand."

74. In the N-Town "Entry into Jerusalem," the disciples themselves are expositors. Peter, e.g., scolds the "Jews" and the audience: "That som of yow be blynd, it may not be denyid, / For hym that is youre makere, with youre gostly ey ye xal not knowe" (398–99). An earlier East Anglian dramatic example of the expositor is the "Doctor" who appears at the end of the Brome *Abraham and Isaac* to provide a moralizing gloss for "lernd and lewyd." See Davis, *Non-Cycle Plays*, 56–57.

75. Gibson, *Theater of Devotion*, 37. On the population of immigrants from the Low Countries in East Anglia, see also Gottfried, *Bury St. Edmunds*, 109, and Sylvia Thrupp, "A Survey of the Alien Population in England in 1440," *Speculum* 32 (1957): 262.

76. David Wallace, "In Flaundres," *Studies in the Age of Chaucer* 19 (1997): 63–91.

77. Ibid., 84.

78. "Igitur circa Ierusalem allegoricam quae est militans ecclesia, sciendum quod declinavit multum a perfectione prima in prelatis & clericis, & etiam religiosis, & similiter in principibus & lacis sibi subiectis. Similiter temporibus modernis multum defecit in numero fidelium." Nicholas of Lyra, "Postilla Moralis on Lamentations," in *Biblia Sacra cvm Glossis*, 4:179. On the ecclesiopolitical background of Lyra's exegesis, see Hailperin, *Rashi*, 199–200.

79. On the commodification of the sacrament, see Beckwith, "Ritual, Church and Theatre," 69.

80. For an "inclusive" interpretation of the Corpus Christi procession in the Croxton Play, see Beckwith, "Ritual, Church and Theatre," 77–79.

81. Gibson, *Theater of Devotion,* 38.

CHAPTER 6.   THE MIXED LIFE IN MOTION:
WISDOM'S DEVOTIONAL POLITICS

1. J. Raine, ed., *Testamenta Eboracensia* (Durham: Surtees Society, 1836–1902), 2:220–29. On Chaworth's extraordinary library, see Thorlac Turville-Petre, "Some Medieval English Manuscripts in the North-East Midlands," in *Manuscripts and Readers in Fifteenth-Century England,* ed. Derek Pearsall (Cambridge: D. S. Brewer, 1983); Ralph Hanna III, "Sir Thomas Berkeley and His Patronage," *Speculum* 64 (1989): 878–916; and John Block Friedman, *Northern English Books, Owners, and Makers in the Late Middle Ages* (Syracuse, N.Y.: Syracuse University Press, 1995), xii–xiii.

2. All citations to the *Seven Poyntes* are from Henry Suso, "*Orologium Sapientiae* or *The Seven Poyntes of Trewe Wisdom* Aus MS. Douce 114," ed. C. Horstmann, *Anglia* 10 (1888): 323–89. For Suso's original version of this passage, see Henry Suso, *Wisdom's Watch upon the Hours,* ed. and trans. Eric Colledge (Washington, D.C.: Catholic University of America Press, 1994), 258–60. For the relationship of this text to Suso's Latin *Horologium* and an assessment of the problems with Horstmann's edition, see Roger Lovatt, "Henry Suso and the Medieval Mystical Tradition in England," in *The Medieval Mystical Tradition in England,* ed. Marion Glasscoe (Exeter: Exeter University Press, 1982), 47–62.

3. Lovatt, "Henry Suso," 57–59.

4. Like the contemporary *Chastising of God's Children,* which draws on Ruusbroec's *Spiritual Espousals* as well as Suso, the *Seven Poyntes* is directed to a religious female reader by the translator but shortly after its production also circulated among laypeople.

5. In his 1912 University of Chicago dissertation, Walter Kay Smart established the direct Middle English and Latin sources that appear in *Wisdom,* including *The Seven Poyntes,* Hilton's *Epistle on the Mixed Life* and *Scale of Perfection,* the *Novem Virtutes,* and the Pseudo-Bernardine *Tractatus de Interiori Domo.* Walter K. Smart, *Some English and Latin Sources and Parallels for the Morality of Wisdom* (Menasha, Wis.: George Banta Publishing, 1912).

6. "When the work of writing this was finished, the Disciple was gripped by a certain human fear of jealous men. Prompted by envy, they are as busy now as ever to misrepresent or destroy completely what others do, however good it may be. They call divine charisms superstitious imaginings, and they say that holy revelations are brainsick illusions. Like men who have never tasted the fruits of the Holy Spirit, they dismiss the deeds of the holy fathers as idle fictions." Suso, *Wisdom's Watch,* 58–59. "Post completum vero huius operis laborem, dum timore quodam humano teneretur, ne ab aemulis, qui nunc quoque sicut olim invidia stimulante facta quaeque, licet bona, depravare aut penitus annullare non desistunt, divina charismata appellantes superstitiosa figmenta, et sanctas revelationes fantasticas deceptiones sanctorumque gesta patrum esse dicunt narratorium fabulosum, tamquam homines, qui non

gustaverunt ea, quae sunt Spiritus Sancti." Henry Suso, *Heinrich Seuses Horologium Sapientiae: Erste kritische Ausgabe unter Benutzung der Vorarbeiten von Dominikus Planker, O.P.,* ed. Pius Kunzle (Freiburg: Universitätsverlag Freiburg Schweiz, 1977), 371.

7. "So on another day, when the lector at table was reading from the sapiental books, he heard Wisdom praised as follows: 'Wisdom is more beautiful than the sun, and above all the order of the stars; being compared with the light, she is found before it. Her have I loved, and I have sought her out from my youth, and I have desired to take her for my spouse; and I became a lover of her beauty.' . . . So when he had heard these words, the youth began to burn for love of her, and said silently to himself: "Truly, if you search every land, you cannot find her like for grace" (Suso, *Wisdom's Watch,* 66–67). "Altera quoque die, cum lector mensae libros sapientales legeret, audivit commendari sapientiam in hunc modum: Sapienta *speciosior sole et super omnem dispositionem stellarum; luci comparata, invenitur prior. Hanc amavi et exquisivi a iuventute mea et quaesivi mihi sponsam assumere, et amator factus sum formae illius. . . .* His itaque auditis iuvenis aestuare coepit eius in amore dicebatque intra se: 'Certe, si omnes terras lustraveris, huic similem in gratiis non poteris invenire' " (Suso, *Heinrich Seuses Horologium Sapientiae,* 375).

8. On the styles of devotion among the gentry in this period, see Malcolm Vale, *Piety, Charity and Literacy among the Yorkshire Gentry, 1370–1480,* Borthwick Papers 50 (York: St. Anthony's Press, 1976); Jeremy Catto, "Religion and the English Nobility in the Later Fourteenth Century," in *History and Imagination: Essays in Honor of H. R. Trevor-Roper,* ed. Hugh Lloyd-Jones, Valerie Pearl, and Blair Worden (London: Duckworth, 1981), 43–55. On the wide circulation of both Henry Suso's and Walter Hilton's writings based on manuscript evidence, see Michael Sargent, "The Transmission by the English Carthusians of Some Late Medieval Spiritual Writings," *Journal of Ecclesiastical History* 27 (1976): 225–40, and "Walter Hilton's Scale of Perfection: The London Manuscript Group Reconsidered," *Medium Aevum* 52 (1983): 189–216; and Vincent Gillespie, "Vernacular Books of Religion," in *Book Production and Publishing in Britain, 1375–1475,* ed. Jeremy Griffiths and Derek Pearsall (Cambridge: Cambridge University Press, 1989), 317–44.

9. Roger Lovatt, "Henry Suso," 58. Although it is beyond the scope of this chapter, much fascinating work along the lines of Lovatt's article is being done on what English translations of Latin spiritual works suppress and on the role of various religious orders in the dissemination of the vernacular texts. See, e.g., Kantik Ghosh, "Manuscripts of Nicholas Love's The Mirror of the Blessed Life of Jesus Christ and Wycliffite Notions of Authority," in *Prestige, Authority, and Power in Late Medieval Manuscripts and Texts,* ed. Felicity Riddy (Cambridge: D. S. Brewer, 2000).

10. For an account of the manuscripts, see Eccles's introduction in *The Macro Plays,* ed. Mark Eccles, ETTS (Oxford: Oxford University Press, 1969), xxvii–xxxvi. See also David Bevington's facsimile edition of the Macro manuscript, *The Macro Plays* (New York: Johnson Reprint Co., 1972).

11. All page citations to this work are from Walter Hilton, "Epistle on the Mixed Life," in *English Mystics of the Middle Ages,* ed. Barry Windeatt (Cambridge: Cambridge University Press, 1994), 108–30.

12. For the most forceful statement of this position, see Jonathan Hughes's problematic *Pastors and Visionaries: Religion and Secular Life in Late Medieval Yorkshire* (Cambridge: D. S. Brewer, 1988), esp. 251–97. For more careful treatments of Rolle, mystical experience, and ideas of the "mixed life," see Nicholas Watson, *Richard Rolle and the Invention of Authority* (Cambridge: Cambridge University Press, 1991), 195–256.

13. For a related text in Latin that demonstrates the ascetic aspirations of a similar kind of early-fifteenth-century reader, see W. A. Pantin, ed., "Instructions for a Devout and Literate Layman," in *Medieval Learning and Literature,* ed. J. G. Alexander and M. T. Gibson (Oxford: Oxford University Press, 1976), 398–422.

14. This passage of Hilton's *Epistle* shows his debt to the anonymous English translation of William Flete's *Remedies against Temptations,* which in ch. 7 warns about men and women being tempted to ignore religious obligations in favor of "good sterynges and devoute thoughts and felyngis of meditacions and contemplacions." Eric Colledge and Noel Chadwick, eds., "Remedies against Temptations: The Third English Version of William Flete," *Archivio Italiano per la Storia della Pieta* 5:14 (1968): 203–40.

15. On Rolle's own "bridal mysticism" in his homily *Ego Dormio,* see Watson, *Richard Rolle,* 226–36; see also Vincent Gillespie, "Mystic's Foot: Rolle and Affectivity," in *The Medieval Mystical Tradition in England,* ed. Marion Glasscoe (Exeter: Exeter University Press, 1982), 199–230.

16. Citations from *Wisdom* are according to line numbers in Eccles, *The Macro Plays,* 113–32.

17. See Marion Jones, "Allegory into Drama: Souls in Jeopardy," in *The Revels History of Drama in English,* vol. 1, *Medieval Drama,* ed. A. C. Cawsley et al. (London: Methuen, 1983), 247–62.

18. Marlene Clark, Sharon Kraus, and Pamela Sheingorn, " 'Se in what stat thou doyst indwell': The Shifting Constructions of Gender and Power Relations in *Wisdom,*" in *The Performance of Middle English Culture: Essays on Chaucer and the Drama in Honor of Martin Stevens,* ed. James J. Paxson, Lawrence M. Clopper, and Sylvia Tomasch (Cambridge: D. S. Brewer, 1998), 51.

19. Interesting in this regard is the York priest Robert Est's 1467 will, where, as Lovatt notes, he "bequeathed to one of his relations both a copy of the *Horologium* and also a work of Walter Hilton because as his will explains 'they are bound together.' We might feel that these words symbolise more than a merely physical contiguity." Lovatt, "Henry Suso," 54.

20. Gail McMurray Gibson, "The Play of Wisdom and the Abbey of Saint Edmund," in *The Wisdom Symposium: Papers from the Trinity College Medieval Festival,* ed. Milla Cozart Riggio (New York: AMS Press, 1986), 39–66. See also Gail McMurray Gibson, *The Theater of Devotion: East Anglian Drama and Society in the Late Middle Ages* (Chicago: University of Chicago Press, 1989), 107–35.

21. Milton McC. Gatch, "Mysticism and Satire in the Morality of *Wisdom,*" *Philological Quarterly* 53 (1974): 342–62.

22. Pamela King, "Morality Plays," in *The Cambridge Companion to Medieval English Theatre* (Cambridge: Cambridge University Press, 1994), 255. Alexandra F. Johnston, "Wisdom and the Records: Is There a Moral?" in Riggio, *Wisdom Symposium,* 87–101.

23. On the four main Westminster courts — Chancery, King's Bench, Common Pleas, and Exchequer — see Edward Powell, "Law and Justice," in *Fifteenth-Century Attitudes,* ed. Rosemary Horrox (Cambridge: Cambridge University Press, 1994), 29–41. On *embracery,* the "manipulation of juries and witnesses," see Alan Harding, *The Law-Courts of Medieval England* (London: Allen and Unwin, 1973), 98–99, and John Bellamy, *Crime and Public Order in England in the Late Middle Ages* (Toronto: University of Toronto Press, 1973), 20–22.

24. The text of the *Epistola ad Quemdam Seculo Renunciare Volentem* is in Walter Hinton, *Walter Hilton's Latin Writings,* ed. John P. Clark and Cheryl Taylor (Salzburg, Austria: Institut für Anglistik und Amerikanistik, Universität Salzburg, 1987), 1:245–98. The *Epistola* survives in two fifteenth-century manuscripts, BL Royal MS 6 E III and Cambridge University Library MS EeVi 7. While there is no hard evidence that the *Wisdom*-playwright knew this text, it is certainly possible given his familiarity with Hilton's English works and related Latin contemplative texts, such as the anonymous *Tractatus de Interiori Domo.* See esp. Clark and Taylor's introduction, 1:1–31.

25. C. T. Allmand, "The Civil Lawyers," in *Profession, Vocation, and Culture in Later Medieval England: Essays Dedicated to the Memory of A. R. Myers,* ed. Cecil Clough (Liverpool: Liverpool University Press, 1982), 155–80. On the cultural interests of the common lawyers, see E. W. Ives, "The Common Lawyers," in the same volume, 181–217.

26. For a wide-ranging discussion of theories of intention in medieval English law, see Richard Firth Green, *A Crisis of Truth: Literature and Law in Ricardian England* (Philadelphia: University of Pennsylvania Press, 1999), 293–335.

27. "Oportet te ergo relinquere studium Iustiniani et forum concistorii iudicalis et intrare scolam Christi per penitciam et cetera exercitia corporalia et spiritualia, cum vera cordis humilitate. Non te retardet metus paupertatis. Semper enim dives est Christiana paupertas." Hilton, *Epistola ad Quemdam,* 262–63.

28. Colledge and Chadwick, "Remedies against Temptations."

29. "[N]on expectavit ab illa confescionem criminum per exprescionem vocis, sed cordis convercionem desiderat et expectat." Hilton, *Epistola ad Quemdam,* 267.

30. "Non enim verbalis est Deus sed realis, nec est spes ponenda in verborum expressione, nec attendit multiloquium ubi sibi offeretur cor purum. Exemplum vide in evangelio. Cum oratis, inquid Christus, 'nolite multum loqui sicut ethnici, qui putant quod in multiloquio exaudiuntur.'" Ibid., 270–71.

31. On the problem of vows and Aquinas's influential categorization of vows and oaths in *Summa Theologica* II-II, Q. 88–89, see Green, *Crisis of Truth,* 294–95.

32. Hilton, *Epistola ad Quemdam,* 296.

33. It is impossible from the text to determine the identity of the author's "suster in Christ," although Minnis assumes that she is an "enclosed nun." A. J. Minnis, "Affection and Imagination in *The Cloud of Unknowing* and Hilton's *Scale of Perfection,*" *Traditio* 39 (1983): 323–66.

34. All page citations to this work are from Walter Hilton, *The Scale of Perfection,* ed. Thomas H. Bestul (Kalamazoo, Mich.: Medieval Institute Publications, 2000), 31.

35. Hilton, *Scale of Perfection,* 89. Hilton's (and Suso's) language of "likeness" derives from Augustine's letter 92, to Italica: "In tantum ergo videbimus, in quantum similes erimus,

quia et nunc in tantum non videmus, in quantum dissimiles sumus. Inde igitur videbimus, ubi similes erimus. Quis autem dementissimus dixerit corpore nos vel esse vel futuros esse similes deo? In interiore igitur homine ista similitude est, qui renovater in agnitione dei secundum imaginem eius, qui creavit eum." Augustine, *Epistulae,* Pars II, ed. Alois Goldbacher, CSEL 34 (Vienna: Tempsky, 1898), 438–39. "We shall see Him then in so far as we shall be like Him, because now we do not see Him in so far as we are unlike Him. We shall see Him then by being like Him. Who is so utterly lacking in intelligence as to say that in the body we either are or will be like God? Consequently, the likeness is in the inner man, 'who is renewed in the knowledge of God according to the image of him that created him.'" Augustine, *Letters,* trans. Wilfrid Parsons (New York: Catholic University Press, 1953), 2:52. This passage from the *Scale* reveals the devotional source of Chaucer's play on God's "privitee" in the *Miller's Tale.*

36. David Bevington, "'Blake and Wyght, Fowll and Fayer': Stage Picture in Wisdom," in Riggio, *Wisdom Symposium,* 18–38.

37. Ibid., 33.

38. Suso, *Wisdom's Watch,* 65, and *Heinrich Seuses Horologium Sapientiae,* 373.

39. Suso, *Wisdom's Watch,* 120. "Rerum altissimarum veritates in sua simplicitate acceptas intellectus humanus capere non potest; et ideo necesse est eas tradere per imagines et consuetas similitudines." Suso, *Heinrich Seuses Horologium Sapientiae,* 422.

40. Suso, *Wisdom's Watch,* 54–55. "Notandum quoque, quod locutio ista quantum ad interrogationem discipuli et reponsionem sapientiae vel econverso solum posita est ad feventiorem modum tradendi. Nec est taliter accipiendum, quasi discipulus fuerit ille talis, de quo sapientia in persona propria solum intenderit, vel qui sapientiam solus prae ceteris tantim amaverit, vel cui sapientia tot et tanta fecerit, sed revera pro quolibet in genere dictum habeatur. . . . Et sic diversimode stilum vertit secundum quod tunc materiae congruit. Nunc etiam Dei Filium et de votae animae sponsum inducit; postea eundem tamquam aeternam sapientiam viro iusto desponsatam introducit." Suso, *Heinrich Seuses Horologium Sapientiae,* 366.

41. For an excellent history of Christian interpretation of the Song of Songs, see Denys Turner, *Eros and Allegory: Medieval Exegesis of the Song of Songs* (Kalamazoo, Mich.: Cistercian Publications, 1995).

42. For contemporary accounts of Edward of York's "good looks" and legendary "licentiousness," see Charles Ross, *Edward IV* (New Haven, Conn.: Yale University Press, 1997), 10, 315–16.

43. Hilton's consideration in *Scale,* book 2, of the "fyve outward wittes" immediately follows his exegesis of the Song of Songs 1:4, *Nigra sum, sed formosa, filie Jerusalem,* one of the sources for this scene of *Wisdom.* Hilton, *Scale of Perfection,* 156–59. See Smart, *Some English and Latin Sources,* 20–22.

44. Bernard of Clairvaux, *On the Song of Songs,* trans. Kilian Walsh and Irene M. Edmonds (Kalamazoo, Mich.: Cistercian Publications, 1971–80), 2:54–55. "Candida proinde Pauli anima erat, et sapientia sedebat in ea, ita ut sapientiam loqueretur inter perfectos, sapientiam in mysterio absconditam, quam nemo principum mundus huius agnovit. Porro in eo hunc sapientiae iustitiaeque candorem nigredo illa exterior de praesentia corporis infirma, de

laboribus plurimis, de ieiuniis multis ac vigiliis, aut operabatur, aut promerebatur. Ideoque et quod nigrum est Pauli, speciousius est omno ornamento extrinseco, omni regio cultu. Non comparabitur ei quantalibet pulchritudo carnis, non cutis utique nitida et arsura, non facies colorata vicina putredini, non vestis pretiosa obnoxia vetustati, non auri species splendorve gemmarum, seu quaeque alia, quae omnia sunt ad corruptionem." Bernard of Clairvaux, *S. Bernardi Opera,* vol. 1, *Sermones super Cantica Canticorum 1–35,* ed. J. Leclercq, C. H. Talbot, and H. M. Rochais (Rome: Editiones Cistercienses, 1957), 166–67.

45. King, "Morality Plays," 253.

46. For descriptions of various corrupt practices associated with maintenance, see Bellamy, *Crime and Public Order,* 1–36.

47. For the letters and petitions concerning this notorious dispute, see Norman Davis, ed., *Paston Letters and Papers of the Fifteenth Century* (Oxford: Oxford University Press, 1971), 1:50–53, 227–33.

48. On the liturgy of the Song of Songs, associated with Trinity Sunday, in *Wisdom,* see Eccles, *Macro Plays,* 207 n. 324.

49. Clark, Kraus, and Sheingorn, "'Se in what stat thou doyst indwell,'" 54–55.

50. The definition "allegoria est alieniloquium" is Isidore of Seville's. See Isidore of Seville, *Isidori Hispalensis Episcopi, Etymologiarum, sive Originum Libri XX,* ed. W. M. Lindsay, I, xxvii, 22 (Oxford: Oxford University Press, 1911).

51. For the Latin version of *Novem Virtutes* that is closest to *Wisdom*'s, see Smart, *Some English and Latin Sources,* 34–37. There is another Middle English version printed in C. Horstmann, *Yorkshire Writers: Richard Rolle and His Followers* (London, 1985), 2:455–56.

b i b l i o g r a p h y

PRIMARY SOURCES

Adso Dervensis. *Adso Dervensis: De Ortu et Tempore Antichristi*. Edited by D. Verhelst. Turnhout: Brepols, 1976.

Aebischer, Paul, ed. *Le mystère d'Adam (Ordo Representacionis Ade)*. Geneva: Droz, 1964.

Alfonso of Jaén. *Alfonso of Jaén: His Life and Works with Critical Editions of the Epistola Solitarii, the Informaciones and the Epistola Servi Christi*. Edited by Arne Jonsson. Lund: Lund University Press, 1989.

Anselm of Canterbury. *Opera Omnia*. 2 vols. Edited by F. S. Schmitt. Stuttgart: Frommann, 1968.

———. *Major Works*. Edited by Brian Davies and G. R. Evans. Oxford: Oxford University Press, 1998.

Aquinas, Thomas. *Summa Theologica Diligenter Emendata de Rubeis, Billuart et Aliorum*. 6 vols. Turin: Marietti, 1909.

———. *Summa Theologica of St. Thomas Aquinas*. Translated by the Fathers of the Dominican Province. 5 vols. New York: Benziger, 1948. Reprint, Westminster, Md.: Christian Classics, 1981.

Augustine. *Epistulae*. Edited by Alois Goldbacher. CSEL 33–34, 43–44, 56–58. Vienna: Tempsky, 1895–1923.

———. *Letters*. Translated by Wilfrid Parsons. 2 vols. New York: Catholic University Press, 1953.

———. *De Civitate Dei Libri XXII*. Edited by Bernard Domabart and Alphonse Kalb. 2 vols. Stuttgart: Teubner, 1981.

———. *The Literal Meaning of Genesis*. Translated by John Hammond Taylor. 2 vols. New York: Newman Press, 1982.

———. *The City of God.* Translated by Henry Bettenson. Harmondsworth: Penguin Books, 1984.

———. *De Doctrina Christiana.* Edited and translated by R. P. H. Green. Oxford: Oxford University Press, 1995.

Barr, Helen, ed. *Pierce the Ploughman's Crede.* In *The Piers Plowman Tradition.* London: Dent, 1993.

Bartholomaeus Anglicus. *On the Properties of Things: John Trevisa's Translation of Bartholomaeus Anglicus De Proprietatibus Rerum.* 2 vols. Oxford: Oxford University Press, 1975.

Bazire, Joyce, and Eric Colledge, eds. *The Chastising of God's Children and the Treatise of the Perfection of the Sons of God.* Oxford: Blackwell, 1957.

Beadle, Richard, ed. *The York Plays.* London: Edward Arnold, 1982.

Bede. *De Temporum Ratione.* Edited by C. W. Jones. Turnhout: Brepols, 1977.

Berger, David. *The Jewish-Christian Debate in the High Middle Ages: A Critical Edition of the Nizzahon Vetus.* Philadelphia: Jewish Publication Society, 1979.

Bernard of Clairvaux. *S. Bernardi Opera.* Edited by J. Leclercq., C. H. Talbot, and H. M. Rochais. 8 vols. Rome: Editiones Cisterciences, 1957–77.

———. *On the Song of Songs.* Translated by Kilian Walsh and Irene M. Edmonds. 4 vols. Kalamazoo, Mich.: Cistercian Publications, 1971–80.

Bevington, David, ed. *The Macro Plays.* New York: Johnson Reprint, 1972.

Blunt, John Henry, ed. *The Myroure of Oure Ladye.* EETS. London: Oxford University Press, 1873.

Bonaventure. *Itinerarium Mentis in Deum.* Edited and translated by Philotheus Boehner. St. Bonaventure, N.Y.: Franciscan Institute, 1956.

Bridget of Sweden. *Den Heiliga Birgittas Revelationes Extravagantes.* Edited by Lennart Hollmann. Uppsala: Almqvist & Wiksells, 1956.

———. *Sermo Angelicus.* In *Sancta Birgitta Opera Minora.* Edited by Sten Eklund. Uppsala: Almquist & Wiksells, 1972.

———. *The Liber Celestis of St. Bridget of Sweden.* Edited by Roger Ellis. EETS. Oxford: Oxford University Press, 1987.

Capes, William W., ed. *Registrum Johannis Trefnant, Episcopi Herefordensis, 1389–1404.* London, 1916.

Cassiodorus. *Expositio Psalmorum I–LXX.* Edited by M. Adriaen. CCSL 97. Turnhout: Brepols, 1958.

———. *Explanation of the Psalms.* 2 vols. Translated by P. G. Walsh. New York: Paulist Press, 1990.

Chaucer, Geoffrey. *The Riverside Chaucer.* 3d ed. Edited by Larry Benson. Oxford: Oxford University Press, 1988.

Cohen, Menachem, ed. *Miḳra'ot gedolot ha-Keter: Isaiah.* Tel Aviv: Bar-Ilan University Press, 1996.

Colledge, Eric, and Noel Chadwick, eds. "Remedies against Temptations: The Third English Version of William Flete." *Archivio Italiano per la Storia della Pietà* 5:14 (1968): 203–40.

Collijn, Isak, ed. *Acta et Processus Canonizacionis Beate Birgitte.* Uppsala: Almquist & Wiksells, 1924–31.

Collin-Roset, Simone, ed. "Le *Liber Thesauri Occulti* de Pascalis Romanus: Un traité d'interpretation des songes du XIIe siècle." *Archives d'Histoire Doctrinale et Litteraire du Moyen
Age* 30 (1963): 111–98.

David of Augsburg. *De Exterioris et Interioris Hominis Compositione.* Rome: Quaracchi, 1899.

———. *Spiritual Life and Progress.* 2 vols. Translated by Dominic Devas. London: Burns,
Oates & Washbourne, 1936.

Davidson, Clifford, ed. *A Tretise of Miraclis Pleyinge.* Kalamazoo, Mich.: Medieval Institute
Publications, 1993.

Davis, Norman, ed. *Non-Cycle Plays and Fragments.* EETS. Oxford: Oxford University Press,
1970.

———, ed. *Paston Letters and Papers of the Fifteenth Century.* 2 vols. Oxford: Oxford University Press, 1971.

"De Miraculo Hostiae a Judaeo Parisiis Anno Domini MCCXC." In *Recueil des histoires des
Gaules et de la France,* edited by Natalis de Wailly and Leopold Delisle, 22:32–33. Paris:
Palmé, 1865.

Dillon, Viscount, and W. H. St. John Hope, eds. *The Pageant of the Birth, Life and Death of
Richard Beauchamp, Earl of Warwick, 1389–1439.* London: Longmans, 1914.

Dobson, R. B., ed. *The Peasants' Revolt of 1381.* 2d ed. New York: Macmillan, 1983.

Eccles, Mark. *The Macro Plays.* EETS. Oxford: Oxford University Press, 1969.

Forshall, Josiah, and Frederic Madden. *The Holy Bible . . . Made from the Latin Vulgate by
John Wycliffe and His Followers.* 4 vols. Oxford: Oxford University Press, 1850.

Foxe, John. *Acts and Monuments.* 8 vols. Edited by G. Townsend. London: Seeley, Burnside
and Seeley, 1843–49.

Francis of Assisi. *Francis and Clare: The Complete Works.* Edited and translated by Regis J.
Armstrong and Ignatius C. Brady. New York: Paulist Press, 1982.

Gallacher, Patrick J. *The Cloud of Unknowing.* Kalamazoo, Mich.: Medieval Institute Publications, 1997.

Galloway, David, and John Wasson. *Records of Plays and Players in Norfolk and Suffolk,
1330–1642.* Oxford: Malone Society, 1980.

Gerson, Jean. "De Probatione Spirituum." In *Oeuvres completes,* edited by P. Glorieux, 9:177–85.
Tournai: Desclee, 1965.

Gransden, Antonia, ed. and trans. *The Chronicle of Bury St. Edmunds, 1212–1301.* London:
Nelson, 1964.

Guillaume de Lorris and Jean de Meun. *Le roman de la rose,* ed. Daniel Poirion. Paris: Garnier-
Flammarion, 1974.

———. *The Romance of the Rose.* Translated by Charles Dahlberg. University Press of New
England, 1983.

Harper-Bill, C., ed. *Charters of the Medieval Hospitals of Bury St. Edmunds.* Woodbridge: Boydell, 1996.

Helmholtz, Richard H. *Select Cases on Defamation to 1600.* Selden Society Publications. London: B. Quaritch, 1985.

Higden, Ralph. *Polychronicon Ranulphi Higden.* 9 vols. Edited by Churchill Babington and
Joseph R. Lumby. London, 1865–86.

Hilton, Walter. *Walter Hilton's Latin Writings.* 2 vols. Edited by John P. Clark and Cheryl Taylor. Salzburg: Institut für Anglistik und Amerikanistik, Universität Salzburg, 1987.

———. "Epistle on the Mixed Life." In *English Mystics of the Middle Ages,* edited by Barry Windeatt, 108–30. Cambridge: Cambridge University Press, 1994.

———. *The Scale of Perfection.* Edited by Thomas H. Bestul. Kalamazoo, Mich.: Medieval Institute Publications, 2000.

Hoccleve, Thomas. *The Regiment of Princes.* Edited by Charles R. Blyth. Kalamazoo, Mich.: Medieval Institute Publications, 1999.

Hodgson, Phyllis, ed. *Deonise Hid Diuinite and Other Treatises on Contemplative Prayer Related to The Cloud of Unknowing.* EETS. London: Oxford University Press, 1955.

Holkot, Robert. *Super Libros Sapientiae.* Hagenau, 1494.

Horstmann, C., ed. *Yorkshire Writers: Richard Rolle and His Followers.* 2 vols. London, 1895. Reprint, Cambridge: D. S. Brewer, 1999.

———, ed. "*Orologium Sapientiae or The Seven Poyntes of Trewe Wisdom* Aus MS. Douce 114." *Anglia* 10 (1888): 323–89.

Hudson, Anne, and Pamela Gradon, eds. *English Wycliffite Sermons.* 5 vols. Oxford: Oxford University Press, 1983–96.

Hugh of St. Victor. *Didascalicon.* Edited by Charles H. Buttimer. Washington, D.C.: Catholic University Press, 1939.

———. *Didascalicon.* Translated by Jerome Taylor. New York: Columbia University Press, 1961.

Hulme, W. H., ed. *The Middle English Harrowing of Hell and Gospel of Nicodemus.* EETS. London: Oxford University Press, 1907.

Isidore of Seville. *Isidori Hispalensis Episcopi Etymologiarum, sive Originum Libri XX.* 2 vols. Edited by W. M. Lindsay. Oxford: Oxford University Press, 1911.

———. *Allegoriae Quaedam Sanctae Scripturae.* Edited by J.-P. Migne. PL 83. Paris: Garnier, 1850.

Jacobus de Voragine. *The Golden Legend.* 2 vols. Translated by William Granger Ryan. Princeton, N.J.: Princeton University Press, 1993.

Jean de la Rochelle. *Tractatus de Divisione Muliplici Potentiarum Animae.* Edited by Pierre Michaud-Quantin. Paris: Vrin, 1964.

Jerome. *The Principal Works of St. Jerome.* Translated by W. H. Freemantle. 1892. Reprint, Grand Rapids, Mich.: Eerdmans, 1989.

———. *Epistulae.* 2d ed. Edited by Isidorus Hilberg. CSEL 54–57. Vienna: Verlag der Osterreichischen Akademie der Wissenschaften, 1996.

Jocelin of Brakelond. *Chronicle of Jocelin of Brakelond.* Edited and translated by H. E. Butler. London: Nelson, 1949.

[Johannis de Caulibus]. *Meditations on the Life of Christ.* Translated by Isa Ragusa and Rosalie B. Green. Princeton, N.J.: Princeton University Press, 1961.

———. *Meditationes Vitae Christi.* Edited by M. Stallings-Taney. CCCM 113. Turnhout: Brepols, 1997.

Johnston, Alexandra F., and Margaret Rogerson, eds. and trans. *Records of Early English Drama: York.* 2 vols. Toronto: University of Toronto Press, 1979.

Jolliffe, P. S. "Two Middle English Tracts on the Contemplative Life." *Mediaeval Studies* 37 (1975): 85–121.

Kempe, Margery. *The Book of Margery Kempe.* EETS. Oxford: Oxford University Press, 1940.

Kurath, Hans, Sherman M. Kuhn, and Robert E. Lewis. *Middle English Dictionary.* Ann Arbor: University of Michigan Press, 1952–.

Langland, William. *Piers Plowman: The B-Version.* Edited by George Kane and E. Talbot Donaldson. Berkeley: University of California Press, 1988.

———. *Piers Plowman: The C-Version.* Edited by George Russell and George Kane. Berkeley: University of California Press, 1997.

Latini, Brunetto. *Li livres dou tresor.* Edited by Francis J. Carmody. Berkeley: University of California Press, 1948.

———. *The Book of the Treasure.* Translated by Paul Barrette and Spurgeon Baldwin. New York: Garland, 1993.

Love, Nicholas. *Mirror of the Blessed Life of Jesus Christ.* Edited by Michael Sargent. New York: Garland, 1992.

Macrobius. *Commentary on the Dream of Scipio.* Translated by William Stahl. New York: Columbia University Press, 1952.

Martini, Raymond. *Pugio Fidei Adversus Mauros at Judaeos.* Leipzig,1687. Reprint, Farnborough: Gregg, 1967.

Menesto, Enrico, and Stefano Brufani, eds. *Fontes Franciscani.* Assisi: Edizioni Porziuncola, 1995.

Meredith, Peter, ed. *The Mary Play.* 2d ed. Exeter: University of Exeter Press, 1997.

Minnis, Alastair J., and A. B. Scott, eds. *Medieval Literary Theory and Criticism, c. 1100–c. 1375: The Commentary Tradition.* Oxford: Oxford University Press, 1988.

Morris, Richard, ed. *The Pricke of Conscience: A Northumbrian Poem.* Berlin: A. Asher, 1863. Reprint, New York: AMS Press, 1973.

Nicholas of Lyra. *Biblia Sacra cvm Glossis, Interlineari, et Ordinaria, Nicolai Lyrani Postilla, ac Moralitalibus, Burgensis Additionibus, & Tacringi Replicis.* 6 vols. Venice, 1588.

———. "Prologue to the Commentary on the Psalter." In *Medieval Literary Theory and Criticism, c. 1100–c. 1375: The Commentary Tradition,* edited by A. J. Minnis and A. B. Scott. Oxford: Oxford University Press, 1988.

———. "Second Prologue to the Literal Postill on the Bible." In *Medieval Literary Theory and Criticism, c. 1100–c. 1375: The Commentary Tradition,* edited by A. J. Minnis and A. B. Scott. Oxford: Oxford University Press, 1988.

———. *The Postilla of Nicholas of Lyra on the Song of Songs.* Edited and translated by James George Kiecker. Milwaukee, Wis.: Marquette University Press, 1998.

Pantin, W. A., ed. "Instructions for a Devout and Literate Layman." In *Medieval Learning and Literature,* edited by J. G. Alexander and M. T. Gibson, 398–422. Oxford: Oxford University Press, 1976.

Parker, Roscoe, ed. *The Middle English Stanzaic Versions of the Life of St. Anne.* EETS. London: Oxford University Press, 1928.

Quodvultdeus. *Opera*. Edited by E. Braun. CCSL 60. Turnhout: Brepols, 1976.

Raine, J., ed. *Testamenta Eboracensia*. 6 vols. Durham: Surtees Society, 1836–1902.

Richard of St. Victor, *De IV Gradibus Violentae Caritatibus*. Edited by Gervais Dumiege. Paris: Vrin, 1955.

———. *Opera Omnia*. Edited by J.-P. Migne. PL 196. Paris: Garnier, 1880.

———. *Richard of St. Victor*. Edited and translated by Grover Zinn. New York: Paulist Press, 1979.

Riley, Henry T., ed. *Liber Customarum*. In *Munimenta Gildhallae Londoniensis,* vol. 2. RS. London: Longman, Brown, Green, Longmans, and Roberts, 1860.

Rolle, Richard. *The Psalter or Psalms of David and Certain Canticles, with a Translation and Exposition in English by Richard Rolle of Hampole*. Edited by H. R. Bramley. Oxford: Clarendon Press, 1884.

———. *Incendium Amoris*. Edited by Margaret Deanesley. Manchester: Manchester University Press, 1915.

Sayles, G. O., ed. *Select Cases in the Court of the King's Bench under Richard II, Henry IV, and Henry V.* Vol. 7. Selden Society Publications 88. London: B. Quaritch, 1971.

Schmidtke, James. "Adam Easton's Defense of St. Birgitta From Bodleian Ms. Hamilton 7 Oxford University." Ph.D. diss., Duke University, 1971.

Sellers, Maud, ed. *York Memorandum Book Lettered A/Y in the Guildhall Munimaent Room.* 2 vols. Surtees Society Publications. Durham: Andrews, 1912–15.

Servius, Maurus. *Servii Grammatici Qui Feruntur in Vergilii Carmina Commentarii.* 3 vols. Edited by Georg Thilo and Hermann Hagen. Leipzig, 1881–87.

Simmons, T. H., and H. E. Nolloth, eds. *The Lay Folks' Catechism*. EETS. London: K. Paul, Trench, Trübner, 1901.

Smith, Joshua Toulmin, and Lucy Toulmin Smith, eds. *English Gilds*. EETS. London: K. Paul, Trench, Trübner, 1870.

Spector, Stephen, ed. *The N-Town Play*. 2 vols. EETS. Oxford: Oxford University Press, 1991.

Stevens, Martin, and A. C. Cawley, eds. *The Towneley Plays*. 2 vols. EETS. Oxford: Oxford University Press, 1994.

Suetonius. *Works*. 2 vols. Rev. ed. Edited and translated by J. C. Rolfe. Cambridge, Mass.: Harvard University Press, 1997.

Suso, Henry. *Heinrich Seuses Horologium Sapientiae: Erste Kritische Ausgabe unter Benutzung der Vorarbeiten von Dominikus Planker, O.P.* Edited by Pius Kunzle. Freiburg: Universitätsverlag Freiburg Schweiz, 1977.

———. *Wisdom's Watch upon the Hours*. Translated by Eric Colledge. Washington, D.C.: Catholic University of American Press, 1994.

Swinburne, Lilian, ed. *The Lanterne of Light*. EETS. London: K. Paul, Trench, Trübner, 1917.

Tischendorf, K. *Evangelia Apocrypha*. 2 vols. Leipzig, 1876.

Todd, J., ed. *Apology for Lollard Doctrines*. London, 1842.

Trevet, Nicholas. *Commentario a las Bucolicas de Virgilio*. Edited by Aires Augusto Nascimento and José Manuel Díaz de Bustamante. Santiago: Universidad de Santiago de Compostela, 1984.

Virgil. *Aeneid.* Translated by Allen Mandelbaum. New York: Bantam, 1972.
———. *Eclogues, Georgics, Aeneid I–VI.* Edited and translated by H. Rushton Fairclough. Revised by G. P. Goold. Cambridge, Mass.: Harvard University Press, 1999.
Walsingham, Thomas. *Historia Anglicana.* 2 vols. Edited by Henry T. Riley. RS. London: Longman, Green, 1864.
———. *Gesta Abbatum Monasterii Sancti Albani.* 3 vols. Edited by H. T. Riley. London, 1867–69.
Weber, Robert, ed. *Biblia Sacra Iuxta Vulgatam Versionem.* 3d ed. Stuttgart: Deutsche Bibel-gesellschaft, 1983.
Wilkins, D. *Concilia Magnae Britanniae et Hiberniae.* 3 vols. London, 1737.
Wyclif, John. *Sermones.* 4 vols. Edited by Johann Loserth. London: Wyclif Society, 1887–90.
———. *Opera Minora.* Edited by Johann Loserth. London: Wyclif Society, 1913.

SECONDARY SOURCES

Allmand, C. T. "The Civil Lawyers." In *Profession, Vocation, and Culture in Later Medieval England: Essays Dedicated to the Memory of A. R. Myers.* Edited by Cecil Clough, 155–80. Liverpool: Liverpool University Press, 1982.
Aers, David. *Community, Gender and Individual Identity: English Writing, 1360–1430.* London: Routledge, 1988.
Ashley, Kathleen. "Image and Ideology: Saint Anne in Late Medieval Drama and Narrative." In *Interpreting Cultural Symbols: Saint Anne in Late Medieval Society,* edited by Kathleen Ashley and Pamela Sheingorn, 111–30. Athens: University of Georgia Press, 1990.
Astell, Ann. *The Song of Songs in the Middle Ages.* Ithaca, N.Y.: Cornell University Press, 1990.
Aston, Margaret. "Corpus Christi and Corpus Regni: Heresy and the Peasants' Revolt." *Past and Present* 143 (1994): 3–47.
Auerbach, Erich. *Scenes from the Drama of European Literature.* Minneapolis: University of Minnesota Press, 1984.
Badir, Patricia. "Playing Space: History, the Body, and Records of Early English Drama." *Exemplaria* 9:2 (1997): 255–79.
Barr, Helen. *Signes and Sothe: Language in the Piers Plowman Tradition.* Cambridge: D. S. Brewer, 1994.
Baswell, Christopher. *Virgil in Medieval England: Figuring the Aeneid from the Twelfth Century to Chaucer.* Cambridge: Cambridge University Press, 1995.
Beadle, Richard, ed. *The Cambridge Companion to Medieval English Theatre.* Cambridge: Cambridge University Press, 1994.
Beadle, Richard, and Peter Meredith. "Further Evidence for Dating the York Register." *Leeds Studies in English* 11 (1980): 51–55.
Beckwith, Sarah. "Ritual, Church and Theater." In *Culture and History, 1350–1600: Essays on English Communities, Identity and Writing,* edited by David Aers. Detroit: Wayne State University Press, 1992.

———. "*Sacrum Signum:* Sacramentality and Dissent in York's Theatre of Corpus Christi." In *Criticism and Dissent in the Middle Ages,* edited by Rita Copeland, 264–88. Cambridge: Cambridge University Press, 1996.

———. *Signifying God: Social Relation and Symbolic Act in the York Corpus Christi Plays.* Chicago: University of Chicago Press, 2001.

Beichner, Paul. "Absolon's Hair." *Mediaeval Studies* 12 (1950): 222–33.

Bellamy, John. *Crime and Public Order in England in the Late Middle Ages.* Toronto: University of Toronto Press, 1973.

Bennett, William F. "Interrupting the Word: Mankind and the Politics of the Vernacular." Ph.D. diss., Harvard University, 1992.

Berger, David. "Gilbert Crispin, Alan of Lille and Jacob ben Reuben: A Study in the Transmission of Medieval Polemic." *Speculum* 49 (1974): 34–47.

Bevington, David. "'Blake and Wyght, Fowll and Fayer': Stage Picture in *Wisdom.*" In *The Wisdom Symposium: Papers from the Trinity College Medieval Festival,* edited by Milla Cozart Riggio, 18–38. New York: AMS Press, 1986.

Black, Antony. *Political Thought in Europe, 1250–1450.* Cambridge: Cambridge University Press, 1992.

Bloch, R. Howard. *The Scandal of the Fabliaux.* Chicago: University of Chicago Press, 1986.

Bongie, Chris. *Exotic Memories: Literature, Colonialism, and the Fin de Siècle.* Stanford, Calif.: Stanford University Press, 1991.

Bowers, John M. *The Crisis of Will in Piers Plowman.* Washington, D.C.: Catholic University of America Press, 1986.

Boyd, David Lorenzo. "Seeking 'Goddes Pryvetee': Sodomy, Quitting, and Desire in *The Miller's Tale.*" In *Words and Works: Studies in Medieval English Language and Literature in Honor of Fred C. Robinson,* edited by Peter Baker and Nicholas Howe, 243–60. Toronto: University of Toronto Press, 1998.

Brawer, Robert. "The Characterization of Pilate in the York Cycle Play." *Studies in Philology* 68 (1972): 289–303.

Briscoe, Marianne. "Preaching and Medieval English Drama." In *Contexts for Early English Drama,* edited by Marianne Briscoe and J. Coldewey, 150–72. Bloomington: Indiana University Press, 1989.

Burr, David. *Eucharistic Presence and Conversion in Late Thirteenth-Century Franciscan Thought.* Philadelphia: American Philosophical Society, 1984.

———. "Olivi, Apocalyptic Expectation and Visionary Experience." *Traditio* 41 (1985): 273–88.

———. *Olivi and Franciscan Poverty: The Origins of the Usus Pauper Controversy.* Philadelphia: University of Pennsylvania Press, 1989.

Burrow, J. A. *Essays on Medieval Literature.* Oxford: Oxford University Press, 1984.

Bynum, Caroline Walker. *Fragmentation and Redemption.* New York: Zone Books, 1991.

Cahn, Walter. "Architecture and Exegesis: Richard of St.-Victor's Ezekiel Commentary and Its Illustrations." *Art Bulletin* 76 (1994): 53–68.

Cantelupe, Eugene, and Richard Griffith. "The Gifts of the Shepherds in the Wakefield *Secunda Pastorum:* An Iconographical Interpretation." *Mediaeval Studies* 28 (1966): 328–35.

Caruth, Cathy. "Traumatic Awakenings." In *Performativity and Performance,* edited by Andrew Parker and Eve Sedgewick. New York: Routledge, 1995.

Catto, Jeremy. "Andrew Horn: Law and History in Fourteenth-Century England." In *The Writing of History in the Middle Ages: Essays Presented to R. W. Southern,* edited by R. H. C. Davies and J. M. Wallace-Hadrill. Oxford: Oxford University Press, 1981.

———. "Religion and the English Nobility in the Later Fourteenth Century." In *History and Imagination: Essays in Honor of H. R. Trevor-Roper,* edited by Hugh Lloyd-Jones, Valerie Pearl, and Blair Worden. London: Duckworth, 1981.

———. "Religious Change under Henry V." In *Henry V: The Practice of Kingship,* edited by G. L. Harriss. Oxford: Alan Sutton, 1985.

Cawley, A. C. "The Grotesque Feast in the Prima Pastorum." *Speculum* 30 (1955): 213–17.

Clark, John P. H. *The Cloud of Unknowing: An Introduction.* 3 vols. Analecta Cartusiana 119. Salzburg, Austria: Institut für Anglistik und Amerikanistik, Universität Salzburg, 1995–96.

Clark, Marlene, Sharon Kraus, and Pamela Sheingorn. "'Se in what stat thou doyst indwell': The Shifting Constructions of Gender and Power Relations in *Wisdom.*" In *The Performance of Middle English Culture: Essays on Chaucer and the Drama in Honor of Martin Stevens,* edited by James J. Paxson, Lawrence M. Clopper, and Sylvia Tomasch, 43–57. Cambridge: D. S. Brewer, 1998,

Clark, Robert, and Claire Sponsler. "Othered Bodies: Racial Cross-Dressing in the Mistere de la Sainte Hostie and the Croxton Play of the Sacrament." *JMEMS* 29:1 (1999): 61–87.

Clopper, Lawrence. "Lay and Clerical Impact on Civic Religious Drama and Ceremony." In *Contexts of Early English Drama,* edited by Marianne Briscoe and J. Coldewey. Bloomington: Indiana University Press, 1989.

———. *Songes of Rechelesnesse: Langland and the Franciscans.* Ann Arbor: University of Michigan Press, 1997.

———. "English Drama: from Ungodly Ludi to Sacred Play." In The Cambridge History of Medieval English Literature, edited by David Wallace, 739–66. Cambridge: Cambridge University Press, 1999.

———. *Drama, Play and Game: English Festive Culture in the Medieval and Early Modern Period.* Chicago: University of Chicago Press, 2001.

Cohen, Jeremy. *The Friars and the Jews: The Evolution of Medieval Anti-Judaism.* Ithaca, N.Y.: Cornell University Press, 1982.

Coldewey, J. "The Non-Cycle Plays and the East Anglian Tradition." In *The Cambridge Companion to Medieval English Theatre,* edited by Richard Beadle, 189–210. Cambridge: Cambridge University Press, 1994.

Coletti, Theresa. "Reading REED: History and the Records of Early English Drama." In *Literary Practice and Social Change in Britain, 1380–1530,* edited by Lee Patterson. Berkeley: University of California Press, 1990.

Colledge, Eric. "Epistola Solitarii ad Reges: Alphonse of Pecha as Organizer of Bridgettine and Urbanist Propaganda." *Mediaeval Studies* 18 (1956): 19–49.

Comparetti, Domenico. *Virgil in the Middle Ages.* New York, 1895. Reprint, Princeton, N.J.: Princeton University Press, 1997.

Copeland, Rita. "Rhetoric and the Politics of the Literal Sense in Medieval Literary Theory: Aquinas, Wyclif and the Lollards." In *Interpretation Medieval and Modern,* edited by Anna Torti. Cambridge: D. S. Brewer, 1993.

Courcelle, Pierre. "Les exegeses chretiennes de la Quatrieme Eclogue." *Revue des Etudes Anciennes* 59 (1957): 294–319.

Cox, John D., and David Scott Kastan. *A New History of Early English Drama.* New York: Columbia University. Press, 1997.

Cutts, Celia. "The Croxton Play: An Anti-Lollard Piece." *MLQ* 5 (1944): 45–60.

Dahan, Gilbert. *Les intellectuels chrétiens et les juifs au Moyen Age.* Paris: Cerf, 1990.

Davis, Nicholas. "The *Tretise of Myraclis Pleyinge:* On Milieu and Authorship." *Middle English Theatre* 12:2 (1990): 124–51.

Desmond, Marilynn. *Reading Dido: Gender, Textuality and the Medieval Aeneid.* Minneapolis: University of Minnesota Press, 1994.

Dobson, R. B. "The Risings in York, Beverley and Scarborough, 1380–1." In *The English Rising of 1381,* edited by R. H. Hilton and T. H. Aston. Cambridge: Cambridge University Press, 1984.

Doyle, A. I. "Remarks on Surviving Manuscripts of Piers Plowman." In *Medieval English Religious and Ethical Literature: Essays in Honor of G. H. Russell,* edited by G. Kratzmann and James Simpson. Cambridge: Cambridge University Press, 1986,

DuBois, Page. *Torture and Truth.* New York: Routledge, 1991.

Duffy, Eamon. *The Stripping of the Altars: Traditional Religion on England, 1400–1580.* New Haven, Conn.: Yale University Press, 1992.

Dutka, Joanna. "Mystery Plays at Norwich: Their Formation and Development." *Leeds Studies in English* 10 (1975): 107–20.

Dyer, Christopher. *Standards of Living in the Middle Ages.* Cambridge: Cambridge University Press, 1989.

Einbinder, Susan L. "Meir ben Elijah of Norwich: Persecution and Poetry among Medieval English Jews." *Journal of Medieval History* 26 (2000): 145–62.

Elliott, Dyan. "The Physiology of Rapture and Female Spirituality." In *Medieval Theology and the Natural Body,* edited by Peter Biller and A. J. Minnis. Rochester, N.Y.: York Medieval Press, 1997.

Ellis, Roger. "Flores ad Fabricandum . . . Coranam: An Investigation into the Uses of the Revelations of St. Bridget of Sweden in Fifteenth-Century England." *Medium Aevum* 51 (1982): 163–86.

Ellis, Roger. *Syon Abbey: Spirituality of the English Bridgettines.* Analecta Cartusianana. Salzburg, Austria: Institut für Anglistik und Amerikanistik, Universität Salzburg, 1984.

Enders, Jody. "Medieval Snuff Drama." *Exemplaria* 10 (1997): 171–206.

———. *The Medieval Theater of Cruelty: Rhetoric, Memory, Violence.* Ithaca, N.Y.: Cornell University Press, 1999.

———. "Dramatic Memories and Tortured Spaces in the Mistere de la Sainte Hostie." In *The Medieval Practices of Space,* edited by Barbara Hanawalt and Michael Kobialka. Minneapolis: University of Minnesota Press, 2000.

Faith, Rosamond. "The 'Great Rumor' of 1377 and Peasant Ideology." In *The English Rising of 1381,* edited by R. H. Hilton and T. H. Aston. Cambridge: Cambridge University Press, 1984.

Fleming, John. *An Introduction to the Franciscan Literature of the Middle Ages.* Chicago: Franciscan Herald Press, 1977.

Fletcher, Alan. "The N-Town Plays." In *The Cambridge Companion to Medieval English Theatre,* edited by Richard Beadle, 163–88. Cambridge: Cambridge University Press, 1994.

Forrest, M. Patricia. "The Role of the Expositor Contemplacio in the St. Anne's Day Plays of the Hegge Cycle." *Mediaeval Studies* 28 (1966): 60–76.

Foucault, Michel. "What Is an Author?" Translated by Josué Harari. In *The Foucault Reader,* edited by Paul Rabinow, 101–20. New York: Random House, 1984.

Frank, Robert Worth. "Meditationes Vitae Christi: The Logistics of Access to Divinity." In *Hermeneutics and Medieval Culture,* edited by Patrick J. Gallacher and Helen Damico, 39–50. Albany: SUNY Press, 1989.

Freedman, Paul. *Images of the Medieval Peasant.* Stanford, Calif.: Stanford University Press, 1999.

Friedman, John Block. *Northern English Books, Owners, and Makers in the Late Middle Ages.* Syracuse, N.Y.: Syracuse University Press, 1995.

Fryde, E. B. *Peasants and Landlords in Later Medieval England.* New York: St. Martin's Press, 1996.

Funkenstein, Amos. *Perceptions of Jewish History.* Berkeley: University of California Press, 1993.

Ganim, John. *Chaucerian Theatricality.* Princeton, N.J.: Princeton University Press, 1990.

Gardiner, Harold. *Mysteries' End: An Investigation of the Last Days of the Medieval Religious Stage.* New Haven, Conn.: Yale University Press, 1946.

Gatch, Milton McC. "Mysticism and Satire in the Morality of *Wisdom.*" *Philological Quarterly* 53 (1974): 342–62.

Gellrich, Jesse. *The Idea of the Book in the Middle Ages: Language, Theory, Mythology, and Fiction.* Ithaca, N.Y.: Cornell University Press, 1985.

Ghosh, Kantik. "Manuscripts of Nicholas Love's The Mirror of the Blessed Life of Jesus Christ and Wycliffite Notions of Authority." In *Prestige, Authority, and Power in Late Medieval Manuscripts and Texts,* edited by Felicity Riddy. Cambridge: D. S. Brewer, 2000.

Gibson, Gail McMurray. "Bury St. Edmunds, Lydgate, and the N-Town Cycle." *Speculum* 56 (1981): 56–90.

———. "The Play of Wisdom and the Abbey of Saint Edmund." In *The Wisdom Symposium: Papers from the Trinity College Medieval Festival,* edited by Milla Cozart Riggio, 39–66. New York: AMS Press, 1986.

———. *The Theater of Devotion: East Anglian Drama and Society in the Late Middle Ages.* Chicago: University of Chicago Press, 1989.

Gillespie, Vincent. "Mystic's Foot: Rolle and Affectivity." In *The Medieval Mystical Tradition in England,* edited by Marion Glasscoe. Exeter: Exeter University Press, 1982.

———. "The Cibus Anime Book 3: A Guide for Contemplatives?" *Analecta Cartusiana* 35 (1983): 90–117.

———. "Vernacular Books of Religion." In *Book Production and Publishing in Britain, 1375–1475*, edited by Jeremy Griffiths and Derek Pearsall, 317–44. Cambridge: Cambridge University Press, 1989.

Goldberg, P. J. P. "Craft Guilds, the Corpus Christi Play and Civic Government." In *The Government of Medieval York*, edited by Sarah Rees-Jones, 141–63. York: Borthwick Institute of Historical Research, 1997.

———. "Performing the Word of God: Corpus Christi Drama in the Northern Province." In *Life and Thought in the Northern Church, c.1100–c.1700*, edited by Diana Wood. SCH, Subsidia 11. Rochester, N.Y.: Boydell Press, 1999.

Gottfried, Robert. *Bury St. Edmunds and the Urban Crisis, 1290–1539*. Princeton, N.J.: Princeton University Press, 1982.

Grayzel, Solomon. *The Church and the Jews in the XIIIth Century*, vol. 2, *1254–1314*. Edited by Kenneth Stow. Detroit: Wayne State University Press, 1989.

Green, Richard Firth. *A Crisis of Truth: Literature and Law in Ricardian England*. Philadelphia: University of Pennsylvania Press, 1999.

Hailperin, Herman. *Rashi and the Christian Scholars*. Pittsburgh, Pa.: University of Pittsburgh Press, 1963.

Hamburger, Jeffrey. *The Visual and the Visionary: Art and Female Spirituality in Late Medieval Germany*. New York: Zone Books, 1998.

Hanna, Ralph, III. " Sir Thomas Berkeley and His Patronage." *Speculum* 64 (1989): 878–916.

———. *William Langland*. Aldershot: Ashgate, 1993.

———. *Pursuing History: Middle English Manuscripts and Their Texts*. Stanford, Calif.: Stanford University Press, 1996.

———. "'Vae Octuplex,' Lollard Socio-Textual Ideology, and Ricardian Lancastrian Prose Translation." In *Criticism and Dissent in the Middle Ages*, edited by Rita Copeland. Cambridge: Cambridge University Press, 1996.

Hanning, Robert. "You Have Begun a Parlous Pleye: The Nature and Limits of Dramatic Mimesis as a Theme in Four Middle English Fall of Lucifer Cycle Plays." In *Drama of the Middle Ages: Comparative and Critical Essays*, edited by Clifford Davidson, C. J. Gianakaris, and John Stroupe. New York: AMS Press, 1982.

Harding, Alan. *The Law-Courts of Medieval England*. London: Allyn and Unwin, 1973.

Hardison, O. B., Jr. *Christian Rite and Christian Drama in the Middle Ages*. Baltimore: Johns Hopkins University Press, 1965.

Harvey, I. M. W. *Jack Cade's Rebellion of 1450*. Oxford: Oxford University Press, 1991.

Hilton, R. H. *The English Peasantry in the Later Middle Ages*. Oxford: Oxford University Press, 1975.

Holloway, Julia Bolton. "Brunetto Latini and England." *Manuscripta* 31 (1987): 11–21.

Holsinger, Bruce. "The Vision of Music in a Lollard Florilegium: *Cantus* in the Middle English *Rosarium Theologiae* (Cambridge, Gonville and Caius College MS 354/581)." *Plainsong and Medieval Music* 8 (1999): 95–106.

Hudson, Anne. *Lollards and Their Books*. London: Hambledon Press, 1985.

———. *The Premature Reformation*. Oxford: Oxford University Press, 1988.

———. "'Laicus Litteratus': The Paradox of Lollardy." In *Heresy and Literacy, 1000–1530,* edited by Peter Biller and Anne Hudson. Cambridge: Cambridge University Press, 1994.

———. "Piers Plowman and the Peasants' Revolt: A Problem Revisited." *Yearbook of Langland Studies* 8 (1995): 85–106.

Hudson, Anne, and H. L. Spencer. "Old Author, New Work: The Sermons of MS. Longeat 4." *Medium Aevum* 53 (1984): 220–38.

Hughes, Jonathan. *Pastors and Visionaries: Religion and Secular Life in Late Medieval Yorkshire.* Cambridge: D. S. Brewer, 1988.

Ives, E. W. "The Common Lawyers." In *Profession, Vocation, and Culture in Later Medieval England: Essays Dedicated to the Memory of A. R. Myers,* edited by Cecil Clough, 181–217. Liverpool: Liverpool University Press, 1982.

James, M. R. "Ritual, Drama, and the Social Body in the Late Medieval English Town." *Past and Present* 98 (1983): 3–29.

Jeffrey, David L. "Franciscan Spirituality and the Rise of Early English Drama." *Mosaic* 8 (1975): 17–46.

Johnson, Willis. "Between Christians and Jews: The Formation of Anti-Jewish Stereotypes in Medieval England." Ph.D. diss., University of California, Berkeley, 1996.

Johnston, Alexandra F. "Wisdom and the Records: Is There a Moral?" In *The Wisdom Symposium: Papers from the Trinity College Medieval Festival,* edited by Milla Cozart Riggio, 87–101. New York: AMS Press, 1986.

Johnston, F. R. "English Defenders of St. Bridget." In *Studies in St. Birgitta and the Brigittine Order,* 2 vols. Analecta Cartusiana 35:19. Lewiston, N.Y.: Edwin Mellen Press, 1993.

Johnston, F. R. "The English Cult of St. Bridget of Sweden." *Analecta Bollandiana* 103 (1985): 75–83.

Jones, Marion. "Allegory into Drama: Souls in Jeopardy." In *The Revels History of Drama in English,* vol. 1, *Medieval Drama,* edited by A. C. Cawley, Marion Jones, Peter F. McDonald, and David Mills. London: Methuen, 1983.

Jordan, William C. *The French Monarchy and the Jews.* Philadelphia: University of Pennsylvania Press, 1989.

Justice, Steven. *Writing and Rebellion: England in 1381.* Berkeley: University of California Press, 1994.

Kaske, R. E. "The *Canticum Canticorum* in the *Miller's Tale.*" *Studies in Philology* 59 (1962): 479–500.

Kendall, Ritchie. *The Drama of Dissent: The Radical Poetics of Nonconformity.* Chapel Hill: University of North Carolina Press, 1986.

Kerby-Fulton, Kathryn, and Denise Despres. *Iconography and the Professional Reader: The Politics of Book Production in the Douce Piers Plowman.* Minneapolis: University of Minnesota Press, 1999.

King, Laura S. "'A Good Bowrde': The *Second Shepherds' Play* and the Defense of Drama in Late Medieval England." Unpublished manuscript, 1998.

———. "Through a Glass Clerkly: Manipulation of Bridgettine Models in the *Myrroure of Oure Lady.*" Unpublished manuscript, 1989.

King, Pamela. "Morality Plays." In *The Cambridge Companion to Medieval English Theatre,* edited by Richard Beadle. Cambridge: Cambridge University Press, 1994.

Kipling, Gordon. *Enter the King: Theatre, Liturgy, and Ritual in Medieval Civic Triumph.* Oxford: Oxford University Press, 1998.

Kirk, Elizabeth. "Langland's Plowman and the Recreation of Fourteenth-Century Religious Metaphor." *Yearbook of Langland Studies* 2 (1988): 1–21.

Klepper, Deeana. "Nicholas of Lyra's 'Questio de Adventu Christi' and the Franciscan Encounter with Jewish Tradition." Ph.D. diss., Northwestern University, 1995.

Knowles, David. *The Religious Orders in England.* 3 vols. Cambridge: Cambridge University Press, 1948–59.

Kolve, V. A. *The Play Called Corpus Christi.* Stanford, Calif.: Stanford University Press, 1966.

———. *Chaucer and the Imagery of Narrative.* Stanford, Calif.: Stanford University Press, 1984.

Kruger, Steven. *Dreaming in the Middle Ages.* Cambridge: Cambridge University Press, 1992.

Kuczynski, Michael. *Prophetic Song: The Psalms as Moral Discourse in Late Medieval England.* Philadelphia: University of Pennsylvania Press, 1995.

Lacan, Jacques. *Four Fundamental Concepts of Psychoanalysis.* Translated by Alan Sheridan. New York: Norton, 1978.

Lambert, M. D. *Franciscan Poverty: The Doctrine of the Absolute Poverty of Christ and the Apostles in the Franciscan Order, 1210–1323.* London: SPCK, 1961. Rev. ed., St Bonaventure, N.Y.: Franciscan Institute, 1998.

Landes, Richard. "The Massacres of 1010: On the Origins of Popular Anti-Jewish Violence in Western Europe." In *From Witness to Witchcraft: Jews and Judaism in Medieval Christian Thought,* edited by Jeremy Cohen, 79–112. Wiesbaden: Harassowitz, 1996.

Langmuir, Gavin. *Toward a Definition of Antisemitism.* Berkeley: University of California Press, 1990.

Lavin, Marilyn Aronberg. "The Altar of Corpus Domini in Urbino: Paoalo Ucello, Joos Van Ghent, Piero Della Francesca." *Art Bulletin* 49 (1967): 1–24.

Lawton, David. "Dullness and the Fifteenth-Century." *ELH* 54 (1987): 761–99.

Leicester, Marshall. "Newer Currents in Psychoanalytic Criticism, and the Difference 'It' Makes: Gender and Desire in the *Miller's Tale.*" *ELH* 61 (1994): 473–99.

Lepow, Lauren. *Enacting the Sacrament: Counter-Lollardy in the Towneley Cycle.* Rutherford, N.J.: Fairleigh Dickinson University Press, 1990.

Lerer, Seth. "Representyd Now in Yower Syght: The Culture of Spectatorship in Late Fifteenth-Century England." In *Bodies and Disciplines: Intersections of Literature and History in Fifteenth-Century England,* edited by Barbara Hanawalt and David Wallace. Minneapolis: University of Minnesota Press, 1996.

———. "The Chaucerian Critique of Medieval Theatricality." In *The Performance of Middle English Culture: Essays on Chaucer and the Drama in Honor of Martin Stevens,* edited by James J. Paxson, Lawrence M. Clopper, and Sylvia Tomasch, 59–76. Cambridge: D. S. Brewer, 1998.

Lewis, Suzanne. "*Tractatus Adversus Judaeos* in the Gulbenkian Apocalypse." *Art Bulletin* 68 (1986): 543–66.

Lipman, V. D. *The Jews of Medieval Norwich.* London: Jewish Historical Society, 1967.

Logan, F. D. "Thirteen London Jews and Conversion to Christianity: Problems of Apostasy in the 1280s." *BIHR* 45 (1972): 214–29.

Lovatt, Roger. "Henry Suso and the Medieval Mystical Tradition in England." In *The Medieval Mystical Tradition in England,* edited by Marion Glasscoe. Exeter: Exeter University Press, 1982.

MacCormack, Sabine. *The Shadows of Poetry: Virgil in the Mind of Augustine.* Berkeley: University of California Press, 1998.

Maltman, Sister Nicholas. "Meaning and Art in the Croxton Play of the Sacrament." *ELH* 41 (1974): 149–64.

Mann, Jill. *Chaucer and Medieval Estates Satire.* Cambridge: Cambridge University Press, 1973.

McGinn, Bernard. *The Growth of Mysticism.* New York: Crossroad, 1994.

Menache, Sophia. "Faith, Myth, and Politics: The Stereotype of the Jews and Their Expulsion from England and France." *Jewish Quarterly Review* 75:4 (1985): 351–74.

Meredith, Peter. "The Towneley Cycle." In *The Cambridge Companion to Medieval English Theatre,* edited by Richard Beadle, 134–62. Cambridge: Cambridge University Press, 1994.

Middleton, Anne. "The Audience and Public of 'Piers Plowman.'" In *Middle English Alliterative Poetry and Its Literary Background,* edited by David Lawton, 101–23. Cambridge: D. S. Brewer, 1982.

———. "The Passion of Seint Averoys [B.13.91]: 'Devynyng' and Divinity in the Banquet Scene." *Yearbook of Langland Studies* 1 (1987): 31–40.

———. "William Langland's 'Kynde Name': Authorial Signature and Social Identity in Late Fourteenth-Century England." In *Literary Practice and Social Change in Britain, 1380–1530,* edited by Lee Patterson, 15–82. Berkeley: University of California Press, 1989.

———. "Acts of Vagrancy: The C-Version 'Autobiography' and the Statute of 1388." In *Written Work: Langland, Labor, and Authorship,* edited by Steven Justice and Kathryn Kerby-Fulton. Philadelphia: University of Pennsylvania Press, 1997.

Miller, E. "Medieval York." In *The Victoria County History of Yorkshire: City of York,* edited by P. M. Tillot. London: Institute of Historical Research, 1961.

Miller, Mark. "Naturalism and Its Discontents in the *Miller's Tale.*" *ELH* 67 (2000): 1–44.

Mills, David. "Religious Drama and Civic Ceremonial." In *The Revels History of Drama in English,* vol. 1, *Medieval Drama,* edited by A. C. Cawley, Marion Jones, Peter F. McDonald, and David Mills, 152–206. London: Methuen, 1983.

Minnis, A. J. "Late-Medieval Discussions of Compilatio and the Role of the Compilator." *Beiträge zur Geschicte der Deutschen Sprache und Literatur* 101 (1979): 385–421.

———. *Chaucer and Pagan Antiquity.* Cambridge: D. S. Brewer, 1982.

———. "Affection and Imagination in *The Cloud of Unknowing* and Hilton's *Scale of Perfection.*" *Traditio* 39 (1983): 323–66.

———. "Langland's Ymaginatif and Late-Medieval Theories of Imagination." *Comparative Criticism* 3 (1981): 71–103.

———. *Medieval Theory of Authorship: Scholastic Literary Attitudes in the Later Middle Ages.* 2d ed. Philadelphia: University of Pennsylvania Press, 1988.

Miret y Sans, Joaquim. "El procés de les Hosties contra los Jueus d'Osca en 1377." *Anuari de l'Institut d'Estudis Catalans* 4 (1911–12): 59–80.

Morgan, Margery. "'High Fraud': Paradox and Double-Plot in the English Shepherds' Plays." *Speculum* 39 (1964): 676–89.

Mundill, Robin R. *England's Jewish Solution: Experiment and Expulsion, 1262–1290.* Cambridge: Cambridge University Press, 1998.

Newman, Barbara. "Possessed by the Spirit: Devout Women, Demoniacs, and Apostolic Life in the Thirteenth Century." *Speculum* 73 (1998): 733–70.

Nirenberg, David. *Communities of Violence: Persecution of Minorities in the Middle Ages.* Princeton, N.J.: Princeton University Press, 1996.

Nisse, Ruth. "Reversing Discipline: The *Tretise of Miraclis Pleyinge,* Lollard Exegesis, and the Failure of Representation." *Yearbook of Langland Studies* 11 (1997): 163–94.

Olson, Paul A. *Chaucer and the Good Society.* Princeton, N.J.: Princeton University Press, 1986.

Ovitt, George, Jr. *The Restoration of Perfection: Labor and Technology in Medieval Culture.* New Brunswick, N.J.: Rutgers University Press, 1987.

Owst, G. R. *Preaching in Medieval England.* Cambridge: Cambridge University Press, 1926.

———. *Literature and Pulpit in Medieval England.* Cambridge: Cambridge University Press, 1933.

Palmer, Barbara. "'Towneley Plays' or 'Wakefield Cycle' Revisited." *Comparative Drama* (1988): 318–48.

Papka, Claudia Rattazzi. "Fictions of Judgment: The Apocalyptic 'I' in the Fourteenth Century." Ph.D. diss., Columbia University, 1996.

Patterson, Annabel. *Pastoral and Ideology: Virgil to Valéry.* Berkeley: University of California Press, 1987.

Patterson, Lee. *Chaucer and the Subject of History.* Madison: University of Wisconsin Press, 1991.

Pezzini, Domenico. "The Meditation of Oure Lordis Passyon and other Bridgettine Texts in MS. Lambeth 432." In *Studies in St. Birgitta and the Brigittine Order,* Analecta Cartusiana 35:19, 1:276–95. Lewiston, N.Y.: Edwin Mellen Press, 1993.

Powell, Edgar. *The Rising in East Anglia in 1381.* Cambridge: Cambridge University Press, 1891.

Powell, Edward. "Law and Justice." In *Fifteenth-Century Attitudes,* edited by Rosemary Horrox. Cambridge: Cambridge University Press, 1994.

Prior, Sandra. "Parodying Typology and the Mystery Plays in the *Miller's Tale.*" *Journal of Medieval and Renaissance Studies* 16 (1986): 57–73.

Quinn, William A. "Chaucer's Janglerye." *Viator* 18 (1987): 309–20.

Rembaum, Joel. "The Talmud and the Popes: Reflections on the Talmud Trials of the 1240s." *Viator* 13 (1982): 203–23.

Rees-Jones, Sarah. "York's Civic Administration, 1354–1464." In *The Government of Medieval York: Essays in Commemoration of the 1396 Royal Charter,* edited by Sarah Rees-Jones, 108–40. York: Borthwick Institute of Historical Research, 1997.

Resnick, Irven M. "The Falsification of Scripture and Medieval Christian and Jewish Polemics." *Medieval Encounters* 2 (1996): 344–80.

Reynolds, Susan. *An Introduction to the History of Medieaval English Towns.* Oxford University Press, 1977.

———. *Kingdoms and Communities in Western Europe, 900–1300.* Oxford: Oxford University Press, 1984.

Riggio, Milla Cozart, ed. *The Wisdom Symposium: Papers from the Trinity College Medieval Festival.* New York: AMS Press, 1986.

Roach, Joseph. *Cities of the Dead: Circum-Atlantic Performance.* New York: Columbia University Press, 1996.

Robinson, J. W. "A Commentary on the York Play of the Birth of Jesus." *JEGP* 70 (1971): 241–54.

Roney, Lois. "The Wakefield First and Second Shepherds Plays as Complements in Psychology and Parody." *Speculum* 58 (1983): 696–723.

Ross, Charles. *Edward IV.* New Haven, Conn.: Yale University Press, 1997.

Rowe, Katherine. "'God's Handy Worke': Divine Complicity and the Anatomist's Touch." In *The Body in Parts: Fantasies of Corporeality in Early Modern Europe,* edited by David Hillman and Carla Mazzio. New York: Routledge, 1997.

Rubin, Miri. *Corpus Christi: The Eucharist in Late Medieval Culture.* Cambridge: Cambridge University Press, 1991.

———. "Desecration of the Host: The Birth of an Accusation." In *Christianity and Judaism,* edited by Diana Wood, SCH 29, 169–85. Oxford: Blackwell, 1992.

Salter, Elizabeth. *English and International Studies in the Literature, Art and Patronage of Medieval England.* Edited by Derek Pearsall and Nicolette Zeeman. Cambridge: Cambridge University Press, 1988.

Sargent, Michael. "The Transmission by the English Carthusians of Some Late Medieval Spiritual Writings." *Journal of Ecclesiastical History* 27 (1976): 225–40.

———. "Walter Hilton's Scale of Perfection: The London Manuscript Group Reconsidered." *Medium Aevum* 52:2 (1983): 189–216.

Schibanoff, Susan. "Botticelli's Madonna del Magificat: Constructing the Woman Writer in Early Humanist Italy." *PMLA* 109 (1994): 190–206.

Schmitt, Jean-Claude, and Jérôme Baschet. "La 'Sexualité du Christ.'" *Annales* 46 (1991): 337–46.

Shklar, Ruth [Ruth Nisse]. "*The Book of Margery Kempe* and the Power of Heterodox Thinking." *MLQ* 56:3 (1995): 277–304.

Sicard, Patrice. *Diagrammes medievaux et exegese visuelle.* Turnhout: Brepols, 1993.

Simpson, James. "Ethics and Interpretation: Reading Wills in Chaucer's *Legend of Good Women.*" *Studies in the Age of Chaucer* 20 (1998): 73–100.

Skinner, Quentin. *The Foundations of Modern Political Thought.* 2 vols. Cambridge: Cambridge University Press, 1978.

Smalley, Beryl. *The Study of the Bible in the Middle Ages.* Oxford: Blackwell, 1952. Reprint, University of Notre Dame Press, 1964.

Smart, Walter Kay. *Some English and Latin Sources and Parallels for the Morality of Wisdom.* Menasha, Wis.: George Banta, 1912.

Somerset, Fiona. "Professionalizing Translation at the Turn of the Fifteenth Century: Ullerston's Determinatio, Arundel's Constitutions." In *The Vulgar Tongue: Medieval and Postmedieval Vernacularity,* edited by Fiona Somerset and Nicholas Watson, 145–57. University Park: Pennsylvania State University Press, 2003.

Spector, Stephen. "Time, Space and Identity in the Play of the Sacrament." In *The Stage as Mirror: Civic Theatre in Late Medieval Europe,* edited by Alan Knight. Cambridge: D. S. Brewer, 1997.

Spencer, H. Leith. *English Preaching in the Late Middle Ages.* Oxford: Oxford University Press, 1993.

Sponsler, Claire. *Drama and Resistance: Bodies, Goods, and Theatricality in Late Medieval England.* Minneapolis: University of Minnesota Press, 1997.

Stacey, Robert C. "The Conversion of Jews to Christianity in Thirteenth-Century England." *Speculum* 67 (1992): 263–83.

Starn, Randolph, and Loren Partridge. *The Arts of Power: Three Halls of State in Italy, 1300–1600.* Berkeley: University of California Press, 1992.

Stevens, Martin. *Four Middle English Mystery Cycles: Textual, Contextual, and Critical Interpretations.* Princeton, N.J.: Princeton University Press, 1987.

Strohm, Paul. *Hochon's Arrow: The Social Imagination of Fourteenth-Century Texts.* Princeton, N.J.: Princeton University Press, 1992

———. "The Trouble with Richard: The Reburial of Richard II and Lancastrian Symbolic Strategy." *Speculum* 71 (1996): 87–111.

Swanson, Heather. "The Illusion of Economic Structure." *Past and Present* 121 (1988): 29–48.

———. *Medieval Artisans: An Urban Class in Late Medieval England.* Oxford: Blackwell, 1989.

Thomson, J. A. F. *The Later Lollards: 1414–1520.* Oxford: Oxford University Press, 1965.

Thrupp, Sylvia. "A Survey of the Alien Population in England in 1440" *Speculum* 32 (1957): 262.

Turner, Denys. *Eros and Allegory: Medieval Exegesis of the Song of Songs.* Kalamazoo, Mich.: Cistercian Publications, 1995.

Turville-Petre, Thorlac. "Some Medieval English Manuscripts in the North-East Midlands." In *Manuscripts and Readers in Fifteenth-Century England,* edited by Derek Pearsall. Cambridge: D. S. Brewer, 1983.

Twycross, Meg. "Transvestism in the Mystery Plays," *Middle English Theatre* 5:2 (1983): 123–80.

Vale, Malcolm. *Piety, Charity and Literacy among the Yorkshire Gentry, 1370–1480.* Borthwick Papers 50. York: St. Anthony's Press, 1976.

Viroli, Maurizio. *From Politics to Reason of State: The Acquisition and Transformation of the Language of Politics, 1250–1600.* Cambridge: Cambridge University Press, 1992.

Voaden, Rosalynn. *God's Words, Women's Voices: The Discernment of Spirits in the Writing of Late-Medieval Women Visionaries.* York: York Medieval Press, 1999.

Von Nolcken, Christina. "Piers Plowman, the Wycliffites, and Pierce the Plowman's Creed." *Yearbook of Langland Studies* 2 (1988): 71–102.

Wallace, David. "In Flaundres." *Studies in the Age of Chaucer* 19 (1997): 63–91.

Walsh, P. G. "'Golias' and Goliardic Poetry." *Medium Aevum* 52 (1983): 1–9.

Warren, Ann. *Anchorites and Their Patrons in Medieval England* Berkeley: University of California Press, 1985.

Watson, Nicholas. *Richard Rolle and the Invention of Authority.* Cambridge: Cambridge University Press, 1991.

———. "Censorship and Cultural Change in Late-Medieval England: Vernacular Theology, the Oxford Translation Debate, and Arundel's Constitutions of 1409." *Speculum* 70 (1995): 822–64.

———. "Conceptions of the Word: The Mother Tongue and the Incarnation of God." *New Medieval Literatures* 1 (1998): 85–124.

———. "The Middle English Mystics." In *The Cambridge History of Medieval English Literature,* edited by David Wallace. Cambridge: Cambridge University Press, 1999.

Weimann, Robert. *Shakespeare and the Popular Tradition in the Theater: Studies in the Social Dimension of Dramatic Form and Function.* Baltimore: Johns Hopkins University Press, 1978.

White, Paul Whitfield. "Reforming Mysteries' End: A New Look at Protestant Intervention in English Provincial Drama." JMEMS 29:1 (1999): 89–120.

Whitehead, Christiana. "Making a Cloister of the Soul in Medieval Religious Treatises." *Medium Aevum* 67 (1998): 1–29.

Whitney, Elspeth. *Paradise Restored: The Mechanical Arts from Antiquity through the Thirteenth Century.* Philadelphia: American Philosophical Society, 1990.

Winterbottom, Michael. "Virgil and the Confiscations." *Greece and Rome,* 2d ser., 23 (1976): 55–59.

Woolf, Rosemary. *The English Mystery Plays.* Berkeley: University of California Press, 1972.

Yuval, Israel Jacob. *Shene goyim be-vitnekh: Yehudim ve-Notsrim—dimuyim hadadiyim* [Two nations in your womb: Perceptions of Jews and Christians]. Tel Aviv: Am Oved, 2000.

Zizek, Slavoj. *The Sublime Object of Ideology.* London: Verso, 1989.

Ruth Nisse
is associate professor of English at
the University of Nebraska-Lincoln.